In this important book, insightful thinkers—from ⎢ *to geographers and planners—explore one of t* *results of our dazzling technological advances: an increasingly attenuated sense of place. Just decades ago, such a book would have been superfluous; today it is essential in a rapidly globalizing and digitizing world.*

BRUCE COLE
Senior Fellow, Ethics and Public Policy Center
Former Chairman, National Endowment for the Humanities

Both liberals and conservatives celebrate, each for their own reasons, the freedoms that modern life gives us, but we all too easily forget that to be liberated from one set of constraints is to become captive to another. Neither nostalgic nor polemical, Why Place Matters *illuminates the "mind-forg'd manacles" of modern mobility, and in so doing teaches us why learning to love where we live—and, so to speak, learning to live where we live—is critical to human flourishing.*

ROD DREHER
Author of The Little Way of Ruthie Leming

Cities are the crucibles of modern civilization. This unique and thought-provoking collection of essays will be crucial for helping anyone who cares about cities understand how they do or do not meet human needs in this new century. I will refer to this collection again and again.

ROD GOULD
City Manager, Santa Monica, California

In our age of increasing rootlessness and digital disembodiment, this splendid book shows us how to think our way back, practically and philosophically, to the solid ground of place—the home, the neighborhood, and the city.

STEVEN LAGERFELD
Editor, The Wilson Quarterly

WHY PLACE MATTERS

NEW ATLANTIS BOOKS

Adam Keiper, Series Editor

PREVIOUS VOLUMES:

Merchants of Despair:
Radical Environmentalists, Criminal Pseudo-Scientists,
and the Fatal Cult of Antihumanism
Robert Zubrin

Neither Beast nor God:
The Dignity of the Human Person
Gilbert Meilaender

Imagining the Future:
Science and American Democracy
Yuval Levin

In the Shadow of Progress:
Being Human in the Age of Technology
Eric Cohen

www.newatlantisbooks.com

Wilfred M. McClay &
Ted V. McAllister, *editors*

WHY PLACE MATTERS

Geography, Identity, and Civic Life in Modern America

New Atlantis Books

ENCOUNTER BOOKS · NEW YORK · LONDON

First American edition published in 2014 by Encounter Books,
an activity of Encounter for Culture and Education, Inc.,
a nonprofit, tax exempt corporation.
Encounter Books website address: www.encounterbooks.com

Manufactured in the United States and printed on
acid-free paper. The paper used in this publication meets
the minimum requirements of ANSI / NISO Z39.48-1992
(R 1997) (*Permanence of Paper*).

FIRST AMERICAN EDITION

LIBRARY OF CONGRESS
CATALOGING-IN-PUBLICATION DATA
IS AVAILABLE FOR THIS TITLE

ISBN 978-1-64177-117-7 (paperback)
ISBN 978-1-59403-718-4 (ebook)

CONTENTS

TO PAUL K. CONKIN,
HISTORIAN AND TEACHER
EXTRAORDINAIRE

AND TO THE MEMORY OF
HENRY HOPE REED,
TIRELESS WARRIOR FOR
THE CAUSE OF URBAN BEAUTY

Preface

WILFRED M. MCCLAY & TED V. MCALLISTER

TO SAY THAT "place" matters is, to some extent, to swim against the principal currents of our times. The globalization of commerce, and the technologies of communication and transportation that have made that globalization possible, make it so easy to move people and products, ideas and styles, that it sometimes seems as if the world is in fact becoming placeless. The tenuous and fungible nature of place in our times is as evident as the phone vibrating in our hands: when we answer, our first question to the caller is likely to be, "Where are you?" and the answer the caller gives us could plausibly be almost anyplace from Manhattan to Mumbai to the house next door. What more powerful evidence is there that place doesn't matter anymore? Isn't stressing the importance of place in our lives just a symptom of backward-looking nostalgia?

But place does still matter. Whether we like it or not, we are corporeal beings, grounded in the particular, in the finite conditions of our embodiment, our creatureliness. So is everything else, even if we sometimes forget the facts of the matter, or get caught up in the power of our own digital illusions. The "cloud" in which untold billions of digital interactions are occurring as you are reading this is not a cloud in the sky; it is the illusion of a cloud, a fantasy, a metaphor whose plausibility is grounded in and sustained by an army of servers, ungainly looking physical objects that are very much sitting right here on the ground, vulnerable to hurricanes, tornadoes, fires, and other calamities. In losing "place" entirely, and succumbing to the idea that a website can be a place and that digital relationships can substitute for friends and family, we risk forgetting this reality of our embodiment, risk losing the basis for healthy and resilient individual identity, and risk forfeiting the needed preconditions for the cultivation of public virtues. For one cannot be a citizen without being a citizen of some place in particular; one cannot be a citizen of a website, or a motel. And if these dangers are real and present ones, surely we are not helpless to address them. Surely there are ways that intelligent people, and intelligent public policy, can begin to address them constructively, by means of reasonable and democratic innovations.

The essays in *Why Place Matters* have in common a view that the recovery of "place" in our personal and public lives is a matter of central importance, but the editors have not otherwise sought to impose a party line. Indeed, we have sought to encourage debate rather than skirt it; hence the range of views represented is wide, often suggesting dramatically different paths forward.

For example, the reader will encounter architect Philip Bess's humane and philosophically grounded urbanism, which seeks to conceptualize the ideal city as a carefully planned vehicle for the fulfillment of the good life; poet Dana Gioia's exuberant celebration of creative, diverse, and disorderly Los Angeles as far more of a "place" than it gets credit for being; philosopher Roger Scruton's call for aesthetic constraints to make city centers more attractive and therefore livable; and architectural historian Witold Rybczynski's wise admonition that the city with a healthy sense of place is one that prudently respects the promptings of the market and the choices of consumers, while also honoring the momentum of history by remembering that "adaptation . . . is always better than invention" and that cities should not imagine they ever have the power to start from scratch.

Similarly, the subject of cosmopolitanism, as a principled enemy to the centrality of place, is treated differently by different authors. Political theorist Mark T. Mitchell attacks cosmopolitanism frontally, as a betrayal of the most fundamental human longings, and seeks to formulate a "humane localism" that will be free of the fear of the "other." The historian and critic Russell Jacoby, while much friendlier to cosmopolitanism in many respects, points to the ways in which it promises far more than it delivers, and how, by inducing a placelessness that leads to resentment and violence, it may ironically serve to foster the very particularistic hatreds that it was created to escape. And for the eminent geographer Yi-Fu Tuan, a Chinese immigrant scholar who rose to the top of his profession as a brilliant student of the structure and phenomenology of place, there is a ceaseless tension between local and cosmopolitan values, between hearth and cosmos—a tension that is inherent and not to be resolved in favor of one or the other. Even such a nuanced position as Tuan's also, in its own way, affirms the enduring importance of the particular and the local.

Other essays perceptively examine the psychological and social effects of mobility (Schulman, Rosen), the ways in which public policy would benefit from greater place-consciousness and greater empowerment of local participatory institutions (Toth, Schambra, Brown, Peterson, McAllister, McClay), and the ways in which a revival of local history could lead to civic and individual renewal on a surprising scale (Amato). All the essays have in common a desire to vindicate a sense of place as something essential to the well-being of all men and women.

These are some of the concerns addressed in *Why Place Matters*. We and our contributors are convinced that the erosion of place is an issue of profound importance, one that goes to the most fundamental purposes of human society. We hope the essays in this book will begin to make the case for that proposition.

Why Place Matters

WILFRED M. MCCLAY

THE MOST FAMOUS WORDS about the city of Oakland, California came from the pen of Gertrude Stein. There was, she declared, no "there" there.[1] This line has been widely understood as a casually dismissive judgment upon that city, and it has been used and reused countless times, as a barb directed at a variety of objects. Unfortunately, her quip is also the chief thing that many people, particularly non-Californians, are likely to know about Oakland. Its better-off neighbor Berkeley, home of the most eminent of the University of California campuses, and always eager to demonstrate its cultural *élan*, has even created a gently witty piece of public art called "HERETHERE" that plays on Stein's words.[2] The installation stands at the border of the two cities, with the word "HERE" on the Berkeley side, and the word "THERE" on the Oakland side. As you might expect, Oaklanders don't much like it. There has even been a T-party rebellion, so to speak, in which an intrepid army of knitters covered up the "T" on the Oakland side with a huge and elaborate tea-cozy.[3] This is how they conduct cultural warfare in the Bay Area, where some people clearly have too much time on their hands.

Yet the irony of it all is that when Stein penned those words in her autobiography, they were not meant as a snappy put-down. She was thinking of something entirely different. Oakland had been extremely important to her when she lived there as a child, as a rare stable place in an unsettled and peripatetic upbringing. But when she discovered later in life that her childhood home there had been torn down, leaving her with nothing familiar to return to, Oakland lost its meaning for her. The blooming, buzzing confusion of the city no longer had a nucleus around which she could orient it. Saying that there was no "there" there was a poignant way to express this personal disorientation—a disorientation felt by many of us in the modern world, particularly when the pace of change causes us to lose our grip on the places that matter most to us.

There is no evading the fact that we human beings have a profound need for "thereness," for visible and tangible things that persist and endure, and thereby serve to anchor our memories in something more substantial than our thoughts and emotions. Nor can we ever predict in advance the points at which our foundational sense of place will be most vulnerable, though surely a childhood home is a very likely candidate. In any event, when one of those anchors disappears or changes, as it did for Stein, we are left alone, bereft and deserted, our minds and hearts burdened by the weight of uprooted and disconnected memories which can no longer be linked to any visible or tangible place of reference in the world outside our heads. So the memories wither in time like cut flowers, and the more general sense of place, of "thereness," is lost with them, like abandoned farmland slowly reclaimed by the primeval forest.

THE PLACES OF OUR LIVES

Although "place" is the most general of words, the things to which it points are very specific. "Place" as a concept is highly abstract, but places in particular are concrete, palpable, intimately meaningful. Each place is different. Each of us comes from just such a particular and unreproducible somewhere, and considers some place (or places) "home."

Each of us knows, too, that "a sense of place" is as much an achievement as a given condition. Although one could argue that a "place" is ultimately merely a point on some coordinate system, such a flat-footed assertion misses the inherently phenomenological character of place. Which explains why not all places are equal, and some places seem to us to be more fully "places" than others. In a frenetically mobile and ever more porous and inexorably globalizing world, we stand powerfully in need of such stable and coherent places in our lives—to ground us and orient us, and mark off a finite arena, rich with memory, for our activity as parents and children, as friends and neighbors, and as free and productive citizens.

And we know that the sense of place, even when it is very strong, is also very fragile and easily lost. Stein's famous line about Oakland is testimony to that. By the same token, the ghostly imprint of a sense of place may persist even when the physical conditions for it have vanished, like the sensations that linger after a limb has been amputated. Such is the utterly quotidian incident described in a haunting little column that Verlyn Klinkenborg wrote several years ago for the *New York Times*, a demonstration that the sense of place can apply especially powerfully to the most commonplace and unremarkable things. The column was a response to the closing of a Korean market in his neighborhood—not an event of obvious importance, and yet Klinkenborg found himself maintaining "a mental map" of the place:

> I know just where the seltzer is in a store that no longer exists. I can walk straight to the dried pineapple, but only in the past. Some part of me had quietly made an inventory of the necessities— the analgesics and toothbrushes and small shampoos—that had migrated to the front counter, which was a drugstore in itself. There are other places to buy all these things, and not far away. But there is still a perfectly good Korean market in my head.
>
> We carry with us these footprints of vanished places: apart-

ments we moved out of years ago, dry cleaners that went out of business, restaurants that stopped serving, neighborhoods where only the street names remain the same. This is the long-gone geography of New York. I look up at the buildings and try to imagine all the lives that have passed through them.[4]

We are sometimes left, he concludes, in the strange position of "knowing our way around a world that can no longer be found."[5]

What Stein's and Klinkenborg's accounts share is their depiction of an ordinary but disquieting phenomenon: the translation of *place* into *space*—the transformation of a setting that had once been charged with human meaning into one from which the meaning has departed, something empty and inert, a mere space. We all have experienced this, some of us many times. Think of the strange emotion we feel when we are moving out of the place where we have been living, and we finish clearing all our belongings out of the apartment or the house or the dorm room—and we look back at it one last time, to see a space that used to be the center of our world, reduced to nothing but bare walls and bare floors. Even when there are a few remaining signs of our time there—fading walls pockmarked with nail holes, scuffs in the floor, spots on the carpet—they serve only to render the moment more poignant, since we know that these small injuries to the property will soon be painted over and tidied up, so that in the fullness of time there will be no trace left of us in that spot.

BLURRING DISTINCTIVENESS

One should not be too melodramatic about this. Such changes and transitions, however painful they may sometimes be, are part of a healthy and dynamic human existence. What is different now is not that they happen but that they have become so pervasive, reflecting a social and psychological fluidity that seems to mark our times. As we have become ever more mobile and more connected and absorbed in a panoply of things that are not immediately present to us, our actual and tangible places seem less and less important to us, more and more transient or provisional or interchangeable or even disposable. The pain of parting becomes less, precisely because there is so little reason to invest oneself in "place" to begin with. Sometimes it almost seems as if we are living like plants without roots, drawing our sustenance not from the earth beneath our feet but from the satellites that encircle us and the computer clouds that feed and absorb our energies.

It has not always been thus, of course; and we forget how recently things were, as they had been from the beginning of time, almost entirely different. It was not much more than a century ago that the lives of most Americans were confined within a narrow local radius, in what historian Robert Wiebe revealingly called "island communities."[6] The ability of these island communities, and the individuals who comprised them, to communicate across large distances was limited by the vast seas of space and time—by the distances that separated them, and the immense time it took to traverse those distances. The term "real time," to the extent it would have had any meaning at all, referred to strictly local time, measured by reference to the sun's reaching its zenith at that particular location. Far from being a puzzle or an enigma, one's "place in the world" was a given for a great many, if not most, men and women. With rare exceptions, the person that one became and the life that one lived were inextricably linked to the geographical location where one was born and raised. Such factors remained even if one moved, as Americans always have, since one's origins lingered on as a structural mold of one's worldly existence, nearly as hard and fast as one's biological makeup. One could only move so far, and so fast.

But a cascading array of technological and social innovations has, with astonishing speed, rendered those considerations obsolete. Inexpensive travel and instantaneous telecommunications have almost eliminated the isolation of provincial life everywhere in the world, and resulted in the unprecedented mobility of both individuals and entire populations, the blurring of national identities and porousness of boundaries, and the relentless global flow of labor, capital, and goods. All these forces erase distances and erode barriers that had formerly been considered an inescapable part of the human condition. And the term "real time" now refers, not to local time, but to its opposite—the possibility of near-universal simultaneity, so that, for example, I can have a lively conversation in "real time" with anyone on any part of the planet.

This revolution shouldn't be a surprise to us, since it has been coming at us steadily ever since the invention of the locomotive and the telegraph. And make no mistake, there is much to celebrate in these developments. They give crucial support to one of the most powerful and fundamental, and universally appealing, of all American ideas: the idea of freedom. We embrace freedom because we believe fervently in the fullest breadth of individual human possibility, and share a deep conviction that no one's horizons in life should be dictated by the conditions of his or her birth. Nothing is more quintessentially American than that conviction. But interestingly, the word "place" rarely plays any role in this freedom narrative, and in fact, what role it plays tends to be negative. One's place of origin is seen as an impediment, something to be overcome. "Place" may even point toward notions of social hierarchy that Americans generally find anathema. Many of us can still remember when the idea of "knowing your place" was used to promote racial segregation and the social and legal subordination of women.

But very little of that is relevant anymore, and it would be a grave error to think that the problems of the past are the same as those today. We now have a new set of problems, which have been engendered precisely by our dazzling achievements. One of those problems is the widespread sense that something is now seriously out of balance in the way we live. All the technological wizardry and individual empowerment have unsettled all facets of life, and given rise to profound feelings of disquiet and insecurity in many Americans. No one can yet reckon the human costs of such radical changes, but they may turn out to be far higher than we have imagined.

Accompanying this disquiet is a gnawing sense that something important in our fundamental human nature is being lost, abandoned or sacrificed in this headlong rush, and that this "something" remains just as vital to our full flourishing as human beings as it was in the times when we had far fewer choices on offer. Could it be the case that the global-scale interconnectedness of things may be coming at too high a price? Could it be the case that the variety and spontaneous diversity of the world as we have known it for all the prior centuries of human history is being gradually leveled and effaced, and insensibly transformed into something standardized, artificial, rootless, pastless, and bland—a world of interchangeable airport terminals and franchise hotels and restaurants, a world of smooth surfaces designed to facilitate perpetual movement rather than rooted flourishing? A world of space rather than place, in which there are no "theres" there?

Could it be the case that one of the chief things neglected by this pattern of ceaseless movement is precisely the opportunity to live dignified and purposeful lives of self-government and civic engagement, the kind of lives that thinkers since the time of Aristotle have regarded as the highest expression of human flourishing? Is the living of such lives even conceivable in a world without "theres"?

These concerns should not be confused with feelings of nostalgia, such as one finds in sentimental discourse about lost "community," often emanating from individuals who would not for a second tolerate the kind of constraints on individual liberty that "thick" communities of the past always required. For better or worse, while a wholesale rollback of modernity may be conceivable as a thought experiment, it is simply not a serious practical option. But that does not mean accepting an unacceptable status quo, in which human flourishing itself is rendered impossible. Instead, we should seek to discover how, given the American people as they are, and American economic and social life as it now exists—and not as those things can be *imagined* to be— we can find means of resisting the steady homogenization of the world. This means cultivating a strong sense of place wherever we find it— and thereby cultivating the human goods that depend upon an enduring sense of place and are impossible without it.

———————

LIVING "*PLACES*"

In both its literal and its figurative meanings, "place" refers not only to a geographical spot but to a defined niche in the social order: one's place in the world. Thus, when we say that we have "found our place," we are speaking not only of a physical location, but of the achievement of a stable and mature personal identity within a coherent social order, so that we can provide an answer to the questions: "Who are you? Where did you come from? Where is your home? Where do you fit in the order of things?" Hence, it is not surprising that a disruption or weakening in our experience of geographical place will be reflected in similar disruptions in our sense of personal identity. The two things go together.

But any effort to affirm the importance of place brings us into tension with the same disorienting forces that are shrinking and transforming our world. A national government and a global economy always tend in the direction of consolidation and uniformity, toward the imposition of a universal standard. A stress upon the importance of "place" represents a counterforce to these huge structural tendencies. For place is always grounded in the particular, even the provincial. Such affirmation is not mere attachment to the abstraction of "place" but to *this* place, scaled to our innate human sensibility: toward *specific* hometowns and neighborhoods and countrysides and landscapes, each having its own enveloping aura of thoughts and desires and memories—that is to say, its own history, its own customs and traditions, its own stories, its foodways and folkways, its relics, and its own burial grounds.

Furthermore, what makes a "place" is not merely a loyalty to its past, but the vitality of its present, and the lure of its future. Far from being static, a "place" must be a node of continuous human activity: political, economic, and cultural. These are the forces that make a living "place" different from a museum. A living "place" has to offer scope for the creative energies of its people.

We should not imagine that the erosion of "place" is an "optional" issue, or an "aesthetic" one, the sort of concern best taken up when times are flush and there are less pressing items on our plate. Nor should we dismiss a renewed emphasis on "place" as fanciful, or backward-looking, or fetishistic, a foolish and futile attempt to resurrect something whose time has passed. Instead, it can be argued that, like it or not, we must recover a more durable and vibrant sense of place if we are to preserve the healthy dynamism of our society as it now exists, and promote the highest measure of human happiness and flourishing. Or, to put it in the words of historian William Leach, "People require a firm sense of place so they can dare to take risks. A society whose common store of memories has been beaten down or shattered is open to further disruption; for such a society cannot defend or protect itself from the stronger incursions of those who know what they want and how to get it."[7]

A firmer sense of "place," in short, may be an essential basis of our freedom, and the necessary grounding for a great many other human goods. Simone Weil wrote eloquently of the human need for roots[8]; but roots cannot be summoned down from the clouds, transported over a fiber-optic network, or carried around in a suitcase. They have to find some "there" that can become an enduring "here" for them.

The abandonment of such roots in the quest to inhabit some technologically simulated stratosphere of pure fluidity, to be at once all things in all places, and thereby escape once and for all every imprisoning feature of the particularities that have been given to us, including ultimately the limitations of our bodies themselves, will carry a fearsome hidden cost. "We exist by distinction," said George Santayana, "by integration round a specific nucleus according to a particular pattern."[9] Let that nucleus be lost—as it became lost for Gertrude Stein—and so too are we.

GPS and the End of the Road

ARI N. SCHULMAN

Few things are more self-evident than the fact that our era's reliance upon increasingly powerful and pervasive digital technologies is playing an important role in reshaping our experience of place. But exactly how and why is this happening, and with what specific effects? Ranging widely through literature and popular culture, and drawing on the insights of philosopher Edward S. Casey among others, Ari N. Schulman explores how it is that the rise of GPS and other new technologies for "location awareness" and "augmented reality" paradoxically militates against a deeper awareness of place, which is a form of consciousness that must in some sense be gotten by and through the particularities of our own experience. Such a loss of awareness not only changes our sense of place, but threatens to deprive the experience of journeying, that most archetypal of human quests, of its primal meaning.

> *Whither goest thou, America, in thy shiny car at night?*
>
> JACK KEROUAC[1]

EACH GENERATION reimagines the allure of the unknown world, and reinvents the means of discovering it. The greatest journeyer, Odysseus, traveled by ship, beset by monsters and the whims of the gods, seeking not new lands or conquests but only to return home. Later way-farers yearned for odysseys of their own; but since the Old World was by then pretty well tamed and charted, the old gods vanquished and the dragons fought back to the corners of the maps, they set out on horse-back in shining armor, seeking after a quest for questing's sake. The fin-est of these knights errant, Don Quixote, readily acknowledged that he'd taken to the road because it was better than the inn.

The Age of Exploration that drew Europe to the Americas made the world seem, at least at first, bigger and more mysterious. The ensuing conquests and technical innovations seemed to open new frontiers just as quickly as they closed old ones: the exploration and charting of the unknown continent gave way to pioneers and pros-pectors; the taming of the West gave way to settlers. Even once the Americas had been crisscrossed with rails and paved roads, a new age of discovery was opened—the age of personal discovery celebrated in the mythology of Kerouac and the open road. The horizon of the unknown is constantly shifting, but not necessarily receding.

If each successive era has closed an old realm of exploration while opening up another, then what are we to make of the innovations in navigational technologies that have just gotten underway in earnest over the last ten years? The rise of digital mapping and the Global Positioning System (GPS) has seemed to come upon us almost as a matter of course, blended in with the general dawning of the digital age and in itself relatively unremarked—but it has in a blink ushered in the greatest revolution in navigation since the map and compass.

The conception of GPS by the U.S. military began in the 1960s. Satellites with extremely precise onboard clocks constantly send out packets of information containing the time and coordinates at which they were sent; navigation devices here below receive the signal and calculate the transit time and distance. By combining information from several satellites, accurate and precise coordinates for the naviga-tion device can be calculated. In 1983, a navigational error sent Korean Air Lines Flight 007 into restricted Soviet airspace, where a fighter plane shot it down, killing all 269 people aboard; subsequently, President

Reagan directed that GPS be opened up for civilian use once it had been fully implemented. This occurred in the early 1990s, when a network of satellites was put in place.

Just as GPS was coming online, digital mapping applications were coming into widespread use. The first widely popular Web-based mapping application was MapQuest, launched in 1996; it also automatically generated driving directions. MapQuest has since been eclipsed by Google Maps, which upon its 2005 premiere provided dramatic innovations in ease of use—as well as satellite and aerial images of the entire world, of sufficiently high resolution in many populated areas to see people walking down the street. In 2007, Google enhanced its maps with Street View, which added panoramic street-level photographs of almost all public roads in major U.S. cities (and is now expanding to include smaller cities, rural areas, and cities around the world). These applications have also spawned versions designed, appropriately enough, for users of mobile devices; Google Maps has been available as a mobile app since the year of its launch, and Apple released a competing app in 2012. Many related applications have risen to prominence as well, most notably Yelp, a website and app designed to improve digital maps by uniting them with the kind of restaurant and business information once found in phonebooks and travel guides.

Digital maps and GPS receivers were combined in the late 1990s to create relatively inexpensive, commercial GPS navigation devices. Aside from their obvious military and industrial applications, these have become widely used as in-car navigational aids. A screen, typically a bit larger than a smartphone and mounted on the dashboard of the car—or, in many new cars, built into the dashboard itself—displays a live-updated map around the user's current location, along with instructions on how to reach his destination. Global sales of GPS navigators number in the tens of millions each year, according to industry analysts, and in 2012, TomTom, one of the leading manufacturers, estimated that one-quarter of cars in the United States and Europe have the devices.[2] Meanwhile, annual sales of GPS-enabled smartphones are expected to reach nearly a billion in 2014.[3]

Digital mapping and GPS are just the beginning of a much larger revolution in technologies designed to facilitate our interactions with places and travel between them. But it is astounding how quickly these technologies have already changed one of the most basic aspects of our existence: the way we move through the world. When driving down the highway, you can now expect to see, in a sizable portion of the cars around you, GPS screens glowing on dashboards and windshields. What these devices promise, like the opening of the Western frontier, and like the automobile and the open road, is a greater freedom— although the freedom promised by GPS is of a very strange new sort.

NO SIGNPOSTS IN A STRANGE LAND

The machine which at first blush seems a means of isolating man from the great problems of nature, actually plunges him more deeply into them. As for the peasant so for the pilot, dawn and twilight become events of consequence. His essential problems are set him by the mountain, the sea, the wind.

ANTOINE DE SAINT-EXUPÉRY[4]

Not long ago, I moved from my native home of Austin, Texas to the Washington, D.C., area. Austin has its share of driving woes: congestion, incomplete frontage roads, discontinuous streets with a single name, and potholes that ought to shame a warm, prosperous city. Still, it was where I learned to drive and navigate—so when GPS devices became popular, I never found much use for them.

But driving in the Washington metro area is a very different experience. The traffic is so dense it would have made Kerouac abandon his car for the subway. Even when the roads are clear, the layout itself is labyrinthine: ironically for a city that began with a central, geometric plan, in mid-navigation it is sometimes tempting to believe that the map of the surrounding area was generated by tossing spaghetti noodles at it and building roads where they lay. In fact, Eastern cities in general, because they long predate the automobile era, are less than optimally designed for traveling in cars. The problem is compounded by the inexplicable dearth of street and route signage in the Washington area. At any rate, soon after I moved, it became clear to me that, if ever there were a case to be made for GPS devices, the Washington area would be it.

So recently, I got a GPS device: an adorable little thing called a Garmin nüvi 350 ("nüvi" seemingly derives from "navigator"; "nävi" would probably have been too on-the-nose, and a bit too suggestive of a certain moony faith). The touch-screen affixes to the windshield; when I want to go somewhere, I just type in the address. It consults its on-board map database, and in just a few seconds, the screen view changes to show me a representation of my car as if I were following behind myself in a helicopter, watching in special goggles that show a symbolic map of the area ahead, with my route through it highlighted in purple. As I drive, my car stays centered on the screen as the imaginary helicopter follows behind, the view updating every couple of seconds. The device also relays directions to me turn-by-turn: at every moment it displays onscreen what my next turn will be, and as I approach the turn, a computer voice announces it.

This setup sounds simple enough: like asking for directions beforehand, only the navigator knows *every* route, and I don't have to worry about remembering the directions or experiencing that stock shame of pulling over and asking for help if I forget them. GPS particularly seems like a godsend in a cluttered suburban outpost, where even a seemingly simple two-step direction can turn out to be a monster. For example, consider the instruction "take Arlington Boulevard to Leesburg Pike south," which involves navigating Northern Virginia's notorious Seven Corners—a seven-way intersection with seven traffic lights, two levels, 150-degree turns into merging traffic, and signs that refer almost exclusively to state and federal route numbers but not the familiar local street names.

Thinking I can now rely just on the GPS's instructions, at Seven Corners I discover just how measly they are: "bear left onto Leesburg Pike," "continue right"—but which left, and which right? There are many turns within a small angle to choose from, and the instructions aren't specific enough. And the screen isn't much help either: the two-second lag time in updating and the lack of resolution below sixty feet or so become real impediments when attempting to negotiate several successive tight intersections. Even when I make the correct turn on my first attempt, I immediately find myself in another intersection, and in the wrong lane to make the next turn I need, because I only knew about one turn at a time.

Similar scenarios play out again and again in the area's many complicated intersections, particularly Washington's traffic circles. At Dupont Circle, for example, one must quickly choose between ten different exits off the circle, which is divided into an inner and outer ring by a concrete island, each ring having two lanes. Maneuvering through the circle is a feat in and of itself using one's own spatial reasoning and the paltry street signage provided. But when I attempt to obey the GPS, it becomes nearly impossible: the device just can't provide information detailed or fast enough to reliably let me know which turn to take. Attempting to negotiate the inner and outer rings, the multiple traffic lights at odd angles, and the pedestrians darting in and out of traffic all over the place would be enough of a challenge without also having to translate the lagging on-screen map to the circle I'm spinning around.

This sort of situation typifies driving with a GPS in D.C. It's pretty easy and convenient to do when a trip involves only a few turns, well-spaced apart on wide, clear roads. But just the situations that would seem to make GPS indispensable in this area are the ones that make it most difficult to use. Just following the GPS in these dense spots itself requires an almost hypnotic attention to it. But what makes this particularly vexing is all of the other, non-navigational things that must be paid attention to. Here, the lack of signage about street names and route information seems to be compensated for by signs every few yards for changing speed limits and special traffic zones; attending to all this to avoid breaking the law is difficult enough, not to mention dealing with frequent construction, closed roads, and pedestrians and drivers who each think they have the right of way.

Even when (as is usually the case) I am able to correctly follow the directions, I often find myself unsure of the current speed limit and my own speed; careening towards the rear end of the car ahead and only realizing it at the last moment; having to look around to take stock of where cars are when I suddenly need to swerve across several lanes; entering a school or construction zone without having realized it; or approaching a closed lane or a stopped car with barely enough time to swerve or stop. Driving in this way with a GPS often becomes downright hazardous or dangerous, and wracks my nerves. Instead of the best place in the country to make use of a GPS device, it seems it must be one of the worst.

'FAILURE TO PAY FULL ATTENTION'

It's just the danger when you're riding at your own risk.
DIRE STRAITS[5]

The problem I've encountered in using a GPS device is one of which the manufacturers are well aware, because every time I turn on the device, I'm greeted with a warning that "Failure to pay full attention to the operation of your vehicle could result in death, serious injury, or property damage. You assume total responsibility and risk for using this device." This is a standard disclaimer of technological apologists generally, high technologists and firearms defenders alike: we just make the thing; how you choose to use it is up to you. Apropos as that claim may be for arguments about legal culpability, devices are still designed for a particular mode of use. The way GPS devices are designed to be used requires learning a new sort of multitasking, because it separates what were formerly two intertwined acts, or two aspects of the same act, into the two distinct acts of *driving* and *navigating*—which must now be performed separately but simultaneously, in real time.

Attesting to this problem is the slew of "news of the stupid" stories about GPS errors that have made their way through the press in recent years. In 2009, New York state reported that it was cracking down on the rash of truck drivers who use GPS to find new but pro-hibited routes and end up crashing into low overpasses.[6] The same year, a Swedish couple was bound for the isle of Capri, but a typo on their GPS led them instead to the northern Italian town of Carpi, one letter and four hundred miles away. (A tourism official in Carpi noted, "Capri is an island. They did not even wonder why they didn't cross any bridge or take any boat.")[7] Another widely reported story was of a couple who, instructed by their GPS, nearly died on a remote Ore-gon road when they became stuck in the snow for three days.[8] Sadly, many other such stories involve fatalities.

Aside from the growing mounds of anecdotal evidence, there is some research to support the idea that GPS navigation weakens driv-ing ability, and that, as researchers at Cornell found, it leads drivers to become detached from their physical surroundings, as "the virtual environment becomes the primary environment with which the user engages."[9] A 2008 review by the National Highway Traffic Safety Administration found that "the mere presence of a navigation system in a vehicle might encourage increasingly frequent and unnecessary use of the system, including browsing through lists of attractions."[10] Another study, conducted by researchers at Aalborg University in Denmark, found that screen-based navigation "led to a decrease in driving performance" compared to drivers who only listened to spo-ken directions from their GPS devices.[11]

Most of this research, however, is small-scale and qualitative, or only compares different types of digital navigation systems to each other. As of yet, there seem to be no firm numbers on how driving performance using GPS navigation compares to internalized naviga-tion, nor are there any comprehensive statistical studies on the effects of GPS on accident rates. But one 2008 survey found that GPS devices had contributed to 300,000 crashes in the United Kingdom, and over a million drivers veering dangerously while following GPS direc-tions.[12] And a 2007 Dutch study found that GPS devices increased traffic accident casualties, and "purposely put the driver into a situa-tion of unacceptable social behavior."[13]

In the popular attention drawn to GPS horror stories, the common conclusion is that they indicate a woeful over-reliance on GPS. But these worries are usually about what we are to do when the technology *fails*. These are easy for defenders to answer by claiming, justifiably, that the technology is still young and only bound to improve, and that this is no more a claim against it than it is against cars, which also break down.

The more significant lesson of these stories and statistics ought to be that GPS devices, as we use them, erode our judgment and faculties, making us worse drivers. Consider the act of driving with the aid of a map or other directions learned (at least partially) before undertaking a trip. Researchers at McGill University have identified two basic ways that people navigate.[14] One involves learning the spatial relationships between various landmarks and destinations and forming a sort of mental map; the other involves memorizing sequences of turns, with landmarks serving as cues. This is an old and well-known division, but either alternative requires paying careful attention to your surrounding environment when navigating: you have to notice the landmarks, sense the distance passed, and match these up to your internalized directions. These necessary objects of attention in navigation, as it happens, overlap with those of driving, particularly insofar as they reside in the same visual space. Paying attention to where you are and where you're going is bound up in the same act of spatial perception as paying attention to other cars around you, where you are in a lane, the curve of the road ahead of you, the presence of barriers or pedestrians, and so on.

There is an idea popular in technophilia, dating back at least to Marshall McLuhan, that some technologies may be considered an "extension" of our own minds or selves. Scott Adams, sounding not unlike the drones who spin corporate techno-jargon in his comic strip *Dilbert*, has said just such a thing about GPS devices, claiming that they are part of our "exobrain" (and that this means that "technically, you're already a cyborg").[15] It's a pretty picture: GPS gives us additional abilities in physical space; therefore it extends our abilities into space; therefore it *is* an extension of *us*, or of our minds or brains. More precisely, as Adams puts it, "your regular brain uses your exobrain to outsource part of its memory, and perform other functions."

This notion of an "exobrain," like most extensions-of-man ideas, is essentially meaningless, as *all* technology "outsources" some functions from humans and so in some sense extends our capabilities. But if we are charitable to the "extended mind" claim, we can see it as an attempt to articulate the peculiar way we use some technologies—that is, we can see it as grasping at the idea of *instrumentality*: the usage of tools that becomes so intuitive that they seem to function as an organic element of our native bodily agency. Using a device as an instrument contrasts with operations that require conscious thought, such as programming a computer or working a complicated control panel.

Among the best examples of such "extensions of our mind" are our cars, which, properly designed and properly learned, can be operated so intuitively that we feel as if they were *bodily* extensions of ourselves in the physical world. This is a well-known principle among race-car drivers, but the same is true, if less consciously acknowledged, of competent nonprofessional drivers. Ask a student driver to parallel park or negotiate a tight turn, and he will nervously tell you that he has no idea how far the *car* extends in front of and behind him; but ask a person who has been driving for a while, and he can easily tell you how close *he* is to some object, as if he were the car. Similarly, an experienced driver on the highway will know at all times where the cars are in his vicinity—which ones are steady with him, and which are approaching or pulling away, even and especially those outside his immediate field of vision; checking his mirrors before changing lanes should only be a matter of verifying what he already knows. Without having to consciously meditate upon the fact, the driver of an automobile learns to assimilate it, so that it becomes the site of his physical agency in the world. He drives, that is, as if the car were his own body—and so achieves a remarkable though commonplace feat of human instrumentality.

In this sense, the GPS navigation device is quite the opposite of an extension of our minds; in fact, in adding a mediator between our own actions and the physical world, it shrinks us back into ourselves, reintroducing the division between the person and the vehicle, and between the vehicle and the world, that is experienced by the student driver. When we are constantly taking immediate directions from GPS, a car largely ceases to be a vehicle *of ourselves*, in the sense in which a vehicle is not just a means of self-transportation but a medium of self-realization. The car becomes much less a habitual extension of our own physical agency and much more a *thing before us* that we must command.

DRIVING'S END

> *Here's a couple of things America got right: cars and freedom.*
> DODGE COMMERCIAL[16]

In truth, our trust in the American driver has long been on the decline; the changes wrought by GPS navigation are only the latest in a long series of efforts to crutch his abilities. All of the recent brouhaha about "distracted driving" has deepened a growing distrust we already have of ourselves as drivers, leading auto manufacturers to devise systems not to make us better drivers, but to take more and more of the responsibilities of driving out of our hands. The last decade has seen a proliferation in automobile features—first in luxury cars, but now increasingly in standard models—that notify the driver of looming obstacles or if he veers out of a lane, or that will even automatically stop the car if an impending collision is detected.[17] Some new cars will alert the driver if they sense, based on braking, acceleration, and steering patterns, that the driver has lost his own alertness, whether through drowsiness, drunkenness, or distraction.[18] And the next generation of so-called "smart cars" will communicate with each other wirelessly, far extending the power of the car to direct the driver and automatically take control to avoid collisions.

But this attitude goes back even further, to choices made decades ago in the design of the U.S. traffic system. A 2008 *Atlantic* essay by John Staddon describes how, in place of driver immersion, the American system emphasizes signage that goes beyond road labels to specify every small detail of how drivers should drive. He argues: "The more you look for signs, for police, and at your speedometer, the less attentive you will be to traffic conditions. . . . A more systematic effort to train drivers to ignore road conditions can hardly be imagined. By training drivers to drive according to the signs rather than their judgment in great conditions, the American system also subtly encourages them to rely on the signs rather than judgment in poor conditions, when merely following the signs would be dangerous." Moreover, "as cars become safer, drivers tend to take more risks," and "often undercut well-intentioned safety initiatives." While acknowledging the effectiveness of many safety systems, such as seatbelts and airbags, Staddon proposes shifting U.S. traffic policy from its emphasis on micro-directing drivers through signage to the British system, which emphasizes and encourages driver attention and judgment, and, Staddon claims, has a much lower accident rate.[19]

It is necessary neither for cars nor roadway systems that technical progress come at the expense of driver skill—and neither must this be true of the new technology of navigation. It is notable that, as detailed in *The New Yorker*, the turn-by-turn system that has become the norm in GPS navigation devices is in fact a technological regress, a reversion to the form of road maps provided to the earliest automobile drivers.[20] The turn-by-turn model neglects one of the greatest achievements of the highway system: any long trip, no matter where the start and end points or what the distance in between, can usually be described in just a few major steps. In part, this is achieved through the system of route numbers: interstates, federal highways, state highways, and all the other roads with numbers give the illusion that they are discrete roads, when in fact they are joined together from numerous different roads— many of which were around before they were incorporated into a route system—and are better understood as guarantees of moving simply between major points. One route number may span dozens of roads with different local names, while any one segment of a road may implement several different route numbers. It is a brilliant means of imposing order, comprehensibility, and ease of use, of creating a system of networks out of the roadway's tangled, ever-shifting web of concrete. Using this system, you can get, say, from Little Compton, Rhode Island, to Boston's Logan Airport in just four steps: 77 to 24 to I-93 to I-90—as long as you pay attention. But computer navigation systems don't take advantage of this: Google Maps, for example, breaks up the same trip into eighteen steps, varying in length from 230 feet to 30 miles—which is too much to try to internalize.

One can imagine a navigation technology that would group such steps together, showing only the major necessary steps of a path, while perhaps including the smaller street details for reference; portions of trips that involve a few short turns or distances of mere hundreds of feet could similarly be grouped together. Such a tool would potentially permit the convenience of existing navigation technology, but would actually supplement and encourage rather than impede and weaken our own judgment and navigational skill. Such a program would likely be simple for even novice developers to create using the public interface for Google Maps. And GPS devices could be designed similarly, with the added benefit of portability, to aid users in *learning* where they are driving, rather than feeding them instructions from the dashboard. In short, such designs might begin to show how navigation technology could work for us like maps but better—like running shoes rather than crutches. (A redesigned version of Google Maps, still in beta version when this book went to press, in fact makes significant progress toward condensing its written step-by-step directions, though it still lacks a corresponding visual display designed to make directions easy to learn.)

But rather than nudging us toward greater independence and reclaimed skills, the future of driving seems to point in the opposite direction—toward the sense that we are becoming obsolete as drivers, and so toward granting us ever less control. Enter the dream of the driverless car. The technology has made great strides in recent years due to competitions sponsored by DARPA, the research agency of the U.S. Department of Defense. And alongside this, Google has been developing autonomous cars for commercial use and quietly testing them out on populated streets and highways with regular traffic. Futuristic as it sounds, the major technical hurdles to the fully-*auto*-mobile have already been met using cameras, GPS navigation, and artificial-intelligence software. The *New York Times* reported in October 2010 that "[Google's] test cars have driven 1,000 miles without human intervention and more than 140,000 miles with only occasional human control," with only one accident, caused by another driver.[21] Although most technology forecasters agree that commercial availability is still many years away, Google has already begun lobbying for its legalization; in 2011, Nevada became the first state to pass such a law, and Florida and California soon followed suit.[22] Meanwhile, the idea has begun to gain popular traction, with many advocates citing the potential gains in efficiency and safety.

Given the decline of the human driver, robotic driving, once we are sure of its reliability, seems to be the natural next step. There indeed seems to be something strange—superfluous, even—in the current human–GPS–car setup, in which people are already mostly just relaying information from one machine to another, only adding in some extra input and error correction. The problems I encountered at Seven Corners and Dupont Circle did not owe to a shortcoming in the technology so much as in human-computer communication. More than inefficient and error-prone, it seems beneath our stature to be relegated to this role—and so only appropriate for us to step out of the loop.

One can anticipate a few concerns about the likely transition to driverless cars. There are those doomed concerns about over-reliance. There may be skepticism that full automation won't work in rural or extreme conditions—but of course manual driving, like horseback riding, would likely stick around in niche applications. Then there are the "neuro"-concerns, which bring us back to the already-ongoing debate over GPS: Many claim that GPS may be "bad for our brains" because it causes us to stop using them for certain functions; navigational skill is associated with the hippocampus, and the McGill team has found that using GPS may contribute to its atrophy. This can lead to a decay in—wait for it—spatial reasoning skills.[23] Poor hippocampal health is also associated with dementia and decline in memory function, including Alzheimer's disease.

But it is hard to muster too much sympathy for our hippocampi. Any tools we use shift the balance of power in our brains. And it is not as if we can't think up yet another technological fix to this apparent problem: in order to maintain hippocampal health, members of the McGill team have begun to develop a sort of treadmill for the GPS age—an exercise regimen that involves using a computer program to navigate around a virtual building.[24] At worst, GPS would seem to join a long line of technologies that have relieved us from burdensome tasks that also gave us some incidental health benefits attainable by other means. Of course, the idea of navigational exercise seems frankly silly, not to mention a bit of a drag: people already tend to be lax about going to the gym, and one of the researchers admits that the navigational exercise regimen is "boring!" It is no coincidence that our rising need to go to the gym has accompanied a shift in the primary meaning of the word "exercise" from "the action of employing a faculty in its appropriate activity" to "bodily exertion for the sake of maintaining physical fitness."

Surely, however, these all seem like problems we can figure out. Any argument made solely on the grounds of health, safety, or practicality as to why we should drive or navigate ourselves seems unlikely to persuade over the long term. Automated navigating and driving relieve us from great burdens, and the notion of driverless cars seems to appeal on a fundamental level to what we want out of technology today. One writer argues that "working people will be anxious for the freedom to work granted by robocars" and young people may someday "be unwilling to set foot in a car that doesn't allow them to tune out and immerse themselves in their electronics."[25] And Sebastian Thrun, the leader of the Google research team, describes the main goal thusly: with self-driving cars, we can "text twice as much while driving, without the guilt."[26]

There is a hint in these claims of some stronger truth that the neuro-concerns are grasping at. The decline of driving, and of finding our own way around, means that we are losing a broad set of skills and practices. And while it is true that the *rise* of driving itself spelled the decline of other skills and practices, driving also opened up in their place a wide range of new faculties for us to exercise—new modes of excellence, and novel, exciting, adventurous ways of experiencing the world. But if the glorious future consists mostly of things like getting to text more, oughtn't we wonder what new skills, what novel forms of adventure, are taking the place of what is being lost with the decline of driving and navigation?

LOCATION AWARENESS

Isn't it strange how this castle changes as soon as one imagines that Hamlet lived here? As scientists we believe that a castle consists only of stones, and admire the way the architect put them together.

NIELS BOHR, to Werner Heisenberg,
at Kronborg Castle[27]

At a 2009 technology conference, Brad Templeton of the Electronic Frontier Foundation lectured on the promise of autonomous vehicles; when asked by a member of the audience whether a society that didn't have to pay attention to the world would be affected in its perceptual and cognitive abilities, he responded: "I don't think that's a bug. I think it's a feature."[28] After all, he said, we would be freed to read or be otherwise productive in the car. Of course, one might object that there are ways in which paying attention to the world is a "feature" and not a "bug": surely, for one thing, there are things in the world worth paying attention to.

To this objection, there is an entire branch of developers of GPS-based technology who would respond: why yes—and there's an app for that. GPS technology now not only shows users how to get where they are going, but increasingly can suggest where they should go in the first place. These are popularly known as "location-awareness" technologies. For example, Yelp, used by tens of millions of people, provides general information and user-generated reviews for restaurants, businesses, parks, and destinations of all sorts. It has an application for GPS-enabled smartphones that can tell you the best places nearby to eat, shop, sightsee, and so forth. Lonely Planet and other tour-book publishers have released apps along the same lines.

Similar software exists for sightseeing, allowing smartphone users to learn about the sites they are visiting as well as nearby attractions. The app HearPlanet reads audio recordings of Wikipedia entries for places as you approach them, and boasts that it "is like having a professional tour guide always by your side—no matter where you are." The GeoTour app advertises, "Imagine visiting a new city. Your iPhone knows where you are, it's guiding you to the town's hot spots, and it's automatically entertaining you with multimedia relevant to your surroundings." Similar purpose-built devices are now increasingly being used at national parks, historical sites, and other points of interest.[29] The devices, like the smartphone apps, are used as automated tour guides: walk a trail at a park, come to a landmark, and the device, able to sense your location, will play an audio recording or display on-screen information telling you exactly why you should find the site interesting.

Location awareness, of course, is also social. The enormously popular app FourSquare, with over forty million users by 2013,[30] turns venturing around a city into a sort of game, where users compete with each other by "checking in" with their phones at certain venues and receiving "badges," thereby learning also where their friends are and have been. Loopt, another popular app, runs constantly in the background, allowing users to post updates about what they are doing, and to receive alerts about what nearby friends are doing. Other developers are working on a sort of ideal realization of this people/location-optimization ethos: an app that would allow people to take videos of parties they are attending, upload them to YouTube, and then use the app to find other videos of nearby parties to determine whether they should stay where they are or leave for someplace that's really hopping. Other apps like Grindr and Tinder, which boast millions of users, facilitate casual encounters of a more intimate nature, allowing users to find other users on nearby phones who are interested in, to put it delicately, turning two sets of GPS coordinates into one.[31]

It is worth noting that that is not the only way location-aware technology is developing. Some of these new technologies encourage users to really engage with places—to attempt to discover places for themselves. For example, one group of Japanese researchers has proposed a GPS navigation system for tourists that requires them to take a more active role in touring, using the device to plan on their own what route to take, in hopes of "creat[ing] accidental encounters."[32] In another vein, a practice known as "geocaching" has arisen, in which people hide objects and post their GPS coordinates online so that others may seek and discover them.

A similar attitude is at work in a practice called "geotagging," in which photographers place their photos online by marking on a digital map the place where they were taken. Google's popular website Panoramio, for example, pins on a digital map many millions of user-submitted photos from around the world, and many newer, GPS-enabled cameras will automatically embed coordinates into photos. (As it happens, in a former life as a software developer in Austin, I created an early geotagging website known as the Austin Map Project. The site was meant as a side project in art and localism rather than a serious venture. But, like many other people who have developed location-based software, I hoped that the site would help deepen its users' relationship with place—one place in particular—by allowing us to, as it were, look *through* the map into what it both represents and conceals. Through photography, I hoped also that it would elicit a certain sort of exploration, encouraging us to seek out new and hidden places, and, more importantly, new views on the familiar.[33])

The future of location-based technology, however, seems headed in a different direction. The next generation, and logical conclusion, of location-awareness technology is called "augmented reality." Smartphones now come enabled not only with GPS, but with video cameras, and typically also with sensors that enable the phone to know where it is pointing. Combining these abilities, augmented-reality applications allow you to hold up your smartphone to, say, an unfamiliar city street, of which it will show you a live video feed, with information boxes hovering over points of interest to show you customer reviews, historical data, photographs, coupons, advertisements, and the like. One such augmented-reality app is called Layar because it allows you to see reality "layered" over, either with fanciful images or with helpful bubbles of information telling you what to see and why. In 2013, Google introduced Google Glass, which allows users to view such information on a pair of eyeglasses worn all day, thus eliminating even the burden of holding up one's arm. (Contact lens versions are sure to follow within a few years.)

The great and simple promise of these technologies is to deliver to us the goods of finding things in the world in the most efficient way possible. After Brad Templeton: their feature is to find the most interesting things in the world, and to explain why they are interesting, while eliminating the apparent bug that most of the things we encounter seem pretty boring. Moreover, location awareness and augmented reality, paired with GPS navigation, transmit us to these interesting places with the minimum possible requirement of effort and attention paid to the boring places that intervene. We can get where we're going, and see what we want to see, without having to look.

ON THE ROAD

The air was soft, the stars so fine, the promise of every cobbled alley so great, that I thought I was in a dream.

JACK KEROUAC[34]

If we are to take seriously the promise these technologies make to facilitate our experience of new places, we must understand not only the technologists' view, but our own, and ask how the new technology of location fits in with what we hope to get out of travel. And there is no greater sage for those hopes in the American conscience than Jack Kerouac. While *On the Road*'s reputation rather outstrips the literary merits of the book itself, the mythology surrounding it taps into our deeper aspirations for the possibility, freedom, and adventure granted by travel, and deserves to be taken seriously in understanding what we seem to want out of travel today.

The mythology of the road has come to be wrapped up in our desire to imagine ourselves as part of stories like Kerouac's, to experience them for ourselves, and so to partially emulate them in our own journeys. How, then, would the new technology of location affect an *On the Road* today? Can we imagine its characters, and by extension ourselves, escaping into the Western night, navigating by GPS and choosing where to go with Yelp, supplied with surrounding-relevant multimedia by GeoTour, encountering city streets with their iPhones held up and overlaying the view, and still having the same adventure? Something about this image is absurd. The reason why might become more clear if we step back and consider *On The Road*'s forerunner in American wayfaring legend, the classic *Adventures of Huckleberry Finn*.

Mark Twain's tale is one of the great depictions of discovery through travel. The power of this depiction comes not just from Twain's storytelling skill, but from the element he chooses to give structure to the story: the river, which conveys Huck and Jim through one scene of adventure after another. T. S. Eliot found this device so powerful that he dubbed it "the River God," claiming that "a river, a very big and powerful river, is the only force that can wholly determine the course of human peregrination."[35] For Huck and Jim, this determination of their course becomes a source of hope, of the possibility of escape from their wretched lives: for Jim, it is a hope for freedom from the miseries of slavery, and for Huck, from his life under a poor, abusive father. And they hope not just to escape their old lives but to find new ones—a broader moral hope that can be felt by the readers who enter imaginatively into the story, who come to apprehend this possibility for discovery and renewal in themselves.

Huck Finn arrived at a curious moment—set twenty years before the Civil War but published twenty years after, when the wild frontier, on whose edge the novel was set, was quickly vanishing. For many of its contemporary readers, the novel could provide not just imaginary access to that source of discovery, but a reminder of their own actual experiences of the very same regions, and of at least the possibility for setting out on a similar adventure themselves. By the middle of the twentieth century, however, the Mississippi had been dammed and locked, its banks developed, tamed, and civilized. It was no longer open for us as it had been for Huck and Jim and their real-life contemporaries.

It was this void that Kerouac stepped in to fill. The open road—the one suitable for travel by automobile—was a product of the technological and civilizational progress that closed off the sort of discovery depicted in *Huck Finn*. But that progress also opened up a new mode of travel, filled with new opportunities for discovery: while the frontier had been closed in its original sense, in another sense, it had been newly opened.

If the displacement of *Huck Finn*—its relegation to the realm of imagination—was what made *On the Road* possible, it was also what made it necessary: the citizens of the automobile age still needed a River God. It was Kerouac who reincarnated that god, in the form of The Road, showing how the possibility for revelation can be achieved even when the means is much more under human control, and the things discovered more tamed by human hands and populated by human affairs. There was still, Kerouac showed us, something wild in the West that was won.

It is this struggle with civilization that is the subtext of *On the Road*, as much as of *Huck Finn*. The protagonists of *On the Road*, Sal Paradise and Dean Moriarty (fictionalized versions of Kerouac himself and fellow-traveler Neal Cassady), set out to find freedom and adventure, and through those some elusive truth. The novel chronicles miles of wayfaring, spontaneous settlings down and lightings out again upon the road. But in truth, there is a deep tension underlying it. As in *Huck Finn*, it expresses a desire to escape from civilization; and the freedom championed in *On the Road* is often viewed as an expression of defiance against the strictures and mundanities of civilization. Yet the story's means of freedom are parasitic upon civilization—not only in using its vehicles, often stolen, but in using roads, a product of its tendency toward order. And the travelers always have civilization nipping at their heels—the raft on the river only a step ahead of the settling on the shores; the highways feeding the same homogenization from which they provide escape.

It is another paradox of both books that the supposed escape from civilization in large part consists of escape *to* civilization, or at least to its lesser-known boroughs. In each case, their travels are set against the grandeur of the natural world, but the scenes of their adventures are composed of unknown people in unfamiliar places. The "promise of every cobbled alley" is wrapped up in the possibility of the stranger—more fully, the chance encounter with the mysterious stranger in the enchanted place.

Seen in the right way, what the two novels show us is not the virtue of quitting civilization, but the freedom that comes from finding our own way through a world that is not of our own making—and with it, a glimpse of the possibility of reaching out beyond our everyday selves into something greater. And the progression from *Huck Finn* to *On the Road* suggests that the advance of technology and civilization need not spell the end of this possibility, but just the shift of its scenes.

Why, then, is it so hard to imagine some form of this journeying as occurring today? In part it is because of that homogenization of place enabled by the open road—the lessening of its difference and so its significance. More fundamentally it is because the mode of travel on the rise today is antithetical to the mode found in *On the Road* and its predecessors. Rather than being filled with adventure and the possibilities of freedom, the GPS-enabled, location-aware adventures of Sal and Dean or Huck and Jim somehow sound dreary before they have begun, filled with anticlimax, boredom, and restlessness. How can this be, when what these technologies seem to promise is a way of freshly opening up the world?

GREAT EXPECTATIONS

*. . .why think about that when all the golden land's ahead of you
and all kinds of unforeseen events wait lurking to surprise you
and make you glad you're alive to see?*

JACK KEROUAC[36]

Location awareness and augmented reality would seem, in fact, to be
a vastly more powerful incarnation of that classic travel aid, the tour
book or travel guide. Certainly travel would not mean what it does
today without the accrued human wisdom of the great sights and
points of interest in the world collected in these volumes, and now
brought to us electronically. The idea implicit in both is that places
and points of interest have some set value, as it were, that can be
entered into a data bank, used to inform our choice of destination,
and received by us on our arrival.

Perhaps the most valuable of these destinations, from the perspective of the American if not the world traveler, is the Grand Canyon.
The sight is awe-inspiring in a way that centuries of recounted visita-
tion to it have never adequately been able to put into words. And yet
some visitors to the canyon have discovered there a certain crack in
the guidebook façade. Take, for example, the recent account of travel
writer Henry Shukman, who admits that he was "disappointed" the
first time he saw the canyon: after enduring a long traffic jam in the
drive from Los Angeles, "When we eventually managed to park, and
walked to the rim, the scale of the sight off the edge was so great it was
hard to muster a response. It was so vast, and so familiar from innumerable pictures, it might just as well have been a picture."[37]

Many other writers over the years have made similar remarks
about their travels to other places: William Least Heat-Moon, in his
travelogue *Blue Highways* (1983), recounts that New Mexico's Mogol-
lon Rim "was a spectacular place; the more so because I had not been
anesthetized to it by endless Kodachromes."[38] Yi-Fu Tuan, in *Space
and Place* (1977), agrees that a place "may lack the weight of reality

because we know it only from the outside—through the eyes as tourists, and from reading about it in a guidebook."[39] Alain de Botton, in *The Art of Travel* (2002), claims that "where guidebooks praised a site, they pressured a visitor to match their authoritative enthusiasm, and where they were silent, pleasure or interest seemed unwarranted."[40] Tuan concludes: "The fleeting intimacies of direct experience and the true quality of a place often escape notice because the head is packed with shopworn ideas. The data of the senses are pushed under in favor of what one is taught to see and admire."[41]

The novelist Walker Percy anticipated these observations in his 1958 essay "The Loss of the Creature" (collected in *The Message in the Bottle*). He begins with the question: do modern tourists see the same sight today at the Grand Canyon as García López de Cárdenas, the first European to discover it, did when he first stumbled out of the mesquite upon the gaping expanse?

> The thing is no longer the thing as it confronted the Spaniard; it is rather that which has already been formulated—by picture postcard, geography book, tourist folders, and the words *Grand Canyon*. . . . If it looks just like the postcard, [the tourist] is pleased; he might even say, "Why it is every bit as beautiful as a picture postcard!" He feels he has not been cheated. But if it does not conform, if the colors are somber, he will not be able to see it directly; he will only be conscious of the disparity between what it is and what it is supposed to be. He will say later that he was unlucky in not being there at the right time. The highest point, the term of the sightseer's satisfaction, is not the sovereign discovery of the thing before him; it is rather the measuring up of the thing to the criterion of the preformed symbolic complex.[42]

Percy outlines a number of ways in which the sightseer might avoid this disappointment, each of which involves avoiding his expectations of the place. One such strategy is "getting off the beaten track."[43]

Or he can take the beaten track but in an unbeaten sort of way: Percy notes the feeling of good fortune when a family visits the canyon and, finding it unexpectedly empty, can report to friends, "We had the whole place to ourselves."[44] Henry Shukman chose just such a strategy on his return trip to the canyon: he went during the winter, when, as a park ranger told him, "You'll more or less have the place to yourself."[45] In a more extreme example, Percy describes the effect of a hypothetical national disaster or global near-apocalypse, in which the infrastructure for "seeing" the canyon is ruined, and the visitor there is able to recover that sense of awe about the canyon—to *see* it as if for the first time.[46]

In short, Percy says, the sightseer "sees the canyon by avoiding all the facilities for seeing the canyon."[47] Our assumption is "that the Grand Canyon is a remarkably interesting and beautiful place and that if it had a certain value P for Cárdenas, the same value P may be transmitted to any number of sightseers."[48] But this is belied by our experience, as the accounts of the travel writers and the general appeal of strategies like "getting off the beaten track" attest. As William Least Heat-Moon discovered during an unexpected detour, "little is so satisfying to the traveler as realizing he missed seeing what he assumed to be in a place before he went."[49]

What Percy and these other writers are getting at is that just as important as *what* we see in the world is *how* we go about seeing it. We are adept at identifying points of interest, but pay scant attention to the importance of our approaches to exploring them; our efforts to facilitate the experience of place often end up being self-defeating. What Percy's strategies aim to do, in part, is to put the traveler into a state of willingness and hunger to encounter the world as it is, to discover the great sights with the freshness, the newness, that is so much of what we seek from them. Alain de Botton also describes this attitude as the solution to the guidebook problem, and identifies it as the mode of *receptivity*.[50]

Practices like geocaching and geotagging rely on this receptivity. Geocaching asks the user to be an active participant in seeking, and to seek something unknown. Viewing geotagged photography may impel us to go forth into the world and seek with our own eyes what the images present to us, thus claiming them in some way for ourselves. It is a tricky balance: as always, photographs, especially when so readily viewed at the very places they were taken, hold the potential to substitute for rather than deepen our own awareness. But these practices at least give some idea as to how location-based technologies can encourage us to orient ourselves to the world in its primary, phenomenal sense—as a realm of places.

But GPS navigation, in its present form, seems to do quite the opposite: it dulls our receptivity to our surroundings by granting us the supposed luxury of not having to pay attention to them at all. In travel facilitated by "location awareness," we begin to encounter places not by attending to what they present to us, but by bringing our expectations to them, and demanding that they *perform* for us as advertised. In traveling through "augmented reality," even the need for places to perform begins to fade, as our openness to the world gives way to the desire to paper over it entirely. It is an admission of our seeming distrust in places to be sufficiently interesting on their own. But in attempting to find the most valuable places and then secure that value from them, the places themselves become increasingly irrelevant to our experiences, which become less and less experiences *of* those places we go.

This is a large part of why *Huck Finn* or *On the Road* as enacted today sound so dreary. Where Percy, in another essay, describes Huck and Jim as "reposing . . . all hope in what may lie around the bend," we can hardly imagine them doing so when what lies around the bend is displayed at all times on a screen before them.[51] Nor can we imagine Sal and Dean dreaming the promise of every cobbled alley, or of all kinds of unforeseen events lurking to surprise them, when they are striving to make sure that events *are* foreseen, and nothing is a surprise. The technology that is meant to facilitate travel deadens the spirit of discovery that draws us to the experience—moreover, it traduces that spirit: *dis*-covery, the removal of the things that paper over our vision so as to reveal the truth of the world, gives way to covering the world over deliberately, and calling that enhanced revelation.

SPACE AND PLACE

> *To see what is in front of one's nose needs a constant struggle.*
> GEORGE ORWELL[52]

The strategies that Percy describes for avoiding the tourist's dulled experience all involve subverting our expectations of a place in some way or another. But these strategies still require a consciousness of our expectations: getting off the beaten path is a negotiation (even if a contrarian one) with the pre-formed idea of a place, rather than with the place itself. And soon enough, getting off the beaten path becomes incorporated into the approved, expected experience: witness the advertisements for SUVs and sporting gear that now use that phrase as a slogan. Indeed, the presumption of location-aware technologies is that place can be a sort of consumer artifact, a packaged item in a showroom awaiting evaluation and purchase.

But this presumption doesn't fit our actual experiences of place. In his essay "How to Get from Space to Place in a Fairly Short Stretch of Time," Edward S. Casey, a professor of philosophy at Stony Brook University, disassembles the ideas we have piled atop our experience of place, suffocating our understanding of it. Our Cartesian and Newtonian mindset regards *space* as the inert medium of the universe onto which *places* cling: "space is absolute and infinite as well as empty and *a priori* in status," while places are "the mere apportionings of space, its compartmentalizations," and the sensory experiences of sight, sound, smell, and so forth are mere "secondary qualities."[53] Space, we might say, is like the empty walls of a house, and place the furniture and paintings added later as decoration. Visiting places and traveling through the world must then be like touring a giant museum, gazing at the pictures and artifacts. This is the mode of travel presupposed by the users of location-awareness technology: it tells them, first, where to go, and second, what to see in what they are looking at—permitting them to leave without ever stepping outside the confines of the guided and certified experience, and into actual exploration.

But however useful and appropriate the Cartesian formulation is for our mathematical understanding of space, the quality of our experience is quite different. As Casey observes, places are not secondary things in the world, because we cannot grasp the abstract realm of "space" except *in* and *through* whatever particular place we occupy at any given time. When we describe the universals of which a place is a part, it is as an abstraction from these so-called "secondary" qualities that are actually first in our experience. In short, as Casey says, "We come to the world—we come into it and keep returning to it—as already placed there."[54]

This primacy of our qualitative experience indicates that even the notion of "receptivity" only begins to account for our engagement with sights and places. As Casey notes, "perception is never entirely a matter of what Kant calls 'receptivity,' as if the perceiving subject were merely passive." And, echoing another philosopher, Casey adds in his book *The Fate of Place* (1998) that "the perceiver's body is not a mere mechanism for registering sensations but an active participant in the scene of perception."[55]

Indeed, the very notion of *engagement* means that we cannot treat places as mere sensory data, as *sights*: we cannot truly experience places simply by arriving and gazing at them, even if attentively. Being in a place, rather, means *doing* in it. But places are not mere bundles of stuff to do—activity tables in a museum to supplement the paintings—any more than they are mere accretions of stuff to see. A place is a realm of affairs for Nature and for humans; the term of our first entry into a place is recognizing our individual potential to be involved in those affairs. When we sense that potential, it manifests as a sort of *invitation* to enter into them—a "solicitation to action," as Matthew B. Crawford puts it—a beckoning to discovery, of the place and of our selves, through what we might encounter there and how we might face it. This is the element crucial to seeing a place: discerning what it invites us to do and answering the challenge.

The demand that a place first makes of us is to be able to *move* in it as our bodily selves. The tourist at the Grand Canyon has a far better chance of "seeing" the canyon if he goes for a hike in it than if he stands gazing at the rim, mightily attempting to behold it (even though he can, in a literal sense, see more of it from the rim). This motion need not be directly a matter of the body; any machine that a person enters and controls as a vehicle of his own powers will do: whether he drives an airplane, a car, or a wheelchair, some relationship between agent and place is formed. As the aviator Antoine de Saint-Exupéry discovered, each of these machines functions as a different sort of body that permits an encounter with different aspects and scales of a place.

Central to the demand to move in a place is the demand to find one's way through it. It is the most basic requirement for gaining access to a place—physical access to its features, but also access to those features as experientially meaningful. It is one of the results of learning to "internalize" a map or a set of directions through a place: the qualities of the place itself become "internalized," taking on new meaning for the traveler. In internalizing bird's-eye directions, one gets the lay of the land, the depth and configuration of space, that helps tie together the disparate components of a place into a whole; in internalizing landmark-based directions, the sites and features of a place gain significance. It is a crucial part of our first real entry into the revelation of place—a revelation that must be worked for, achieved in stages and through struggles; that can never be simply told or taught.

Through this struggle, place gains an experiential shape. The features of a particular place begin not just to look different from the features of another place, but to *feel* different and *mean* something different. Go to a city and find your way to somewhere new; take a walk or a drive through the streets of Washington, D.C., and you will begin to *feel* how it is a different place from Austin or San Francisco or New Orleans or Paris—how your possibilities for action are different and so too your possibilities for being. Finding your way around is how you begin to escape the realm of mere location and sight, wresting from it *place* and that elusive *sense* of the place.

In short, finding our way around engages us in the way we need to snap us out of the alienation facing Percy's tourist at the Grand Canyon, and to form instead the basis for a connection with the place: a purposive encounter with it whereby we can "get at it." For López de Cárdenas, as for the natives who came before him, it was impossible for the canyon to be a mere *sight* because it was a tremendous obstacle; a thing that must be conquered to pass; a possible site for injury and death, or for shelter, food, and water; an opportunity for riches, prospect, and conflict. Its features—a towering crag, a boulder, a valley, a thick of brush, the river at its core—were apprehended in terms of passability and possibility. Only relatively recently has it even become possible to regard the Grand Canyon as merely a sight—to stumble groggy off a tour bus right at the edge, without any sense of having traversed the distance there, and be faced with the challenge of perceiving the thing in itself.

Something like the sight that faced López de Cárdenas is still available to us; but it is and must be a struggle to *see* it. When we circumvent, by whatever means, the demand a place makes of us to find our way through it, we deny ourselves access to the best entry we have into inhabiting that place—and by extension, to really *being* anywhere at all. One *Wired* magazine writer noted at the conclusion of an essay lauding location awareness, though without any apparent sense of irony, this qualification: "I had gained better location awareness but was losing my sense of place."[56] Indeed, there is a doublethink at work in regarding GPS and the technologies built upon it as engendering "location awareness," when their aim is to permit us to traverse a place with the minimum necessary awareness of it—to shrink place, as the name suggests, into the mere location best fit for experience by a disembodied machine.

———

THE VOYAGE HOME

I wish I were a freeway, laid out clearer than a bright day.
I'd run right open down this causeway like brand new.

TIFT MERRITT[57]

The driver on the open road, the world out ahead with unending possibility for him, and he in charge of his own path through it, has for decades been the very image of American freedom. But today the automobile seems more a trap than a source of liberation. This owes in no small part to the ever-growing headaches of congestion, and to legitimate concerns over the environment and safety (though driving fatalities per capita have been on the decline for at least twenty years[58]). Still, it is worth noting the curious inversion in our understanding of "freedom": the ideal of the free person may soon be the one who, to go where he pleases, need not participate in getting there nor even know how, while the person who drives and finds his own way around seems slavish. The freedom of the automobile era, the Kerouacian variety, is a freedom *for* certain ends in the world, while the newer freedom is defined negatively, as a freedom *from*—from the burdens of getting around, but not for anything especially (except, apparently, working, texting, and other glories of the smartphone).

Considering how distant that freedom-for may feel to us today, and how prone its spirit is to abstraction from the realities of travel, it may already seem an irrelevant idealization, rather like the Romantic notions of the sublime and the wild-eyed traveler. Indeed, it seems hard to find much of practical value in what Walker Percy considers, in the titular essay of *The Message in the Bottle*, the purest opportunity for discovery and renewal: that given to the castaway who washes up on an island after a shipwreck, who has forgotten his past and is given a blank slate for a new life.[59] This ideal seems to have little to tell us about the more ordinary travels of the regular person, and especially about the mundane, everyday applications in which today's technologies of place are mostly put to use.

But the castaway points us also in another direction. Amy A. Kass, in her essay "The Homecoming of Penelope," notes that upon the return home of Odysseus, it is not he but surprisingly his wife whose reaction is described as being like the way a shipwrecked sailor welcomes the shore. For the Greeks, Kass notes, "to forget who you are and to forget home . . . are one and the same. . . . One's relations to home make one who and what one is."[60] And so for Penelope, who loses the habits and convictions attaching her to her household when Odysseus is lost at sea, the homecoming is hers as much as his. It is not a single event, but the beginning of the process by which she can, as Kass puts it, begin to reweave the loosened threads of home.

In another time and place, we might expect that Penelope would have sought relief from the ennui of her home life by setting out on a journey of her own—and perhaps she would have found it, *Eat, Pray, Love*-style. But she shows us that the salvation of Percy's castaway—the break from alienation—is available not just in escaping from everyday life but in finding a way to reclaim it. This struggle with home lies at the heart of the struggle with civilization in *Huck Finn* and *On the Road*. We seek the revelation of truth, beauty, and possibility in the world; and we seek to know our place in it. But often it seems that one can only come at the expense of the other: the regularity of home, where we find our attachments, blocks us from newness and possibility, obscuring our view of the revelatory.

Perhaps this opposition, too, is born of preexisting expectations, some other lingering Romantic influence that equates the revelatory with the aesthetic sublime. In contrast to that tradition, there is a school of art, exemplified by the late American painter Andrew Wyeth, whose subject is not the pristine but the ordinary, even the run-down, the ugly. Yet there is something remarkable and beautiful in Wyeth's depictions—a transfiguration of the ordinary. His works offer a window not into the point at which we escape the everyday and ascend into a more pure realm, but the point at which the quotidian opens up and, not *in spite of* but *through* itself, becomes something more. It requires the acceptance of frustration and inexcitement on the path to seeing it; but Wyeth shows us that it is there to see for those with the vision and the patience.

Take *Evening at Kuerners* (see facing page), a painting he made of the dingy farmhouse of his neighbor, set from across a small stream in the last light of day. The painting is drab, even bleak, but hauntingly beautiful. Contained in it is the suggestion of two elsewheres: the inside of the farmhouse, whose lonely inhabitance is suggested by a light in the window; and the unseen beyond, past the hill, suggested by the trees against the last light of a wintry gray sky. It hints that what we long to encounter by venturing elsewhere ultimately points back to what we yearn to find in the everyday, at home.

Percy's novel *The Moviegoer* (1961) describes such experiences, at home and abroad, as encounters with "the singularities of time and place." His protagonist recollects a childhood trip to Chicago:

> Not a single thing do I remember from the first trip but this: the sense of the place, the savor of the genie-soul of the place which every place has or else is not a place. . . . [O]ne step out into the brilliant March day and there it is as big as life, the genie-soul of the place which, wherever you go, you must meet and master first thing or be met and mastered.[61]

And later, when his uncle sends him back to the city on a business trip:

> Chicago. Misery misery son of a bitch of all miseries. Not in a thousand years could I explain it to Uncle Jules, but it is no small thing for me to make a trip, travel hundreds of miles across the country by night to a strange place and come out where there is a different smell in the air and people have a different way of sticking themselves into the world. It is a small thing to him but not to me. It is nothing to him to close his eyes in New Orleans and wake up in San Francisco and think the same thoughts on Telegraph Hill that he thought on Carondelet Street. Me, it is my fortune and misfortune to know how

Andrew Wyeth, *Evening at Kuerners* (1970)
Drybrush on paper. ©Andrew Wyeth. Private collection.

the spirit-presence of a strange place can enrich a man or rob a man but never leave him alone, how, if a man travels lightly to a hundred strange cities and cares nothing for the risk he takes, he may find himself No one and Nowhere.[62]

Places *beckon* us to experience them, and ourselves as through them. But our lives now seem headed towards being carried out on some other plane of existence: today, as a marketing analyst notes in the trade journal *Advertising Age*, young consumers are interested in digital technology that "allows [them] to transcend time and place."[63]

It is this aspiration that we find frustrated when we speak today of feeling "disconnected": we mean we are disconnected not from the place where we are standing, but from that realm of virtual transcendence, that place that is no place. Hence we want access to it wherever we go—we demand (and increasingly get) wireless connectivity even in places far and wild, at campgrounds and national parks and remote destinations. And yet at the same time we strangely speak of the thrill of "disconnecting for a while"—as if disconnecting is required for reconnecting.

If feeling "connected" for us means inhabiting the virtual realm, then what we most long to connect to is not what is in front of our eyes. When we speak of feeling "disconnected," then, we are confessing that we have become displaced: we are losing interest in and forgetting how to inhabit real places on their own. This displacement produces restlessness—but of a very different sort than the restlessness that motivates the traveler to go forward into the world. In fact, this restlessness is *opposed* to the traveler's impulse: it seeks its relief not in the real world but the virtual. It is not like what Percy's traveler to Chicago feels—for his anxiety is *of* the place, over who he might be there, whether he might emerge from it changed, and the risks of what that newness might mean. Rather, our anxiety is based in having begun to disengage from this realm of worldly possibilities, but finding ourselves still left with the task of being in the world.

It is tempting to believe that the trouble is simply that our digital technology has until recently been itself blind to place, and that consequently GPS and location awareness offer a way to reconnect with places. But this hope is belied by that peculiar habit of the user of GPS and location-awareness technology: he checks first with the device to find out where he is, and only second with the place in front of him to find out what *here* is. Consider the example of a hiker who is guided by GPS and a location-awareness app, and who enters a valley where his device has no reception. Will he suddenly feel alienated, as if his connection to the place has been lost? Or is it likelier that he will feel a nervousness that is actually a quizzical sense of excitement—the excitement of unknown risk and adventure, experiences that can be found now only at the fringes? Suddenly he is faced with the thrilling anxieties and possibilities of *being in place*. Location awareness, especially when it becomes augmented reality, enshrines the individual in a shell of fancy where he may distract himself from these anxieties—where he is free from them—but at the cost of what he is free for, of the freedom given to him as an earthly being to inhabit the world, and as a human being to forge his path through it.

If the adventures of Huck and Jim, and Sal and Dean, seem impossible under this new mode of travel, it is not just because they would be blocked from encountering places, but more fundamentally because they would be blocked from encountering themselves in those places. Just as our dogma about how to "really see a place" supposes that a place is some vital essence independent of us, the modern task of "finding yourself" supposes that we are some vital essence independent of the world. It directs us to seek after this essence in itself, obscuring from us the truth that *who we are* is bound up in *what we do*—not so much the work or entertainment we choose, but how we act and what we make of ourselves from what we are given. The "reposing of all hope" that Percy describes only partly lies in what may be presented to us around the bend; the rest lies in how we may act in response to what is presented, and who we may become.

How can the traveler sense these dual potentials when the most basic thing he can do in a place—explore it for himself, find his way through it—becomes so little an exploration of possibilities, of *realization* through them? The traveler may sense this gap, but the loss is liable to seem to the user not some consequence of a particular device he holds, escapable by leaving it at home, but an alteration of the world itself—a deflating sense that the optimal path through it has already been determined and recorded, the journey taken, the world emptied of anything new to see or do.

There was already a sense, in *Huck Finn* and *On the Road*, that something in the air was becoming so thick that it threatened to entrap the human spirit. This reached a frantic intensity for Kerouac, whose characters had to be almost constantly on the move, as if they might otherwise get stuck in place like bugs in amber. Today Sal and Dean could not move fast enough to escape what has congealed in the landscape before them. This is why, if Kerouac's work succeeded Twain's as the American fable of wayfaring, today there is no clear successor to Kerouac. There are a number of genres popular today that try to recapture the journeyer's spirit of discovery, but while earlier works could still depict an escape *within* civilization, today's travelers leave ordinary civilization altogether. Post-apocalyptic tales like Cormac McCarthy's *The Road*, along with the rising cult of zombie fiction, recapture a sense of newness of our world by depicting a disaster-stricken version of it (recalling Percy's recommendation). Science fiction lets us escape to other, new worlds (where even cowboy-style frontiers are available again, as in the short-lived TV series *Firefly*). And of course the hugely popular fantasy genres recapture a spirit of adventure and discovery—but only through fantasy.

A smaller subset of recent fiction relies on a much older setting for stories of discovery, the one Percy looked to in "The Message in the Bottle": the castaway who washes up on an island. The 2000 film *Cast Away* is a fine example, avoiding the phoniness of reality-TV competitions like *Survivor* by making its protagonist a genuine castaway, a wayfarer against his will. But like *Robinson Crusoe*, *Cast Away* is less about discovery than about the doldrums of survival. Another example, the television series *Lost*, eliminates the doldrums and focuses on the mysterious, filling its island with strange people and fantastical things, guaranteeing the stranded islanders (and their viewers) new discoveries around every bend. But *Lost* had to sustain its mystery by relying on the supernatural, and by setting the story on an island so remote as to be apparently impossible to locate by ordinary cartography. The fact that our tales now have to resort so fully to the strangeness of works like *Lost* and *The Road* to generate stories of discovery suggests that we feel unable to find them in our own thoroughly mapped world.

It is by now an old idea in futurology, originating with Alvin Toffler, that modern man exists in a state of constant shock at the changing landscape of the technological world—akin to "culture shock," but as ceaseless as the progress of technology.[64] But in reality, we quickly become accustomed and adjust ourselves to the technologies that ever more form the fabric of our interaction with the world—and so their novelty rapidly fades. And then we find our experience of moving through the world is not one of perpetual awe and wonderment, but of boredom and restlessness.

We seem likely only to continue to misunderstand the source of our disappointment—as some inherent shortcoming in the world, rather than a problem in how we place ourselves in it. And our demand will continue to be for it to perform better for us—or, since we cannot make it do that, to seek with ever greater insatiability after images to distract us from reality; rather, to "augment" it, to overlay it with the interestingness it seems to lack on its own. But in consuming these images, the traveler gives up all hope of escaping the plight of the tourist. The harder he seeks to contrive the experience for which he is searching, the further it slips from his grasp. For what the journeyer truly seeks is just that which cannot be contrived.

Place-Conscious Transportation Policy

GARY TOTH

In the America of the past half-century, the song of the open road is increasingly likely to have been sung on an interstate highway. Indeed, no aspect of the American transportation system is by now more fully entrenched, and yet also more lingeringly controversial and resented, than the Interstate Highway System. Transportation planner Gary Toth here argues that this enormous project, for all its virtues, epitomized a view of transportation policy that emphasized movement over destination, that prioritized roads and road-building over the well-being of the places to which those roads are taking us. He believes the time has come for transportation policy to be rethought, and to reverse some of those errors.

I STARTED WORKING at the New Jersey Department of Transportation (NJDOT) in 1973, right out of college, as a civil engineering trainee. For the first twenty years of my career as a transportation engineer, I bought into the prevailing ethos of the profession that the solution to congestion was to build more and bigger roads. The mission of transportation planning, we believed, was simply accommodating the demands of traffic, whether on local streets or on state and national highways. We felt we were not doing our jobs properly unless

48

enough lanes were added to ensure free-flowing traffic 24/7/365. The quality of life in communities and the condition of the environment were someone else's business; our job was to move cars and trucks as smoothly and rapidly as possible.

Gradually my faith in this "wider, straighter, faster" paradigm of traffic planning began to change. This occurred while I was in charge of a new unit at NJDOT that had been created to meet with communities, business owners, public agencies, and other community stakeholders to seek their support for various road projects. We were supposed to reduce community resistance, which was beginning to delay and even cancel projects. But as time went on, it became clear to me that the real point of transportation projects should be building successful communities and fostering economic prosperity.

HOW DID WE GET INTO THIS JAM?

Prior to the introduction of the automobile, the American conception of what constitutes a good road was vastly different than it is today. Serving the community and creating an efficient and livable pattern of development were central to the aims of street design. Transportation was fully integrated into land use planning.

The growing popularity of automobiles after 1910 created pressure for the federal government to become more directly involved in financing roads. Spurred on by cries of "Get farmers out of the mud," Congress passed the Federal Aid Road Act of 1916, which made continuous funding available for states to make road improvements.[1] Motorists and other organized interests began to apply intense pressure to build more highways. In the 1930s, many American officials visited the German Autobahn network and returned with a sense of urgency that we needed to create a national system of high-speed freeways. This ultimately led to federal legislation in 1944 to establish the Interstate Highway System and in 1956 to fund it, which ignited the great road-building era of the 1950s, 60s, and 70s.

Today, it is fashionable to vilify transportation planners for ignoring the negative effects of large-scale road-building on our communities. However, two men at the top of the transportation field during the years the Interstate Highway System was formed—Thomas H. MacDonald, chief of the federal Bureau of Public Roads, and his top aide, Herbert S. Fairbank—warned, in a 1944 report issued to President Roosevelt by the National Interregional Highway Committee, that thoughtless planning and improperly placed roads "will become more and more of an encumbrance to the city's functions and an all too durable reminder of planning that was bad."[2] They recognized that a shift of population to the suburbs was beginning to take a toll on cities.

Unfortunately, the federal government ignored MacDonald and Fairbank's vision of connecting highway development to a broader regional planning approach. As late as 1947, at the annual meeting of the American Association of State Highway Officials, MacDonald urged his colleagues to do whatever they could to reverse politicians' refusal to subsidize mass transportation. Repeatedly, however, Presidents Roosevelt, Truman, and Eisenhower, along with Congress, ignored these sensible recommendations for an integrated and balanced transportation network in the various federal highway bills that were enacted.

Starting in the 1950s, the transportation industry mobilized in an unprecedented way to deliver a mandate for a new generation of highways that would eliminate hassles and obstacles to the rapid flow of traffic. Planning in the United States became dominated by transportation engineers, while citizens, advocacy groups, and planners in other fields saw their influence decline. The transportation profession was remarkably successful in convincing two generations of politicians, developers, construction industries, special-interest groups, and the public about how things should be done. With blinders fully on, the transportation planners and the nation at large ignored mounting evidence of the unintended consequences of this huge road-building campaign.

EFFICIENCY FOR AUTOMOBILE TRAFFIC, AND ITS CONSEQUENCES

By the early 1990s, when the Interstate Highway System—one of the biggest construction projects in human history—was essentially completed, congestion in urban areas was still growing worse, and community opposition to new road projects was stronger than ever. Within the transportation profession, there was a dawning recognition that something was inherently wrong with the way we were thinking about and designing highways.

Not knowing any other way to operate, however, the transportation profession continued to plan new road projects in the same old way—using a formula that, though it may seem arbitrary now, had by then become standard: attempt to meet peak demand by ensuring the free flow of traffic up to the thirtieth-busiest hour of the year. When the inevitable resistance from affected communities arose, state departments of transportation found that invoking the "national interest"—which had worked so well to override community objections during the years of Interstate Highway construction—was no longer effective in pushing through the projects. By the 1990s, citizen opposition was able to bring many projects to a standstill.

Meanwhile, evidence was mounting that the wider, straighter, and faster approach was not solving the problem. The Texas Transportation Institute, in its Urban Mobility Reports, has shown that over the last two decades of the twentieth century, congestion indicators spiraled out of control; for instance, the 2005 report reveals that between 1982 and 2003 the average delay for every person using motorized travel during rush-hour traffic had tripled.[3]

This was occurring because of the way street and road networks were being planned. New highway capacity made spread-out development possible, which was creating congestion faster than transportation agencies could widen or replace failing highways. Furthermore, mass transit could not feasibly serve the sprawling suburbs, and street design made biking and walking all but impossible. All of these factors caused vehicle trips and vehicle miles to explode at a much faster rate than population growth. Transportation professionals and state departments of transportation watched these problems worsen, but stood aside and did nothing, believing that their job was building roads and that land-use planning was someone else's responsibility.

As a result, construction costs for adding new traffic capacity have been escalating sharply, at exactly the same time that our aging transportation infrastructure demands more attention. States are facing steep financial difficulties, exacerbated by the recent recession, and state legislators are loath to speak of raising taxes. Meanwhile, many roads and bridges built in the highway boom years between the 1940s and 1960s have aged to the point of needing major repairs or replacement, creating a towering backlog of fix-it-first projects. All of these factors make it far less likely that even the most determined state departments of transportation can build their way out of congestion.

As congestion has worsened in a transportation system focused on high-speed travel, so have other social problems. The ever-increasing vehicle miles traveled annually in the United States is closely connected to the major problems of energy and environmental policy. At the same time, our nation's public health indicators are taking a nosedive. The Centers for Disease Control and Prevention reports that, between 1960 and 2005, the obesity rate among American adults rose from 13 percent to 35 percent. Until about 1989, most states had an obesity rate below 10 percent, but by 2009, all but one state had an obesity rate over 20 percent, and nine states had an obesity rate above 30 percent.[4]

The CDC has emphasized the role of inactivity in this rapid deterioration of public health, and warns us that our increasing lack of fitness brings major health problems in addition to obesity: diabetes, cardiovascular disease, increased symptoms of depression and anxiety, and poorer development and maintenance of bones and muscles. While some still dispute our transportation system's role in this widening health crisis, studies linking sprawl and obesity are accumulating.

FRESH THINKING ABOUT PLACES AND PLANNING

Today, awareness of the problems with transportation planning is on the rise, attitudes are changing, and the time is ripe for rethinking our approach. There are several changes that can be implemented to improve the way we develop and get around to places:

1. *Target the "right" capital improvement projects.* The first step is to recognize that transportation decisions have a huge impact on community and land-use planning—and vice versa. Major investments in roads should be pursued only in communities and regions with effective land-use plans in place, which will protect the public investment in new highway capacity. With our nation struggling mightily to figure out how to raise funds for infrastructure, we can no longer afford to support land-use practices that consume new highway capacity long before the useful life of the investment. We must invest in ways that will permanently solve our transportation problems, not create new ones that we will then have to raise funds for in only a few years. Meanwhile, the transportation profession itself needs to accept that road projects carry significant social and environmental consequences. Transportation professionals need to heed Thomas MacDonald and Herbert Fairbank's advice from the 1930s, as described by Richard F. Weingroff in the magazine *Public Roads*: "Freeway location should be coordinated with housing and city planning authorities; railroad, bus, and truck interests; air transportation and airport officials; and any other agencies, groups, and interests that may affect the future shape of the city."[5]

2. *Make place-making and far-sighted land use planning central to transportation decisions.* Traffic planners and public officials need to foster land-use planning at the community level, which supports a state's transportation network rather than overloading it.

This includes creating more attractive *places*, in both existing developments and new ones, that people will want to visit. A strong sense of place benefits the overall transportation system. Great places—popular spots with a good mix of people and activities, which can be comfortably reached by foot, bike, and perhaps mass transit as well as cars—put little strain on the transportation system. In Burlington, Vermont, for instance, U.S. Route 7 successfully supports regional through traffic as two lanes in a residential setting, while just two miles south, multiple lanes fail every day due to a lack of thoughtful place-making. Cities like Denver, Charlotte, Portland, and even Los Angeles are now fostering development that provides citizens with choices on travel instead of forcing them onto overcrowded roads. Poor land-use planning, by contrast, generates thousands of unnecessary vehicle trips, creating dysfunctional roads, which further worsens the quality of the places. The locations cited in the 2010 Urban Mobility Report as having the most dramatic increases in congestion over the last two decades are largely those that grew after World War II—when the build-more-lanes ideology was dominant.[6]

3. *Shift away from single-use zoning.* We must begin to phase out planning regulations that treat schools, affordable housing, grocery stores, and shops as undesirable neighbors. The misguided logic of current zoning codes calls for locating amenities as far away from residential areas as possible. Locating essential commercial services along busy state and local highways creates needless traffic and forces local traffic to mix with commuting and regional traffic, thus choking the capacity of the road system. The emergence of form-based zoning codes (FBCs), which essentially remove government regulation of how property is used, allows the free market—instead of government planners in cubicles—to decide on land uses that work best for the community. Instead of imposing regulations on what can be built and where for decades to come, FBCs seek to influence only the

form of development so that it contributes to what the local market decides is important: building heights, parking locations, setbacks from the street, and so forth.

4. *Get more mileage out of our roads.* The nineteenth- and early-twentieth-century practice of creating connected road networks, still found in many beloved older neighborhoods, can help us beat twenty-first century congestion. Mile for mile, a finely woven, dense grid of connected streets has much more carrying capacity than a sparse, curvilinear tangle of unconnected cul-de-sacs, which forces all traffic out to the major highways. Unconnected street networks, endemic to post-World War II suburbs, do almost nothing to promote mobility.

5. *View streets themselves as places.* Streets take up a high percentage of a community's land—nearly a third of the area of parts of some cities. Yet, under planning policies of the past seventy years, people have given up their rights to this public property. While streets were once a place where children played and grownups stopped for conversation, they are now the exclusive domain of cars. Even the sidewalks along high-speed local streets and highways feel inhospitable. But there is a new movement to view streets in the broader context of communities. It's actually a rather simple idea: streets need to be designed in a way that induces traffic speeds appropriate for that particular context. High-speed travel should be left for freeways; the rest of our streets should be designed for speeds that allow businesses and residents to decide on what the market will support and where it will be supported.

6. *Spread transportation investment money around.* If we continue with the practice of chasing big engineering projects as our first choice in solving congestion, most communities will wait decades for a solution to their problems. The huge cost of adding lanes to

existing problem areas and building new roads will allow for only a few congestion hot spots to be fixed each year. In contrast, investments in transportation and land use that support choices on travel and shape development to keep our roads congestion-free will focus our limited funding on better uses. For instance, a scenario-planning study done for the Salt Lake City region in the late 1990s concluded that balanced investment and development would reduce infrastructure needs from $27 billion to $22 billion over two decades.[7] At the same time, congestion would be reduced, economic stimulus increased, and the rural life that Utah residents cherished would not be gobbled up by sprawl.

A NEW APPROACH TO TRANSPORTATION

In the post-World War II era, the transportation profession responded to a mandate from government officials to build a new generation of highways for public mobility and national defense. They should be commended for a job well done. But a new generation of solutions is needed for the twenty-first century, and this well-organized and well-trained profession should apply its talents to helping us adapt to these new realities. We need a new vision of transportation that truly improves our mobility, sustains our communities, protects our environment, and helps restore our physical fitness and health.

The transportation profession can no longer respond to mounting levels of congestion, nor to community and environmental dilemmas, by trying to widen existing roads or build new ones. New highways are now packed with cars almost as soon as they open. And today there is simply not the money available for that kind of large-scale road building. Most states cannot even keep up with the backlog of repair projects.

When I was at NJDOT, we came to realize that the 1950s were long past, and that we needed a new approach to meet the needs of our citizens. New Jerseyans lost their patience with top-down government decision-making. So we began collaborating with the public on solutions that took into account the whole context of communities being served by a particular road, creating an approach known as Context Sensitive Solutions.[8] Like most people, we initially believed that Americans were in love with the automobile and would demand that we continue to provide them with bigger, faster roads separated from shopping and neighborhoods. While we did find this response in some communities, we were surprised by how many more communities firmly supported better land use and community planning.

We Americans may always love our automobiles, but that does not mean we want to spend all day stuck inside them. Transportation systems that afford Americans the option of getting to places without using their cars actually offer more freedom than those that keep people solely dependent on the automobile to get anywhere. And more flexible systems will lighten the fiscal burden on taxpayers, since it will be less necessary for government to raise revenue to help the less fortunate get around. People understand this, and can see that a transportation network that caters exclusively to cars has harmed our communities, compromised our health, fueled the environmental crisis, and made us dependent on foreign oil.

Some critics of this new approach to transportation investment might feel it is too centralized and technocratic. But there is nothing un-American about planning communities as a whole, or acknowledging that roads are just one of the elements that create a livable place. Place-based processes are profoundly democratic: they call for full engagement of citizens and businesses in communities to determine their own future and then inform government of the type of transportation investment that best suits them. In contrast, has there ever been a more top-down approach than that used by transportation agencies over the latter half of the twentieth century? While at the New Jersey Department of Transportation for thirty-four years, I watched community after community, property owner after property owner, feel powerless and helpless as we made decisions that affected their property rights.

A place-based approach to transportation policy is in keeping with America's best traditions. Indeed, a common-sense understanding of place guided the design of our communities until at least 1920. While pre-twentieth-century community planners were by no means perfect, they did create places where transportation was integrated into broader public aims. The roads and bridges in these areas were built to foster economic development and quality of life in the community, not to hamper it.

If we are to embrace the concept of economically sustainable, healthy, and livable communities that serve a diverse population and provide options for mobility, then we must integrate our transportation planning with our larger goals, and we must design our roads for all users. We must allow the people of America to have more say on how their places are shaped. To do so, we can draw on the wisdom of our past to build communities that will flourish well into the future.

"I Can't Believe You're from L.A.!"

DANA GIOIA

One of the obstacles to thinking more clearly about place is our ten-dency to clothe the concept in rigidly idealized or prescriptive forms, as if a locale is only fully a "place" if it has the coherence and order of a Siena, Italy, or the settledness of a New England town. By this standard, a place like Southern California, with its legendary mobility, sprawl, and diversity, is deemed to be less than a "place," and is turned into the butt of countless jokes. But such thinking is as short-sighted as it is shallow. Places are most fully themselves when they serve as a nexus for vibrant human activity, and as poet Dana Gioia argued in the follow-ing address from 2011, by that standard, and if one looks at the evidence, Los Angeles is, and long has been, most emphatically a place like none other on earth: creative, growing, decentralized, fascinatingly contra-dictory, a dynamic model of the future with an impressive past.

I AM SIXTY YEARS OLD, and, by happy coincidence for our topic today, I have spent exactly half of my life in California and half of it elsewhere—in New York, Washington, Boston, Rome, and Vienna. I was born and raised in California, specifically in southwest Los Angeles County in the town of Hawthorne. For many years I lived in Northern California, and this fall I shall return from Washington, D.C.

to teach at the University of Southern California. I plan to stay here permanently. So I speak to you as a native son and cultural product of a city whose only cultural advantage, according to Woody Allen, "is being able to make a right turn on a red light."[1]

Such abuse bothers me not at all. I am used to it. Wherever I've gone over the years, I've always identified myself as a Californian and an Angeleno, which I assure you is an excellent conversation opener in artistic and intellectual circles. *Everyone* has an opinion about L.A., especially in New York City and Cambridge, Massachusetts. If you ask people about Moscow or Beijing, London or Toronto, you will probably get a brief and perfunctory response. But everybody's opinion of L.A. is detailed and emphatic. Significantly, one encounters such responses even in foreign countries, because the world has been saturated with images of L.A. from TV and movies. The City of the Angels has been—for almost a century now—a cultural symbol.

If I were to summarize the thousands of opinions I've heard over the years, I could say they fall mostly into five predictable categories. (The quotations are my own paraphrases unless otherwise noted.)

1. *Los Angeles isn't really a city, just sprawling suburbs connected by freeways.* You know the clichés. "It has no downtown." "It has no character." "There's no 'there' there." The town is "nineteen suburbs in search of a metropolis," or, as H. L. Mencken harrumphed, it is "inconceivably shoddy."[2]

2. *Los Angeles is a city of transients.* "No one was born here." "People come to L.A. to pursue their dreams." "No one feels a sense of belonging." "Everything is new, and nothing is built to last." "There is no local character except delusional expectations of sunshine, wealth, and stardom." In the words of a Bertolt Brecht poem that his fellow German exile Hanns Eisler set to music, "Paradise and hell can be the same city."[3]

3. *Los Angeles is shallow and inauthentic.* "All surface, no depth." "Surfers and starlets gliding over the surface of life." "Like a Holly-

wood set, a bright façade, with nothing behind the surface." "The two symbols of L.A. are Disneyland and Hollywood." As the radio comedian Fred Allen said about Southern California, "It's a great place to live—if you're an orange."

4. *Los Angeles is the center of bland, suburban, consumerist culture.* "The worst of materialism combined with credulous faddism." "It lacks the depth of older cities and deeper culture or tradition." "What passes for culture is driven by food and novelty—yoga, transcendental meditation, vegetarianism." As a forgotten journalist of the 1930s described the City of Angels—"that big, sprawling, incoherent, shapeless, slobbering civic idiot in the family of American communities."[4]

5. *Los Angeles has no artistic culture except showbiz, no intellectual life.* "No art, only entertainment as a commodity." "Commercial Hollywood has devoured all the other arts." "It is the land of make-believe." "Everything is surface and show." As F. Scott Fitzgerald said about Hollywood, "It's a mining town in lotus land."[5]

I will address these points shortly, but first let me share a little more of my background, because understanding any place depends on your perspective. Are you looking at it from the inside or the outside? Do you perceive it as home or a stopover?

It is no coincidence that many of the most famous books about Los Angeles were written by visitors and transients. Most of those authors arrived in L.A. looking for paying work in Hollywood, and many quickly left. The souvenirs of their visits include Evelyn Waugh's *The Loved One*, Nathanael West's *Day of the Locust*, F. Scott Fitzgerald's *The Last Tycoon*, Horace McCoy's *They Shoot Horses, Don't They?*, Bertolt Brecht's "Hollywood Elegies," and Alison Lurie's *Nowhere City*. But not everyone in L.A. is just passing through. A couple million of us were born here.

Let me begin with just one native son's story—my own. I was born and raised, as I mentioned, in Hawthorne, a city you all have seen in such movies as Quentin Tarantino's *Pulp Fiction* and *Jackie Brown*. The Beach Boys were born there. Marilyn Monroe went to school there (with my mother). Jim Thorpe, "the All-American," died there. Hawthorne was and remains a poor, rough, ugly town. When I was young, it was populated mostly by Mexicans and Dust Bowl Okies, with a sprinkling of Irish, Italians, and Cubans—all fleeing poverty, politics, and fate. My mother, a mestizo, was born in Hawthorne in 1929. My dad, a Sicilian, had come from Detroit during the Depression in 1932.

My Los Angeles was not Hollywood. It was working-class, highly traditional, family-oriented, very Latin, and mostly Catholic. It was also culturally rich and complex. Like Vladimir Nabokov, I had a happy, normal trilingual childhood—English at home and school, Italian in my larger family, Latin at church in those last pre-Vatican II days. So I knew, as a matter of course, the languages of the New World, the Old World, and the Next World. I also heard Spanish every day on the street and in the homes of friends. I went to twelve years of Catholic schools. In church we sang from Latin hymnals written by St. Thomas Aquinas. In second grade, I began piano lessons with one of the Sisters of Providence. Sister Camille Cecile started me with Bartók's music for children and eventually moved me through Mozart, Beethoven, and Schubert.

So there was—and is—an L.A. culture that has nothing to do with Hollywood, a local culture casual visitors miss. I later went to school in Gardena, which was then a city where half the population was Japanese and had as many Buddhist temples as mainstream Protestant churches. My high school was run by Marianists, a French Catholic order, which consisted of mostly Chinese, Hawaiian, Italian, German, and Mexican priests and brothers.

My friends and I would go to Hollywood, Westwood, or downtown L.A. for classical music, movies, art exhibits, operas, and rock concerts. At classical performances, especially of contemporary works, we heard audience members speaking German, reflecting the migration of German and Jewish artists, intellectuals, and scientists who had fled the Third Reich. To paraphrase the poet Charles Simic, Hitler was their travel agent.[6] They found refuge in L.A. and they stayed.

We took it for granted that a huge number of the people whose work we read, watched, or listened to lived in L.A., or once lived in L.A. To list only a few more "local" artists, writers, and musicians, we knew about Igor Stravinsky, Aldous Huxley, Fritz Lang, Billy Wilder, Jascha Heifetz, Alfred Hitchcock, Lotte Lehmann, Miklós Rózsa, Christopher Isherwood, Thomas Mann, Richard Neutra, Arnold Schoenberg, David Hockney, and Joni Mitchell. Having grown up among immigrants from Italy and Mexico, I felt absolutely at home hearing non-native speakers like Stravinsky and Lang present their work. They were just like my family, where most adults had a foreign accent.

Then there were the American writers: Ray Bradbury, Raymond Chandler, Ross Macdonald, Harlan Ellison, Robert Heinlein, Will and Ariel Durant, Joan Didion, Anita Loos, Chester Himes, M. F. K. Fisher, Charles Bukowski, John Fante, Richard Matheson, Budd Schulberg, Dalton Trumbo, and Theodore Geisel, A.K.A. Dr. Seuss. (We didn't know that the secretive Thomas Pynchon was writing *Gravity's Rainbow* in the nearby city of Manhattan Beach, but we had read *V.* and *The Crying of Lot 49*.)

Many of these writers were not respectable in Eastern literary circles. They were popular authors, writing science fiction and detective novels. Or more precisely, they were innovative authors, transforming these new genres into major literary forms. Whether you liked it or not, Los Angeles was vibrantly alive, rudely inventive, and ecstatically productive. One saw communities created or transformed at a rate unthinkable elsewhere, and imagination took flight without the restraints of established tastemakers. Was it any wonder that the tastemakers elsewhere didn't like it, whatever the "it" was: movies, television, animation, science fiction, detective fiction, vernacular architecture, cool jazz, radio evangelism, pornography, space travel, transcendental meditation, yoga, weight training, health food, or surfing?

L.A. was also in the midst of the West Coast jazz movement. At local clubs like the Lighthouse, Bird in a Basket, or the Chicken Shack, you could hear Charles Mingus, Art Pepper, Chet Baker, Zoot Sims, Hampton Hawes, Dexter Gordon, Shelly Manne, Shorty Rogers, Art

Farmer, Chico Hamilton, Dave Brubeck, Eric Dolphy, and Stan Getz. These Californians were the best-selling jazz artists of the era, though they too were dismissed by New York critics. At least the local scientists got respect—especially from Stockholm. Cal Tech alone had dozens of great figures on the faculty—Richard Feynman, Murray Gell-Mann, Linus Pauling, Robert Millikan, and—it seems inevitable this physicist and seismologist would work in L.A.—Charles Richter.

So it struck me as odd to me a few years later up at Stanford to hear that L.A. was a cultural wasteland. After all, it didn't have an opera company, and Tony Bennett never sang a hit ballad about it. The smug San Francisco attitude was summarized by the popular columnist Herb Caen, once a true cult figure in the Bay Area, who sneered, "Isn't it nice that people who prefer Los Angeles to San Francisco, live there?"

The preference for L.A. didn't seem so bad to me, when these "people" included Stravinsky, Huxley, Bradbury, Hockney, Heifetz, and Hitchcock. Sophisticated San Francisco was the older brother in West Coast sibling rivalry—never mind that L.A. is actually seven decades older—with all the accompanying overlays of history and culture. But in the 1970s it was already clear to Angelenos that San Francisco had fallen behind L.A. in cultural innovation and energy. Beautiful San Francisco had a cultural hierarchy, magnificent architecture, and rich traditions. All L.A. had was enough rude energy and unbridled creativity to change world culture.

Historical origins aside, L.A. was then—and perhaps still is—a young city. Consider the following statistics. In 1900, the population was 102,000; today it is 3.8 million.[7] The Metro area was probably no larger than 200,000 in 1900; now the Southland numbers nearly 18 million souls.[8] (Yes, Angelenos have souls.) During the twentieth century the population of the city increased thirty-six-fold. Los Angeles is now the third-richest city in the world after Tokyo and New York,[9] the second-largest city in the United States,[10] and, of course, the world center for entertainment. It is also the largest Catholic diocese in North America,[11] and is reportedly the biggest book market in the United States.

New Angelenos have come from everywhere, even from within the United States during the initial growth spurt (especially Iowa and Nebraska), and then from the Dust Bowl in the 1930s. But also from Germany, Mexico, the Philippines, Korea, Japan, England, Ireland, Canada, China, and Cuba.

The first European to visit the area that would become Los Angeles was Juan Rodriguez Cabrillo, a Portuguese sea captain working for Spain, who in 1542 found it peopled by Chumash and Tongva Indians (two entirely different tribes and language groups). Cabrillo claimed it for Spain and immediately moved on—simultaneously becoming both L.A.'s first recorded Latino and its first transient. The city itself didn't really start until Father Junipero Serra, a Catalan from Majorca, directed the creation of the San Gabriel Mission in 1771.

In 1781 the town was moved down the San Gabriel Valley, to what is now downtown L.A. The original settlers were Latino, mestizo, and mulatto—drawn from the Americas, Africa, and Europe. Los Angeles has been multicultural since the beginning, and the races have widely intermarried (a social pattern typical of Catholic areas like New Orleans, rather than Protestant ones like the South). This cultural feature has made the city difficult to understand for Easterners and Southerners, who have historically seen U.S. history in terms of Anglo-Saxon Protestant culture and race relations as rigidly black and white.

Los Angeles was a primarily Hispanic city, which briefly became a primarily white city, and is now becoming an entirely mixed city (of Latinos, whites, Asians, and African Americans), which has no majority race.[12] I expect that by mid-century the majority will be mixed-race—like me, an Italian, Mexican, and American Indian, married to a woman who is German and Russian.

This is only one way in which L.A. represents the urban landscape of the future. New Yorkers, as we've seen, often complain that L.A. lacks a downtown. This, of course, isn't true. But it raises the question: what is downtown? Where is Rome's downtown? Where is London's downtown? One even wonders if New York has a specific downtown. If so, where is it? Midtown, Wall Street, Central Park, Times Square?

Isn't New York also a collection of neighborhoods—some high rise, some not—with no single center? Great cities mostly sprawl.

These canards also mischaracterize L.A., the urban areas of which have a population density comparable to New York City.[13] What these critics generally lack the vocabulary to articulate is how L.A.'s urban design is different from that of older Eastern cities—and not simply the design, or the architecture, but the folkways of the population in perhaps the first automotive megalopolis. The British historian Jan Morris described L.A. as "a complex merger of separate settlements."[14] In this sense L.A. resembles London, where dozens of separate cities, villages, and royal properties were slowly blended together by population growth.

In L.A.'s case, these separate settlements tended not to be shaped as squares, but took the form of spokes in a wheel. The true neighborhoods of L.A. are long linear spokes built along the major boulevards. For example, Sunset, Hollywood, and Wilshire run roughly parallel, as do Fairfax, La Cienega, and Central, but each street unfolds as a different world. To a great extent, L.A. is the first city designed—mostly unintentionally, of course—to be experienced by car and not by foot. There are large areas of high-rise development, but most of the city consists of dense, low-rise buildings, once again rather like London. As Quentin Crisp observed, "Los Angeles is New York lying down."[15]

Perhaps to outsiders Los Angeles culture is a bit like digital culture: If you didn't grow up in it, it's hard to understand how it works. New paradigms seem threatening to outsiders. Digital natives and L.A. natives share a contrarian view about how the world might work: less centralized, more populist, more innovative, less bound by the past, and more optimistic. The traditional alternatives have advantages, but the natives (digital or Angeleno) have little interest in moving either back to print culture or back East. When Angelenos talk of moving, it usually isn't to another city, but to the country. L.A. is their urban ideal.

The Los Angeles attitude reminds me of an old joke about American newspapers and their readers: The *Wall Street Journal* is read by the people who run the country. The *Washington Post* is read by the people who think they run the country. The *New York Times* is read by people who think they should run the country and are very good at crossword puzzles. The *Boston Globe* is read by people whose parents used to run the country and did a fine job of it, thank you very much. The *Miami Herald* is read by people who are running another country, but need the baseball scores. The *San Francisco Chronicle* is read by people who aren't sure if there is a country or that anyone is running it. And the *Los Angeles Times* is read by people who wouldn't mind running the country—if they could find the time—and if they didn't have to leave Southern California to do it.

In the twenty-first century, it is absurd to view Los Angeles as a failed attempt to create a nineteenth-century city, like San Francisco or New York. L.A. is entirely and unabashedly itself—one of the paradigms of contemporary urban existence. For better and for worse, L.A. created the most influential model for a new contemporary city. So it is silly to describe what L.A. isn't. We need instead to understand what it actually is. What is L.A.'s reality? I would suggest eight answers:

1. *L.A. is a creative city, not a critical city.* New York remains the undisputed adjudicator of American cultural reputations. There are more dance reviewers, opera critics, fiction editors, visual-arts writers, and prize committees in New York City than the rest of the United States combined. L.A. barely supports a handful of critics for traditional high culture. It doesn't adjudicate taste; it creates it. Let New York write the reviews and give the prizes. Los Angeles creates the popular culture the world loves.

2. *L.A. is an international city.* It looks outward, it looks abroad—rather than back East—to define itself. L.A. pays more attention to Asia, Europe, and Latin America than to the Northeast. It is a world center, not a subsidiary of New York or Washington.

3. *L.A. is a new city.* It is less concerned with the past, and utterly obsessed with the future. Los Angeles has not only invented new arts and industries; it has invented itself as a post-modern city—

not simply for architecture and city planning but also for the arts and culture.

4. *L.A. is a growing city.* It exists in a perpetual state of reorganization. Everything is open to change. Rebuilding is characteristic, of course, of all cities, but few do it as habitually as L.A. This tendency shows a horrifying disregard for the past, but it also displays a huge optimism for the future.

5. *L.A. is a populist city.* It sees no distinction between high and low culture. It distrusts traditional distinctions made elsewhere. It assimilates cultures and peoples in transformative ways. Most of its great artists have worked in what then seemed like disreputable popular media—movies, jazz, detective fiction, science fiction, rock.

6. *L.A. is a decentralized city.* It lacks central planning at all levels. It emerges from the bottom up, rather than the top down. This creates confusion, but also makes it innovative, democratic, and mobile.

7. *L.A. is a contradictory city.* It is both secular and religious, materialistic and spiritual, traditional and avant-garde—with banks and churches, yoga studios and liquor stores, restaurants and weight loss centers facing one another across the streets.

8. *Finally, L.A. is attractive as a viable, contemporary cultural model.* The town is so disorganized, anarchic, and open that it isn't an intimidating model for other growing cities to emulate. L.A. is dense, creative, inclusive, mobile, and mercurial.

My L.A. offers the best of European, Latino, Indian, African American, Asian, and North American culture, in which everything from Hollywood to the Vatican, Buddha to the Beach Boys has its place.

Some people don't like Disneyland or David Hockney, West Coast jazz or sci-fi movies. But you take Norman Mailer. I'll keep Raymond

Chandler. He's more fun, and has a longer shelf life. I agree with Randy Newman—"I love L.A."[16] I'm happy to live in a city capable of inventing both the French dip and the nacho, the skate board and the space shuttle, cool jazz and film noir. The town may be a bit crazy, but it's my kind of crazy. Is it any wonder I'm glad to be home?

Cosmopolitanism and Place

RUSSELL JACOBY

Any advocate for the importance of place soon comes up against the ideal of cosmopolitanism, a philosophy that puts aside narrow particularisms and ethnic or national rivalries, and instead identifies with the needs and outlooks of all humankind. From that perspective, why shouldn't the appeal to place-consciousness be regarded as little more than narrow provincialism? Historian Russell Jacoby suggests one reason why the answer to that question may be more complicated than it seems, and cosmopolitanism should be seen as "both a promise and a danger." Borrowing from the insights of René Girard, Jacoby posits that the great leveling induced by globalization, far from leading inexorably toward a more peaceful world, may have the opposite effect, producing rivalrous anger and resentment rather than harmony. In this view, the cultural distinctions embodied in place and local identity may serve as essential stays against the anxiety of a dangerously fluid world.

THE LITERATURE ON cosmopolitanism is daunting. What can be added to it that has not been said before? Perhaps it is possible to start at its beginning with a reminder that cosmopolitanism once challenged convention and conformity. The idea of cosmopolitanism—or at least the word—is usually traced to the Greek Cynic Diogenes, who when asked where he came from, supposedly answered, "I am a citizen of the world."[1] Little is known of Diogenes that is reliable, but he first came to public attention as a delinquent; he was banished for defacing state coinage. Diogenes was a troublemaker.

He was also a fanatic about equality. When Alexander the Great stood before him and said, "Ask of me any boon you like," Diogenes replied, more or less: Move, you are blocking the light.[2] A later Greek philosopher, Maximus of Tyre, writing in the second century, described him this way:

> He divested himself of all calamitous circumstances, liberated himself from his fetters, and traveled round the earth without restraint, like a bird endued with intellect, fearing no tyrant, compelled by no law, employed by no polity, neither oppressed by the education of children, nor suffering restraint through wedlock, nor detained by agriculture, nor disturbed by military affairs. . . . He, indeed, lived the life of a fearless and free king.[3]

His relationship to cities and civilization seems complicated at best; on one hand Diogenes derided artifice; on the other hand he dwelled in the city and praised its laws.[4] The point is relevant inasmuch as it suggests a contradiction—but perhaps also a solution—to lax ideas about the cosmopolitan. An individual may travel lightly with few commitments to place—but such a person also needs a home base. The world citizen needs to be rooted in the city he sometimes disdains. If Diogenes were the first cosmopolitan, it is good to keep in mind that he was difficult, cantankerous, and perhaps dangerous. To be a cosmopolitan means setting oneself against certain local beliefs and mores—to become, perhaps, an outsider or a permanent stranger.

In fact, the idea of the permanent stranger has been offered as the key to modern cosmopolitanism. Yuri Slezkine in his book *The Jewish Century* (2004) argues that the Jews were the iconic modern people, the cosmopolitans. They were permanent strangers and could operate in various countries and cultures. In the modern age this enabled them to become successful. They could settle anywhere. "Modernization is about everyone becoming urban, mobile, literate, articulate, intellectually intricate, physically fastidious, and occupationally flexible. . . . It is about transforming peasants and princes into merchants and priests, replacing inherited privilege with acquired prestige. . . . Modernization, in other words, is about everyone become Jewish."[5]

There is hyperbole here, but the point can be conceded. Modernization requires cosmopolitanism. To this paean of cosmopolitanism, one might add more philosophical blessings such as found in Kwame Anthony Appiah's book on the subject. He writes in *Cosmopolitanism* (2005) that there are "two strands" in cosmopolitanism: one is that we have obligations towards others who are not related to us, the other is that we take seriously the value of particular human lives. "People are different, the cosmopolitan knows, and there is much to learn from our differences." He notes that the two ideals—"universal concern and respect for legitimate difference"—can conflict, in which case cosmopolitanism becomes a "challenge."[6] While Appiah acknowledges "challenges," his book is largely an appreciative meditation on the virtues of cosmopolitanism.

He is hardly alone. It is easy to multiply references, where philosophers, sociologists, political scientists and others happily characterize and endorse cosmopolitanism as a type of worldly multiculturalism. These approaches are not wrong, but usually drown in truisms and academic argot. For instance, one sociologist defines cosmopolitanism thusly: "Cosmopolitanism involves inter-cultural openness on a transnational stage."[7] Who could be against "inter-cultural openness?" Or in a typically jargon-laced essay, an anthropologist declares that "critical and dialogic cosmopolitanism as a regulative principle demands yielding generously . . . toward diversity as a universal and cosmopolitan project in which everyone participates instead of 'being participated.'"[8]

These formulations typically sidestep the dark or difficult dimension of cosmopolitanism where it is less a blessing than a threat. If as Slezkine argues, Judaism and cosmopolitanism are linked—so is the reverse, as it were. Cosmopolitanism has frequently provoked a response, which has long been linked with anti-Semitism. Stalinists used the term "rootless cosmopolitan" to denounce individuals, mainly Jews, whom they charged were spies with no loyalty to the mother country. A 1949 Soviet denunciation of cosmopolitanism is worth studying. "What is cosmopolitanism?" it asked. "Cosmopolitanism is a denial of peculiarities formed in the course of history in the development of peoples, a denial of national interests, of national independence, and of the state sovereignty of peoples."[9] This Soviet condemnation damned cosmopolitanism as a cover for imperialist and American interests:

> The propaganda of cosmopolitanism serves as a screen for the unbridled activity of the most reactionary forces of Anglo-American imperialism. It is their ideological weapon, with the help of which they are trying to weaken the people's will to defend their national sovereignty. It is not without reason that cosmopolitanism is extolled by all the minions of American imperialism, who grovel before the 'almighty' dollar.[10]

The Stalinist philosophers declare that "it is the primary duty of our cadres of philosophers to be active in fighting to expose fully this cosmopolitan scum."[11]

The Soviet attack on cosmopolitanism evidently cannot be accepted. Yet it can remind us that cosmopolitanism is not just an ideal or an ethic about how to treat strangers; it is inextricably wound up with the reality of globalization—and perhaps economic domination. It is sometimes a promise, but also a threat. Again scholars only make glancing acknowledgments of this reality. They sometimes talk about "cosmopolitanism from below," which suggests the economic forces of globalization that affects struggling populations.[12] Others pursue the pastime of broaching different ways that cosmopolitanism can be theorized—hybridity, particularities, multiculturalism, and so on. But these concepts address the cosmopolitanism of the international traveler or academic, who jets about the world and ponders global differences. Since these are thoughtful scholars, they also recognize the threat or damage of cosmopolitanism, but this recognition is an afterthought, not a central topic to investigate.

In the same vein scholars write endless studies on how diverse groups adapt to global cultural happenings. "Cosmopolitan Malayness operates at all levels of society both in Malay and in a much broader 'transnational' Malay World—a space across which merchants, entrepreneurs and religious reformers continue to travel," writes one anthropologist who studies Malaysia.[13] Another anthropologist studying Indian steel workers comes to the bold conclusion that "what I have tried to suggest . . . is that different segments of the Bhilai 'working class' are markedly different in the degree to which they are cosmopolitan in outlook."[14] Yet these studies rarely confront the destructive dimensions of a global cosmopolitanism; they give short shrift to those who are pushed out of work by the refiguring of the global economy—by outsourcing and such—or who are pushed from one nation to another in search of work. These populations unwillingly register a form of cosmopolitanism (or globalization) in their lives. They do not reflect upon cosmopolitanism; they suffer from it.

This economic and forced cosmopolitanism often brings in its wake a cultural homogenization. Nike and baseball hats, iPods and iPads conquer the world. A thousand, perhaps ten thousand, scholars have argued about the reality of a global culture, and probably most object to terms such as homogenization. If youths from Brazil to Bahrain wear baseball hats and go to McDonald's, so what? McDonald's serves wine in France and prohibits beef in India. That is, diverse local mores undermine and fundamentally alter a single global culture.

Appiah has offered a recent statement of this in his *Cosmopolitanism*. He tells us "that the research supports" the notion that how "people respond" to American television programs "depends on their existing cultural context."[15] He cites a media scholar who interviews students from South Africa, and found that one, Sipho, who followed the American soap opera *Days of Our Lives*, drew lessons relevant to his own life. This happens throughout the world, according to Appiah.[16] "Talk of cultural imperialism structuring the consciousnesses of those in the periphery treats Sipho and people like him as *tabulae rasae* on which global capitalism's moving finger writes its message, leaving behind another homogenized consumer as it moves on. It is deeply condescending. And it isn't true."[17]

Perhaps, but Sipho may not be the proof. This may be a contemporary form of myopic progressivism—negative thoughts are chased away and only what is close is seen. Academics, like everyone else, prefer to study trees rather than forests. One Sipho refutes world forces. Of course, global cultural trends are tempered by local situations—this is obvious—but tempered, not annulled or negated. Why is it condescending to see this? Is it condescending to say that poverty makes people poor and that is not good for their health? The reluctance to admit that they lack the resources for unfolding their lives reveals a fetish of "agency," which is often paraded. Presumably people are always agents of their own fate. To suggest otherwise is supposedly insulting. In any event it is not a case of either/or. The global culture extends its reach and depth everywhere and, of course, is mediated by local situations. But "mediated" does not spell annulled.

THE THREAT OF ASSIMILATION

To what extent does economic and social globalization undermine local identities? As people become more alike, they may feel more threatened. Individuals do not always want to feel alike; sometimes they long to be different. René Girard, the literary critic, can help us fathom this issue. He can help unpack what appears to be a paradox: as people become more alike they do not necessarily become more peaceful, but the opposite—more antagonistic.

For Girard, likeness is the problem, not the solution. He dubs the belief that discord stems from differences a prejudice, a fashionable and false intellectual attitude. He cites an anthropologist who gives the conventional interpretation with its usual jargon that conflict emerges from palpable differences within a group. Structural differentiation, both vertical and horizontal, writes this anthropologist, is the foundation of strife and factionalism. But for Girard, the testimony of literature and anthropology demonstrates the opposite. It is not differences that give rise to conflict, but similarity. In human relationships words like *sameness* and *similarity* evoke an image of harmony. If we have the same tastes, surely we are bound to get along. But what happens when we share the same desires?

For Girard, a single principle pervades religion and literature: "Order, peace, and fecundity depend on cultural distinctions; it is not these distinctions but the loss of them that gives birth to fierce rivalries and sets members of the same family or social group at one another's throats."[18]

Brothers and twins—as a special case—become prime examples for Girard. While brothers share a great deal—the same mother, father, gender—twins share more. Twins are in a sense reinforced brothers whose final objective difference, that of age, has been removed. Girard reverses the traditional attitude about fraternity: we instinctively regard the fraternal relationship as an affectionate one. However, the record is clear from history and literature. The theme of enemy brothers dominates, from Cain and Abel down through Richard the Lionhearted and John Lackland and beyond. It is not only in myth that brothers are simultaneously drawn together and driven apart by something they both desire, a throne, a woman or in more general terms, a paternal heritage.[19]

For Girard fraternal strife dwells at the center of life and literature. Sibling rivalry, in turn, derives from mimetic desire. This is a critical concept; for Girard, desire itself tends to be mimetic (that is, imitative). As individuals, our desires unfold by imitating the desires of those around us. We live and grow by copying not only what people do but what they want. We emulate their language, their gestures, but also their desires. The mimetic aspects of desire, Girard writes in *Violence and the Sacred* (1972), "must correspond to a primary impulse of most living creatures."[20] Herein lies the problem, however. The mimetic impulse engenders rivalry, especially in a universe of limited resources, or where only one-of-a-kind exists: one kingdom or one special mate. If you and I desire the same thing, as we inevitably do, discord arises.

The conflictual implications of mimesis, Girard believes, have always been misunderstood. Freud got much wrong. The son does not desire the mother; he imitates his father and desires what his father desires. Oedipus is essentially the rival of the father, first elbowed out, then victorious. The father and son both desire the throne and wife. Mimesis harbors strife. Mimesis coupled with desire leads automatically to conflict.[21]

Girard is frequently obscure, but his work as a whole functions as a tonic. In challenging the fetish of opposites, he declares that not only is it misleading to believe that opposites give rise to conflict but that the reverse is true, that is, as opposites recede, tensions advance. Too much likeness threatens people. Brothers harbor violence toward each other; they are too close. The stuff that sets people apart—their identifying marks—reflects historical realities. The identities endure only to the extent that their historical foundation endures; and the identities alter as those historical realities alter.

What does this mean in a gritty reality? Girard seldom situates his ideas in a political framework, but this should not prevent us from doing so. In the modern era, the structures that sustain differences and identification generally shift in one direction; they undercut those identifying differences. To repeat Girard's key insight: "Order, peace, and fecundity depend on cultural distinctions.... It is not these differences but the loss of them that gives rise to violence and chaos.... This loss forces men into a perpetual confrontation."[22]

This loss, however, is the story of the modern world, a proposition Girard does not express. People forced into the thrall of industrialization emerge more and more alike. They get stripped of their unique markings. For instance, many groups uphold their identity by virtue of their own language, yet the forces of modernization—schooling, employment, communication—undermine the existence of small language communities. The speakers lack the numbers or the economic clout to maintain their language. This is true of languages spoken by indigenous peoples of the Americas as well as of languages such as Yiddish, once spoken by millions of East European Jews. The languages lose their function in a world economy and vanish or survive only in the laboratories of scholars. *Peasants into Frenchmen* runs the title of a classic book on modernization in France, which partly concerns the victory of the French language over regional dialects once spoken by rural inhabitants outside Paris.[23]

The Girardian insight here gains its force. Likeness does not necessarily lead to harmony. It may elicit jealousy and anger. Inasmuch as identity rests on what makes an individual unique, similitude threatens the self. The double evokes fear. The mechanism also operates on a social terrain. As cultural groupings get absorbed into larger or stronger collectives, they become more anxious and more prone to defend the dwindling identity. The French Canadians amid an ocean of English-speakers are more testy about their language than the French of France. Language is, however, just one feature of cultural identification.

Assimilation becomes a threat, not a promise. It spells homogenization, not diversity. The assimilated express bitterness as they register the loss of an identity they want to retain. Their ambivalence transforms their anger into resentment. They desire what they reject and are upset with themselves as well. The resentment feeds the protest and sometimes the violence. To draw on a philosophical truism, appearance and essence diverge. The identity that feels threatened by surrendering its distinct qualities—rears up as strong. It *appears* robust and aggressive because it *is* weak and vulnerable. In the same way as we might say of an all-consuming egoist that he or she suffers from a weak ego, we could say of the aggressive in-your-face identity that it suffers from a threatened identity. In the current world, the forces of globalization or Americanization—the danger of becoming like everyone else—imperils the self-identity of many societies.

GLOBAL CIVILIZATION AT WAR WITH ITSELF

In the wake of the 9/11 attack on the World Trade Center, the newspaper *Le Monde* interviewed Girard and asked him whether his ideas on mimetic rivalry could be applied to the current international situation. He gave a cautious affirmative. We err, he said, to always look for difference whenever a mimetic rivalry between people and cultures arises. A desire to imitate drives this rivalry. "No doubt terrorism is bound to a world 'different' from ours, but what gives rise to terrorism does not live in that difference," Girard told the editors of *Le Monde*. "To the contrary, it lies in an exacerbated desire for convergence and resemblance.... What is experienced now is a form of mimetic rivalry on a planetary scale.... In Islam we see an effort to mobilize an entire Third World of those frustrated ... in their relations of mimetic rivalry with the West."[24]

In a book written just before 9/11, Girard emphasized the same points. The real secret of conflict and violence, Girard wrote, is the mimetic desire and the ferocious rivalries it engenders. This means that the Third World does not simply reject the West but also attempts, with much ambivalence, to imitate it. The hatred of the West and all it represents is not due to its spirit being truly foreign to these people, according to Girard. On the contrary, the West's ethos is completely familiar to them. Far from turning away from the West, they cannot keep from imitating it, from adopting its values without admitting to themselves what they are doing.[25]

This seems more than half right. Muslims—and not only the fundamentalists—feel threatened by Western economic and cultural power. Insofar as the extreme Islamists sense their world imitating the West, they respond with enmity. It is not so much the other as its absence that spurs anger. Resemblance embitters them. They fear losing themselves by mimicking the West. A Miss World beauty pageant in Nigeria, for instance, spurred widespread riots by Muslims that left hundreds dead.[26] This could be considered a violent rejection of imitation. "It is now on a planetary scale that the game of mimetic rivalry will play itself out," writes a follower of Girard. "The image that appears to emerge—in place of the 'clash of civilizations' slogan invoked by those who do not understand the state of the world—is that of a civil war within a single global civilization."[27]

Malise Ruthven, in his 2002 book *A Fury for God*, underlines the embattled identity of the lead hijacker of 9/11. Mohamed Atta studied architecture and Western city planning, but imitation haunted him. The Islamic metropolises he loved seem organized on principles diametrically opposed to those of Western cities. The old urbanscape boasted narrow alleys with merchants who displayed goods in open booths and often dispensed tea to customers. The new Westernized districts were characterized by broad avenues with sleek stores staffed by cool professionals.[28]

After Atta studied architecture he went to Germany where he wrote a master's thesis on urban planning. This move itself is revealing. Atta was not an outsider to Western education or mores but a successful player. His German thesis advisor had the highest praise for him and considered him a skillful and attentive city planner. "I know him very well and vouch for Mohamed in every respect," he stated in a letter of recommendation.[29] He also noted that Atta believed that modernization threatened the Islamic heritage and that high-rise towers destroyed the warren of alleys and courtyards that had constituted the old cities.[30]

Atta's thesis for his Hamburg studies, which has not been published, is subtitled "Neighborhood Development in an Islamic-Oriental City." It examines an old quarter in Aleppo, one of Syria's oldest and best preserved cities. According to Atta, Western planners were destroying the neighborhood. The cover of the thesis sports opposing photos and maps. An image of a taxi-clogged street is set against one of smiling boys in an alleyway; an aerial view of straight avenues, traffic circles, and high-rises is juxtaposed with one of the honeycombed streets of the old town.[31]

In *Newsweek*, former acquaintances also spoke of Atta's belief that the new high-rise, Westernized apartment buildings undermined the old neighborhoods, with their intimacy and dignity. "It may have been particularly galling to Atta," according to his teachers and former class-mates, "that his own family had moved into an eleventh-floor apart-ment in just such a hulking monstrosity in 1990, as he was graduating with an engineering degree from Cairo University. To Atta, the boxy building was a shabby symbol of Egypt's haphazard attempts to mod-ernize and its shameless embrace of the West."[32] It is all here, imita-tion and the rage at imitation, which spells loss of identity. This might be dubbed cosmopolitanism from below.

NEEDING MORE THAN ROOTS

A loss of identity in a globalized world can be countered by a secure sense of where one belongs and fits. Indeed, as seen by Yuri Slezkine, the modern individual is not only mobile, but also—paradoxically—stable. The Jew like the overseas Chinese or Indian merchants—all of whom incarnate the successfully modern citizen—retain an acute loy-alty to tradition and family, Slezkine writes. They are modern nomads, but nomads who retain something of the "sacredness of the nuclear family and the chosenness of the tribe."[33] They have roots even as they are uprooted. The cultivation of roots allows an individual to thrive; it gives an individual a secure identity in a fluid environment.

Many thinkers have pondered the significance of roots and their loss. The French mystic Simone Weil devoted a book to this subject, *The Need for Roots* (1949). She saw the "disease of uprootedness" as the ailment of the modern age and believed the fall of France before the Nazis could be attributed to this. "The sudden collapse of France in June 1940, which surprised every one all over the world, simply showed to what extent the country was uprooted. A tree whose roots are almost entirely eaten away falls at the first blow."[34]

The agrarian metaphors must be handled with care, however. The fetish of roots and soil has long marked conservative, if not fascist, thought. The cosmopolitan was attacked, it should be recalled, as "rootless" by the Soviet ideologues. What does it mean to be "rooted" in a particular place? Is it a form of nationalism? A loyalty to a real or fictitious past? Weil is not especially helpful. A human being has roots, she wrote, "by virtue of his real, active, and natural participation in the life of a community which preserves in living shape certain particular treasures of the past and certain particular expectations for the future. This participation is a natural one, in that sense it is automatically brought about by place, conditions of birth, profession, and social surroundings."[35] Nor is Weil's own life especially reassuring in what she meant; she was obsessed by the imperative of doing hard physical work on a farm.[36]

Theodor Adorno pilloried Heidegger's jargon of roots and authenticity, the notion that deep philosophizing takes place in peasant huts in cold nights before burning fires. "When on a deep winter night a wild snowstorm rages around the cabin, and covers and conceals everything, then the time is ripe for philosophy. Its question must then become simple and essential," stated Heidegger as cited by Adorno.[37] A study of genocide through the ages is titled *Blood and Soil* and its author, the historian Ben Kiernan, observes that a romantic agrarianism marks many genocidal movements.[38] "Roots" by themselves can hardly be the answer to modern anomie.

Where does this take us? At least we should be wary of the conventional verities about cosmopolitanism and we should challenge lax philosophizing about a dialogic or hybrid world. As an ethic, one can argue about the parameters and meanings of cosmopolitanism. But we should not forget Diogenes, perhaps the first cosmopolitan, whose commitment to global citizenship entailed snubbing local mores or— to give it a more modern spin—nationalist sensibilities. Diogenes was a rebel, and indeed he is sometimes claimed by anarchists as one of their brethren. It is possible to draw a link between Diogenes' critics and the twentieth-century attacks on "rootless cosmopolitanism" by Soviet anti-Semites. The global citizen lacks loyalty to the local entity, which could be a virtue.

Yet to move beyond a philosophical ethics means looking at cosmopolitanism as situated in a world economy and political structure.

Cosmopolitanism must be placed within the economic and social reality in which it exists as both a promise and a danger. Its promise is obvious—we saw it in the recent "Arab Spring": the lure and strength of democratic longings that are obviously abetted by an international media and communications, by a certain globalism. But we should be prepared for the backlash, a fear of loss of an identity. In times when little or no meaningful work is available, cosmopolitanism is thin gruel that mocks the individual. It promises global citizenship and its benefits but delivers unemployment and its poverty. This gives rise to anger and anxiety—and sometimes a violent return to an ethnic and religious identity.

Making Places:
The Cosmopolitan Temptation

MARK T. MITCHELL

Like Russell Jacoby, Mark T. Mitchell sees danger in the uncritical advocacy for cosmopolitanism that pervades contemporary intellectual life. But Mitchell takes the criticism even deeper, arguing that the proper critique of cosmopolitanism has to be grounded in a probing critique of modernity itself, whose emphases upon boundless choice and the plasticity of the human condition undermine the very possibility of human flourishing. Mitchell here proposes a middle ground between the thinness and artificiality of cosmopolitan culture and the moral insularity of tribalism. At the center of such revitalized localism will be the restoration of place and place-making.

WHEN PEOPLE USE the term today in casual conversation, "cosmopolitan" generally refers to a person whose disposition is one of urbane sophistication, not blinkered by the prejudices and limited experience of the provincial, the uneducated, and the narrow-minded. The cosmopolitan exhibits tolerance rather than xenophobia, reason rather than prejudice, universalism rather than localism. The cosmopolitan considers himself a citizen of the world and views other affil-

84

iations as secondary to his universal embrace. He is suspicious of patriotism and fearful of nationalism. He is not a communitarian for his community knows no limits; rather, the embrace of his imagination, if not his actual affections, extends to all humanity.

The word "cosmopolitanism" is, of course, used in a variety of ways. On the one hand, this flexibility points to the usefulness of the term; however, it also invariably creates confusion as various meanings slide past each other making effective communication about the concept frustratingly illusive. Nevertheless, it is possible to tease out several threads. *Ethical cosmopolitanism* is the view that human beings owe moral duties to all other human beings by virtue of a shared moral status. *Political cosmopolitanism* is the view that ideally human beings are (or should be) moving toward a common political organization where common moral goods can best be realized. Finally, *cultural cosmopolitanism* is a consequence of globalization whereby, through mass media and ease of travel, cultural particularities are dissolved into a universal culture. In this essay, I will argue for what I call *humane localism* where both political and cultural cosmopolitanism are rejected while ethical cosmopolitanism is affirmed even as cultural diversity and political decentralization are championed as the best means to achieve human flourishing.

HISTORY OF AN IDEA

The Stoics are generally recognized as the first to fully develop a vision of cosmopolitanism. Cicero, for instance, argued that all men are joined by a common law rooted in reason and ultimately born of God: "Law in the proper sense is right reason in harmony with nature. It is spread through the whole human community, unchanging and eternal, calling people to their duty by its commands and deterring them from wrongdoing by its prohibitions.... There will not be one such law in Rome and another in Athens, one now and another in the future, but all peoples at all times will be embraced by a single and eternal and unchangeable law; and there will be, as it were, one lord and master of us all—the god who is the author, proposer, and interpreter of that law."[1] Here we clearly see Cicero's ethical cosmopolitanism whereby all human beings are understood to participate in a natural order, grasped by reason. We are bound by common moral standards; therefore, we inhabit together a single and unified moral universe. It is important to note, though, that the emphasis is on the moral cosmos. There is no suggestion that a political cosmopolitanism, an actual universal polis, is necessarily entailed in the moral claim.

The Stoic emperor Marcus Aurelius affirmed the law's connection to reason but both secularizes it and emphasizes political cosmopolitanism along with the ethical: "If the intellectual capacity is common to us all, common too is the reason, which makes us rational creatures. If so, that reason also is common which tells us to do or not to do. If so, law also is common. If so, we are citizens. If so, we are fellow-members of an organized community. If so, the Universe is as it were a state—for of what other single polity can the whole race of mankind be said to be fellow-members?"[2] By Marcus's time, of course, the polis as the normative political entity had been replaced by the idea of empire. With this expansive political reality, the ethical and political elements join together into a form of cosmopolitanism that links human beings not only morally but politically as well.

In the modern age, the German philosopher Immanuel Kant is a key figure in history of cosmopolitanism. He memorably argued for an ethical universalism in the form of his categorical imperative. Persons are to be treated as ends and never merely as means. These persons legislate as citizens in a kingdom of ends where each rational creature acts as both legislator and sovereign. However, Kant's ethical cosmopolitanism differs from Cicero's in that reason is severed from nature and man is autonomous. The God of Cicero is replaced by human reason alone. This secularized version of ethical universalism goes hand-in-hand with a political vision. In his essay *Perpetual Peace*, Kant writes: "The peoples of the earth have thus entered in varying degrees into a universal community, and it has developed to the point where a violation of rights [*Recht*] in *one* part of the world is felt *everywhere*. The idea of a cosmopolitan right is therefore not fantastic and overstrained; it is a necessary complement to the unwritten code of political and international right, transforming it into a universal right of humanity."[3] In Kant, both ethical and political cosmopolitanism emerge in stark relief.

One of the foremost advocates of cosmopolitanism today is the German philosopher Jürgen Habermas. For Habermas, the alternatives before us are few and stark. We can either actively and intentionally work to realize the Kantian vision of a peaceful cosmopolitan order or we can descend into an aggressive and likely violent tribalism.[4] As Habermas puts it: "Even if we still have a long way to go before fully achieving it, the cosmopolitan condition is no longer merely a mirage. State citizenship and world citizenship form a continuum whose contours, at least, are already becoming visible."[5]

In addition to Habermas, University of Chicago professor Martha Nussbaum is a leading contemporary advocate of cosmopolitanism. According to Nussbaum, the cosmopolitan is "the person whose primary allegiance is to the community of human beings."[6] Allegiances to Burke's "little platoons" are secondary, and even trivial, for the demands of universal justice trump anything less than universal membership in humanity itself. "If we really do believe that all humans beings are created equal and endowed with certain inalienable rights, we are morally required to think about what that conception requires us to do with and for the rest of the world."[7] Nussbaum realizes that such an expansive claim makes her vulnerable to those who offer up a common-sense objection: Isn't it a good thing that mothers, for instance, prefer their own children over all the other children in the world? Aren't particular affections and affiliations the necessary glue that holds communities together? That makes life sweet? In reply, Nussbaum argues that we can, in fact, justify giving special care for those in our own limited spheres but we must do so in universalist terms. Universal ends, she asserts, are more efficiently realized when individuals attend to the particular individuals within their narrow spheres of influence.[8]

Nussbaum bears her cosmopolitanism like a cross: "Becoming a citizen of the world is often a lonely business. It is, as Diogenes said, a kind of exile—from the comfort of local truths, from the warm, nestling feeling of patriotism, from the absorbing drama of pride in oneself and one's own.... Cosmopolitanism offers no such refuge; it offers only reason and the love of humanity, which may seem at times less colorful than other sources of belonging."[9] Apparently, only the strong and brave lovers of humanity can muster the courage to be cosmopolitans. The rest of us hunker down in the refuge of our patriotism, prejudice, and local pride. Of course, the love of humanity is a curious ideal. How is it possible to love an abstraction? Can one feed humanity? Can one embrace humanity? Can one console suffering humanity? No. One can only love, feed, and console particular human beings. Nussbaum's apparently high-minded assertions bring to mind Ivan Karamazov, who noted that he loves humanity but finds individual human beings downright repulsive.[10]

More recently, Nussbaum has modified her position. "Further thought ... persuaded me that the denial of particular attachments leaves life empty of meaning for most of us."[11] It is striking that such a banal conclusion would require "further thought." One would hope that the lived lives of human beings the world over would make it obvious that a meaningful life necessarily requires "particular attachments." What, after all is friendship?

As a Rawlsian, Nussbaum follows in his metaphysically austere footsteps: "I now think it crucial that the political principles of a decent society not include comprehensive ethical or metaphysical doctrines that could not be endorsed by reasonable citizens holding a wide range of comprehensive doctrines."[12] However, she admits that "the moral sentiments on which Rawls relies are a bit too transparently rationalistic."[13] Given Rawls's neo-Kantianism, I take this an indirect criticism of Kant as well. Thus, while she is less than optimistic about the rationalist flavor of the Rawls–Kant cosmopolitan project, she remains committed to the general ends toward which it strives. Nussbaum ultimately attempts to argue for a "purified patriotism," one that defends the liberal state as the normatively decent society.[14] Nussbaum's purified patriotism, of course, shuns any hint of nationalism or prejudice and instead makes it possible to embrace one's nation only to the extent that it realizes the goals of liberty and equality as understood through the Rawlsian–Kantian framework. Thus, the citizens of a modern liberal state could, in these terms, legitimately express a patriotic love of country while a citizen of any other type of polity throughout human history could not. One is tempted here to accuse Nussbaum of her own brand of provincialism even as she attempts to outline the contours of her cosmopolitanism.

WHICH COSMOPOLITANISM?

In addition to ethical and political cosmopolitanism evident in thinkers such as Kant and Nussbaum, there is another form that, while related, deserves a separate discussion. Some thinkers on both the left and the right have expressed concern about the homogenization of culture. The pervasive influence of the global economy and global politics, and the technological extension of the imagination, make it increasingly possible to see oneself as a citizen of a global culture even as local and particular cultures are drowned in the wave of commonality and sameness. This is "cultural cosmopolitanism," and while neither ethical nor political cosmopolitanism requires cultural cosmopolitanism, both are potentially facilitated by a common culture.

Of course, some degree of cultural cosmopolitanism has always existed. Through travel and exchange, individuals have encountered other cultures and in the process have adopted practices foreign to their native ways. However, this kind of cultural exchange has exponentially increased with technologies developed in the twentieth century. Today a person can travel with relative ease and great speed to virtually any part of the world. The so-called global economy brings people and interests together like never before, even as it fosters common tastes and habits. Cell phones and e-mail have made instant communication possible, and television and the Internet have brought forth a common means of accessing and consuming information on a global scale.

One aspect of this increasingly globalized culture is the necessary triumph of popular culture. Of course, high culture has always been the purview of a minority. It requires work to grasp and the rewards are not immediate. On the other hand, pop culture goes down easily, requires virtually no effort to grasp, and is consumed at the touch of a button. The ascendance of a global pop culture has seriously undermined local folk culture. Folk culture is necessarily tied to a particular locality and is rooted in local skill and participation. Folk music, folk dance, and local arts and crafts require apprenticeship into a particular tradition and a willingness to labor under the auspices of a particular form. For this reason, folk culture can never be cosmopolitan.

This suggests the emergence of a cosmopolitan vision that is not merely the abstract dream of a philosopher but one in which the brotherhood of men can be imagined in concrete terms, where barriers of language, culture, and lifestyle are gradually eroded by the ongoing influence of commercial, communications, and entertainment technologies. Surely this is a practical advance of the Kantian vision, one that can be appreciated not only by a philosopher but by anyone who eats a Big Mac while watching old episodes of *Seinfeld* on the Internet.

Nevertheless, it would be well to ask if there any drawbacks to these various cosmopolitanisms. One way to get a better handle on the contours of this discussion is to consider the different philosophical anthropologies animating the various positions. I would suggest that what we might call modern liberal cosmopolitanism is rooted in a quite different view of human nature than the pre-modern cosmopolitanism of, say, Cicero or Christian natural lawyers. These differences will play a decisive role in helping us grasp the implications of various forms of cosmopolitanism, for at the root, we encounter strikingly different understandings of the notion of limits. There are three elements I want to discuss.

First, nominalism vs. essentialism. The Ciceronian or Thomistic varieties of ethical cosmopolitanism, for instance, are rooted in a normative conception of nature and natures. Human beings, according to this view, share a common nature that is ordered to certain ends. Human flourishing depends on the extent to which individuals conform their actions to the norms rooted in nature. Conversely, nominalism holds that there are no universal natures. Rather there are only individuals who may share biological material and physical attributes but because there is no normative nature linking all human beings together, there exists no common moral order joining human beings in a common moral community. Indeed, we live in a society that elevates the autonomous individual and celebrates individual choice as the apex of human existence. Despising limits and asserting one's freedom is a theme that pervades our cultural consciousness and manifests itself everywhere from advertising to film, from education to, ironically, religion. Autonomous choice, unencumbered by either authority or tradition, is the reigning orthodoxy of our day. This elevation of individual choice is predicated on a nominalist conception of reality, for the greatest latitude of choice is afforded when the constraints erected by nature are destroyed or at least ignored.

It would seem obvious that an essentialist view of human nature provides a robust philosophical grounding for the claim that all human beings are equal in dignity and therefore all human beings owe each other at least the respect afforded by non-interference and in many cases a positive duty to render aid. On the other hand, it is less obvious how a nominalist view of human existence provides an adequate grounding for any view of universal dignity or universal rights. This is not to say that modern thinkers rooted in the nominalist tradition have not tried. Indeed some of the most vociferous advocates of universal rights are those who at the same time deny the existence of norms rooted in an essential human nature. But if ethical cosmopolitanism is facilitated by (and historically rooted in) some form of essentialism, modern claims to universal rights either (a) tacitly and parasitically depend on a version of human nature that they explicitly deny, or (b) attempt to develop an account of rights based on the desire of all to freely *choose* their own ends unconstrained by anything other than a reciprocal respect for the similar choices of other choosers. If the former, then the project is philosophically incoherent. If the latter, then at the very least they are being consistent by grounding their accounts in the fact that we choose; however, it is not immediately clear how the capacity to choose, in itself, implies moral value. To be sure, the novelty of the justification stands in marked contrast with the historically grounded (though metaphysically laden) account provided by essentialism.

Second, secular vs. religious. As Nussbaum makes clear, her Rawlsian conception of society shuns any reliance on "comprehensive ethical or metaphysical doctrines that could not be endorsed by reasonable citizens holding a wide range of comprehensive doctrines."[15] One is left wondering what room that claim leaves for any comprehensive ethical or metaphysical doctrines at all or what, in Nussbaum's mind, constitutes a reasonable citizen. One might be tempted to argue that Nussbaum's metaphysically austere liberalism amounts to a comprehensive ethical and metaphysical doctrine that many reasonable citizens would summarily reject. On the other hand, the ethical cosmopolitanism of the classical and Christian variety was rooted firmly in a religious view of reality.

To be sure, there are plenty of examples of religious belief promoting not ethical cosmopolitanism but rather aggressive tribalism. This fact is not to be ignored. But neither should we ignore the fact that the twentieth century demonstrated with bloody clarity the violent frenzy of an aggressively secular political vision. It seems that neither religion *per se* nor secularism immediately offers a superior vantage point from which to evaluate cosmopolitanism. On the one hand, the theistic vision of Cicero and the more explicitly Christian view developed in the natural law theory of Aquinas grounds its ethical cosmopolitanism firmly in a religious conception of reality. In fact, their moral theories would fall to pieces if the underlying theism were removed.[16] Furthermore, a common religious belief can serve as the primary impetus for a cultural cosmopolitanism that extends as far as the religious belief is shared. On the other hand, Nussbaum and other contemporary secular cosmopolitans argue that comprehensive beliefs tend to divide people in a world where a plurality of religious beliefs and convictions exists. Their solution, then, is to privatize religious belief (if it can't be eradicated) and attempt to articulate a universalist vision bereft of metaphysically controversial views.

Both the religious and secular versions of cosmopolitanism seem to offer promise and danger. Ethical cosmopolitanism and aggressive tribalism or nationalism have been rooted in religious conviction as well as secular commitments. The power and scope of the medieval church suggest at least an aspiration toward political cosmopolitanism, which at times included forced conversions and the exile of unbelievers. At the same time, for much of church history, the political vision has been deferred to the eschatological Day of the Lord at the end of time, thereby defanging political cosmopolitanism. That said, today the most enthusiastic supporters of political cosmopolitanism tend to be the secularists. This is not surprising to many Christian thinkers who have noted that when God is removed from the political and moral calculus of a people, the state naturally steps in to assume the role once occupied by God. If this is so, then the logic of the secularist would naturally extend to the world as a whole thus promoting political cosmopolitanism as an ideal and legitimate goal.

Third, human beings as perfectible vs. as problematic. The classical and Christian conception of human nature finds, at best, a puzzle. For the orthodox Christian, human beings are created in the image of God yet tragically fallen from grace. The *Imago Dei* provides a theological justification for some form of ethical cosmopolitanism, for in this view all are equal before God and therefore all human beings are bound together in a moral universe superintended by God and obligating all. On the other hand, human fallenness suggests good reasons to be skeptical about the ability or willingness of human beings to live in peace. If human beings are capable of moving acts of nobility, courage, and sacrifice, they seem just as willing to engage in acts of violence, self-interest, and greed. This fact has led many to warn against both the consolidation of power that political cosmopolitanism represents as well as the radical individualism that liberalism tends to enjoin. First, the consolidation of power is dangerous, for the greater the consolidation, the greater the opportunity for abuse. James Madison famously rooted his argument for the separation of powers in his belief that human nature is given to abuses of power and therefore no person or institution should possess absolute power.[17] Second, radical individualism is also understood as a problem by those who see in human nature an ever-present dark side. The Puritans of colonial New England, for instance, sought to construct a commonwealth where they could freely worship God, but the commonwealth they fashioned was not one where the autonomous individual was welcomed or even imagined. Because of the sinful tendencies inherent in human nature, the Puritans emphasized strong communities that, among other things, provided a network of accountability for its members as they sought together to live lives that gloried God and regulated the carnal appetites.[18] Such communities were necessarily of a scale where anonymity was impossible and exit was by no means simple. Thus, in the Augustinian view of human nature, political cosmopolitan is a danger to be feared, but so too is a political structure that fails to provide strong community support of virtue.

Political cosmopolitanism seems altogether desirable if we hold that human beings are essentially good and perhaps even perfectible. If consolidated power is nothing to fear, or at worst, a problem that can be mitigated by proper education, liberal institutions, or sheer optimism, then the putative good that such power can accomplish clearly outweighs the potential danger. Nussbaum and Kant share the same dream: a cosmopolitan world of happiness, peace, and justice where ethical norms embrace all autonomous individuals and universal political institutions promote the peaceful interaction of all.

At least one form of ethical cosmopolitanism affirms that human beings are united by a common nature or by knowledge of common moral truth and as a consequence are obligated to treat all human beings with respect. This form of ethical universalism is fully compatible with the claim that we owe special duties to certain individuals either by virtue of unique relationship or proximity. According to this rather modest cosmopolitanism, we owe all human beings respect and ought to affirm the inherent dignity of all. However, a more expansive form of ethical cosmopolitanism—the form advanced by Nussbaum—asserts that we owe positive duties to all human beings regardless of relationship or proximity. The expansive ends of this strong version of ethical cosmopolitanism seem to warrant some kind of political cosmopolitanism. It is for this reason that at least one writer has argued that cosmopolitanism in this form is at heart an imperialist doctrine.[19]

COSMOPOLITANISM AND HUMAN FLOURISHING

If human nature is as the ideological liberal suggests, it is clear that both ethical and political cosmopolitanism are warranted or should at least be the default positions barring other compelling objections. At this point the issue of cultural cosmopolitanism comes into play, for we have yet to inquire if cosmopolitanism in all its forms is suited to human flourishing: does it enhance or detract from the best sort of life? Both ethical and political cosmopolitanism, on their faces, avoid the degradations of tribalism with its insularity and easy recourse to violence. However, it is not at all clear that political cosmopolitanism, with the centralization of power, consciousness, and perhaps culture, is any less fraught with peril than the blinkered existence of the tribe. Let me suggest four arguments against political and cultural cosmopolitanism.

The first is rooted in human psychology. Human beings have a deep and abiding longing to belong. We quite naturally frame our identities, at least in part, according to our various relationships and associations. I am a son, brother, husband, father, neighbor, citizen. These identities help to me to situate myself in terms of self-understanding as well as in terms of action, for a life of virtue is unintelligible if it is abstracted away from the concrete relationships that form the contours of my existence. Furthermore, my need to belong is not fully realized only in terms of human relationships. My relationships with cultural artifacts help to frame my understanding of myself and others.

A particular language, a particular cuisine, a particular geography, climate, manners, stories, songs, metaphors—these all serve to make me who and how I am. While I can imagine my abstracted self as a global citizen or as a brother to all humanity, such an extension requires significant effort and is as unlivable as it is unnatural. The limits of my belonging are determined by the limit of my love—and love, not an abstracted feeling of goodwill, has limits. My imagination can reach beyond my love, but my need to belong is only satisfied when it is co-extensive with my capacity to love. Thus, it appears that local political institutions and local cultures are best suited to human needs and desires.

Second, neither political cosmopolitanism nor cultural cosmopolitanism are suited to the human scale. This is the idea that there exists a scale that is fitting for human flourishing. Depart from the scale and the potential for flourishing correspondingly diminishes. One feature of the human scale is simply biological: we are embodied creatures, therefore we occupy a particular space and time. We are limited, placed creatures, and therefore our existence is in some respects necessarily local. If this is the case, then politics, economics, education, and other vital elements of society must be centered on the local and the placed. This is not to say that components of these institutions cannot extend beyond the local; however, if the local is subsumed by the national or international, the centrality of the local is lost and the principle of human scale is disregarded. In this light the principle of subsidiarity clearly emerges as one naturally suited to addressing matters of human scale while at the same time acknowledging the possibility that some institutions must exceed the local if they are to function as they should. As long as flourishing individuals and healthy local communities are understood to justify the very existence of institutions that extend beyond them, a proper perspective can be maintained. If, however, it ever comes to pass that national and global institutions are thought to be primary and individuals and local communities mere parts or servants of the whole, then the principle of human scale will have been violated and harm will invariably ensue. Thus, whatever else political and cultural cosmopolitanism represent, they are not suited to human beings, for they ignore the limits imposed by human scale.

Third, political and cultural cosmopolitanism is not suited to human nature. One aspect of this is the problem of consolidated power I discussed above. A world community requires an enforcement arm that encompasses the globe. Without absolutely trustworthy leaders, such a power would represent a threat to freedom like no other. But where are such leaders to be found? Until they are, we do well to keep power relatively diffuse. If the centralization of political power is a legitimate concern, we do well to foster political institutions scaled to human needs and human nature. At the same time, cultural cosmopolitanism would clearly facilitate political cosmopolitanism, for cultural variance is one of the main blocks against political unity. Thus, to the extent that political cosmopolitanism is to be feared, cultural cosmopolitanism should be resisted.

Fourth, there is an aesthetic appeal to variety and vibrant difference that cultural cosmopolitanism tends to diminish even as ethical cosmopolitanism equips us with the moral vision to appreciate the vastly different ways other human beings shape their particular places. Cultural cosmopolitanism, which as I have argued is necessarily constituted by pop culture of the lowest common denominator, inevitably leads to a flatness and banality even as its champions celebrate the tolerance they see as integral to it. But tolerance is not the same as universal platitudes about equality or the value-free rhetoric of the enlightened. Indeed, one only tolerates what one does not like. In other words, tolerance is only a possibility in a world of real difference. And real difference helps provide the kind of texture that makes the world the stunningly beautiful place that it is. And even when the beauty is admittedly absent, its absence is noticeable and therefore regrettable. Local differences, particularities, and personalities are what constitutes "local color," and color, after all, is one aspect that contributes to beauty. Remove the local color and something is lost. Remove the local songs, stories, businesses, cuisine, dialects, games, and something very good has been lost, and when lost, they are likely to be gone forever.

PLACE-MAKING

We are all deeply implicated in the liberal project and thus inhabit what is essentially an empire of individual choice. By practice and consciousness we are, as Nisbet put it, "loose individuals."[20] If our lives are constituted by mere choice (or the perception of choice), then we are all cosmopolitans: The communities and traditions we inhabit are chosen, embraced, and rejected based primarily on acts of individual will. We are consumers of cultures not inheritors or caretakers or stewards. Cultures are smorgasbords of alternatives each potentially tantalizing, each an option to be provisionally accepted or rejected and replaced when our interests are diverted by something else. We are eclectics, dabblers, and both our philosophical anthropology and our economy encourages this very outlook.

However, not all cultures are (or have been) confined by this anthropology of liberation. In other words, liberalism, while advertising itself as a traditionless posture that judges the world from a neutral standpoint, is actually a tradition that blinds the liberal to its underlying preconditions. If our human longings are best fulfilled in the context of vibrant local communities, we would do well to consider how best to foster a more rooted existence. We would do well to cultivate the art of place-making. Here are some suggestions.

First, a sense of limits is essential. As I have argued, political limits are an essential means by which power is controlled and local cultures are a vital means by which human beings participate in and perpetuate particular goods. At the same time, ethical cosmopolitanism seeks to embrace the whole of humanity with its moral vision. Are these two views incoherent? They are not so long as the ethical cosmopolitanism is of the weak form that does not entail the claim that all human beings owe equal moral duties to all other human beings without regard to proximity or relation. The moral universalism I am advocating is one rooted in the claim that all human beings are equal in moral worth and inherent dignity. However, our actual moral duties are, to some extent, determined by accidentals of place and therefore ethical cosmopolitanism is a combination of negative moral duties of respect for all and positive duties to particular people within our particular places.

Second, we must come to orient our lives around long term commitments and a recognition of natural duties. Cultural cosmopolitanism lends itself to pop culture, which is, if nothing else, ephemeral and transitory. It demands little and therefore one can easily jump from one facet of pop culture to the next with little trouble. This ease and eclecticism undermines the stability of local communities that necessarily depend on long term affiliations and commitments. A life given to assiduously keeping one's options open will, in the process of avoiding commitments, miss out on the very best kinds of human goods that are only found in the wake of commitment.

Third, limits and long-term commitments can be better realized if we recover the language and sense of providence, vocation, and stewardship. Providence, of course, implies some form of theism that includes at the very least a God who is both concerned about and in some way involved in human affairs. The belief that God has created a world infused with moral norms necessarily implies that certain actions are prohibited while others are enjoined. There exist, prior to any human will, limits on human action. The theological doctrine of vocation requires the antecedent notion of providence, for vocation is the doctrine of calling whereby God calls each person to a particular set of tasks and as a consequence to a particular place. Again, the idea of vocation implies a sort of positive limitation, a natural suitability, that is unique to each person. Finally, the idea of stewardship implies that that the places and institutions we have inherited are gifts to be wisely tended and lovingly passed on to the next generation. But one can only tend well what one understands and ultimately loves. Understanding and love are limited, for only God can understand the entire world or love it in a way that does not become merely an abstraction. Stewardship, then, is necessarily rooted in local affections and particular commitments.

Finally, place-making is an art that requires time and practice. Yet it is an art that is desperately needed if the potentially harmful effects of cultural cosmopolitanism are to be countered. What are some of the features of place-making? Neighborliness is one facet of place-making. As one becomes a good neighbor, one helps to create the small fibers that bind people and places together. Related to neighborliness is friendship, one of the sweetest goods in life and one that is only fully realizable in terms of particularity. One cannot be friends with the world, and Facebook "friending" is at best a parody of the kind of friendship described by Aristotle who argued that friends must live in proximity to each other, for only then can they truly know each other and fully appreciate their shared virtues. Place-making also entails education in local stories, practices, flora, and fauna. As one becomes familiar with the particulars of one's place, one is better equipped to act as a steward and therefore better able to pass on to the next generation that which one has inherited and tended.

What I am suggesting represents something of a third way that avoids the cosmopolitan temptation while at the same time shuns any aggressive tribal reaction. This third alternative, what we might call *humane localism*, appreciates the variety and differences between cultures and thus resists the homogenizing impulse that is so strong in modern liberal democracies. It recognizes that the language of global village represents an abstraction that will never satisfy human longings. It is characterized by a love for one's particular place and the people thereof. Yet at the same time this humane localism is not animated by fear of the other, for by an act of imagination it sees through the inevitable differences and recognizes the common humanity we all share. It recognizes that we are all living souls with needs and longings that bind us together even as the particulars of our own places remind us of our distinctness. In short, humane localism is rooted in respect, not in homogeneity; in love of one's place, not hatred of other places; and in the realization that human flourishing is best realized in the company of friends and neighbors sharing a common place in the world.

Place / Space, Ethnicity / Cosmos:
How to Be More Fully Human

YI-FU TUAN

Concern with human flourishing is the animating spirit of Yi-Fu Tuan's essay, just as it is at the center of all of his work. So too is the concept of place, and its dialectical relationship with the cosmopolitan outlook. Tuan is one of the world's most important cultural geographers, known for his ability to combine the precision of his discipline with a vivid imagination, great reserves of humane empathy, and irrepressible curiosity. He has written insightfully on the difference between "place" and "space," and movingly on the tension between "hearth" and "cosmos" as equally vital sites of human experience. As a Chinese immigrant to America, he has always valued the cosmopolitan perspective, and here he emphasizes it as an essential feature of education. But in his hands, cosmopolitanism takes on a more supple and less dogmatic aspect, in keeping with the breadth of his sympathies.

A QUESTION THAT persistently nags me is: How can a human being be all that he or she is capable of? Much depends on upbringing, on the availability and quality of the school. In the twenty-first century, when in theory any school anywhere in the world can draw on the library and media resources of humankind, what should be in the curriculum? What should be taught so that the young can grow up justifiably self-confident? The politically correct answer might be that, whatever else they are taught, they should be steeped first in the beliefs and practices of their own people. Such rooting guarantees them identity and self-esteem. My answer is the opposite. As I see it, children should, above all, be imbued with the sense that they are heirs to the best in thought and ethics that the entire world has to offer, though, of course, that best may well include local treasures. But I get ahead of myself. To make this conclusion plausible, I need to explore a number of paired terms that have a family resemblance in meaning. They are: place/space, local/global, culture/civilization, and ethnicity/cosmos. I invite you to follow me on a tour of these ideas with the promise that it will lead back to the question of what constitutes a truly empowering school curriculum for the young.

PLACE/SPACE

Several years ago, Spring Harbor Middle School in Madison, Wisconsin decided to set aside a day to celebrate "Environment Day." Rather than regular schoolwork, students were to choose one of four sessions to attend: a boat ride on Lake Mendota, a walking tour through the arboretum, a visit to the cinema to see a nature film, or a talk on "Space and Place" to be given by a retired professor. I was that retired professor and, as you can imagine, few students turned up. How could I possibly interest the few eleven- and twelve-year olds who did turn up? I started by saying something like this. "Place is the familiar—this classroom, for instance. Space is the little known world outside. Those friends of yours who have chosen to go on the boat ride are out there in space, which, though it is exciting, can also be dangerous. Who knows? Their boat might sink. Right?" "Right!" said the students. I continued: "Now, place—this classroom—is safe. Its downside is that it can be boring. Right?" To my chagrin, they shouted, "Yes, this class is boring!" "Wait a minute," I said, "the classroom may be familiar and boring, but isn't it also here, rather than on Lake Mendota, that your mind comes to grips with the distinction between place and space?"

It wasn't difficult to interest my young audience and that's because "place and space" were a common experience for them—and, indeed, for children everywhere. In an affluent suburb, children's intimate place is their own room, beyond which is space, the less frequented parts of the house. In poor neighborhoods, children are well aware of the difference between home ground and the streets, the one relatively safe, the other exciting but dangerous. In another culture and society altogether, say, that of hunter-gatherers, children cannot help knowing the difference between place—the forest clearing where they eat and sleep—and space—the circumambient forest.

Home is a special sort of place—place at its most intimate, with an aura that is hard to describe. Instinctively, we feel that the aura would fade if our critical faculty is too active. Maybe that's why, for many of us, the home of our childhood has the strongest emotive draw. Children do not ask whether the color of the rug matches the wallpaper. They simply soak up what their environment offers. As adults, we can occasionally revert to childhood experience: for instance, when unwell and in bed, we abandon ourselves to the tactilities and odors of rumpled sheets and pillows, and to the caring ambience of the sick room itself. As for the homes we occupy later in life, what is special about them? Certain fond particulars may come to mind, but I submit that what is truly special about home—universally, and not just in this or that society—is that we sleep there. In dreamless sleep, we human beings are at one with the world, a state of existence that we seldom reach awake. In other words, home also satisfies a death wish.

Home is people. Home and people make up the smallest community. Larger ones are, progressively, neighborhood, village, city, and region. In the past, rootedness to place and community at all scales was the rule. An agricultural way of life required it. In modern times, people have the choice to migrate. Many do so. This is a familiar story. Less familiar is that some individuals, though well able to migrate or simply travel, stubbornly resist. I think of Charles Lamb, the essayist, who declared that his "household-gods plant a terrible fixed foot, and are not rooted up without blood."[1] I think of Immanuel Kant, the philosopher, who never left his hometown of Königsberg. I think of Arthur Waley, a scholar of Chinese civilization, who was never tempted to visit China, and of the poet Philip Larkin who opined, "I wouldn't mind seeing China if I could come back the same day."[2]

Note that these homebodies were thinkers and writers. They wanted to be anchored in place, believing that such anchorage allowed their minds to roam freely. Too much traveling could be counterproductive. A cartoon series called "Through History with J. Wesley Smith" satirizes globetrotting. J. Wesley Smith is a man who appears in different historical times, each time as a prig and a scold. In one cartoon, Smith, dressed as a bourgeois merchant, stands before Immanuel Kant, who writes at his desk, and says to him, "You can stick here in this dinky village if you want to, Herr Kant, but I intend to travel and make something of myself!"[3] Traveling can lead to success. It may even broaden the mind, but that's the snag. Minds broadened by travel may become shallow. Yet staying at home is not the answer. It invites timidity and staleness. It stymies growth.

GROWTH

Growth almost always requires a displacement in space, beginning with birth itself. The human fetus is unhappy leaving the womb and howls in protest. Yet it is in the less agreeable environment outside the womb that life can continue and flourish. The same sort of transition is necessary in the later stages of life. Young children, used to home, may at first find kindergarten forbiddingly strange, but they quickly adapt and rejoice in the new setting. In America, eighteen-year-olds willingly leave hometown with its constraints and limitations for the larger world that is the university. Ethnic minorities from poor and under-educated families are an exception. They are reluctant to make the move and the reason often given is that they find the atmosphere of the university alien. In response, the university tries to make itself less alien and more home-like for them. Though well-intentioned, the gesture is not only segregating but patronizing. Why? Because the university sees no need to reassure foreign students in the same way. Rather it pays them the compliment of assuming that they can cope on their own even though they are from a different culture and will be a small minority in the student population. Foreign students naturally welcome tokens of home on campus, but they also know that they are at the university precisely for what they do not find at home—glittering labs, well-stocked libraries, and cutting-edge professors. The challenge to the university, and indeed to society at large, is to find ways of encouraging ethnic minorities to feel the same way, drawn to the university by the same lures. Can it be done in young adulthood? Shouldn't it have been done much earlier? I will return to this question.

Meanwhile, let me supplement these examples of growing up with two from the settled, adult world, one drawn from anthropology, the other from political philosophy. Anthropologist Victor Turner notes a common type of movement in pre-modern times, which he says is from "community" to "communitas." The movement occurs periodically in response to the needs of economic exchange, but not only that. It is also prompted by the desire of the people in a local community—say, a village—for a larger sense of who they are. That larger sense of self villagers find in the market town—the "communitas" of acquaintances and strangers. In the communitas, villagers experience a greater freedom, a more liberating spirit, in the midst of people who are friendly yet do not obligate and constrain them to the degree that kin and neighbors in the village all too often do. The two social orders, community and communitas, have their own strengths and weaknesses.[4] Both are necessary to a people's well-being. Still, it is communitas rather than community that points to growth and the future.

The second example is from the political philosopher Hannah Arendt. She uses the beliefs and values of the ancient Greeks as a point of departure for examining what she calls "the human condition." The Greeks, she notes, distinguished sharply between private and public, privileging the latter. The bias against private is captured by the Greek word *idios*, which means "private" and is the source of our word "idiot." To be private is to be isolated, out of touch, a state that leads to idiocy. The private is also linked to the biological, the needs of the body. A citizen's farmstead, which caters to life, is not considered a suitable permanent habitat for a man if he wishes to reach his full stature. For that, he must be willing to appear in the city's public forum, a place that is indifferent to his bodily well-being. There he debates with his peers in regard to the higher callings, such as the figuration of the ideal city-state. Who is left behind to take care of the farmstead? Women and slaves. The West retained elements of this distinction between the private (women's sphere) and the public (men's sphere) until well into the twentieth century. Women's movements strove and still strive to abolish it.[5]

CULTURE AND CIVILIZATION

The difference between "place" and "space" is one of relative scale: the one small, the other large; the one local, the other possibly global. More specifically, the local is a circumscribed entity such as a village, town, or city that can be more or less visually encompassed. The large, such as a nation-state or empire, is space rather than place; it is space because it cannot be directly perceived and can be encompassed only by the mind. An empire has never been so large as to cover the entire globe, but empires have always had global pretension: thus, Alexander the Great believed that he had conquered the world; the Roman empire saw itself as the entire civilized world; and the Chinese empire called itself *Tian Xia*, meaning "all under heaven."

"Culture" and "civilization" are another pair of terms that imply scale. Culture is the local and the small: we speak of a folk's culture, a village or town's culture. But of the large and complex—city, nation-state, and empire—the term more commonly used is "civilization." These two terms, which found their way into the lexicon in the eighteenth century, were adopted by anthropologists and historians to mark a division of intellectual labor. Anthropologists studied culture, which was understood to be the customs, arts, and beliefs of nonliterate peoples; and historians studied civilizations—their institutional, engineering, and artistic accomplishments. The division proved to be invidious. Anthropologists could not help treating primitive peoples as somehow inferior. Their very use of the ecological model—a model that had been developed earlier to study animal communities—implied as much. Historians, by contrast, treated civilizations with respect. They had no use for the ecological model. How could they when they were trying to understand the achievements of men and women who were their equals and superiors, and of societies such as Periclean Athens and Renaissance Florence that had qualities their own society might envy? Historians could be critical of the actions and policies of their forebears, pointing out their errors and moral failings, but that in itself was a mark of respect. Anthropologists, for their part, refrained from criticizing primitive peoples. In this regard, they followed the example of primatologists, who would not dream of hurling moral judgments on the behavior of the animals they studied.

I have sketched a school of thought that regarded civilization as the acme of achievement. Another school, championed by German thinkers, rose to challenge it. To thinkers like Gottfried von Herder and Oswald Spengler, culture was rich and creative, civilization essentially superficial and sterile. Culture (*Kultur*) was engaged with deep moral questions, whereas civilization fussed over etiquette. Other derogations followed, all of which hinged on the abuse of power—military power foremost, but also cultural power; cultural imperialism, if you like—in the form of vast engineering and architectural projects. An effect of the excessive use of power was to produce a certain dull uniformity in landscapes.

Consider two empires—the Han Chinese and the Roman—that flourished at about the same time. Both boasted extensive road systems in response to military and administrative requirements, but the roads also promoted commerce and the diffusion of household goods and artworks, creating a certain monotony in the general appearance of towns and cities, as well as in their furnishings and accouterments. Imperial road systems were established from above, that is to say, by order of the rulers. Not so, or less so, were city plans and buildings. These achieved an empire-wide sameness through imitation. Such was the case in Han-dynasty China. Provincial towns, to gain prestige, imitated the capital city's cosmic pattern of rectangular walls and rectilinear streets. As for the Roman world, certain forms of aesthetic expression in sculpture and architecture reached such perfection that, for hundreds of years, they were copied everywhere around the Mediterranean Sea.[6]

The American empire is a good example from the modern age. More than two-thirds of the country was surveyed by government fiat starting in 1785; in the course of time, the government's township-and-range system of survey brought about a remarkable consistency to America's Midwestern and Western landscapes. Moreover, thanks to the ease of movement and the desire to move, all sorts of goods and cultural practices diffused over the country such that the country and its citizens acquired a somewhat standardized look. Americans themselves found the standardized look rather dull, compared with the greater variety they could see in Europe. In recent decades, thanks not only to the global movement of peoples and goods, but also to global communication and transaction in cyberspace, landscapes and even mindsets seem more and more alike the world over. There may come a time when only the flora and fauna, the mountains and plains of nature provide that order of contrast our eyes yearn for.

LACK OF VARIATION AND FLATNESS

Other than the lack of variation, another emerging characteristic of the earth's surface is that it can seem strangely flat. What do I mean by flat? I have two meanings in mind. One is temporal. The temporal depth of the urban landscape has diminished in that buildings of different ages, which serve as time-markers, are rarely found occupying the same confined space. If Lewis Mumford were to observe the city today, he would hardly come up with the idea that it is time made visible.[7] Architectural historians have often lamented this progressive flattening of time as old buildings make way for the new. Less often lamented or even noticed is the way speed of communication and motion cuts into our experience of temporal depth. In the past, news that reached me from afar was old news. Now, with instantaneous transmission, all news is contemporary. I live in the present, surrounded by present time, whereas not so long ago, the present where I am was an island surrounded by pasts that deepened with distance.

The second sense of flat is a consequence of the ascendancy of materialist secularism, which is strongly antipathetic to thinking that lacks rigorous empirical grounding or that has an air of paradox. By eliminating the vertical dimension and a touch of the mysterious from our understanding of reality, materialist secularism leaves us with little else than the "flat earth" of common sense and normative science. Methodologically, it is reductionist, inclined to see things in terms of their simpler components. A particularly fond object for reduction is the human mind, which is set aside in favor of the brain, a tangible organ. A consequence of reductionism is to lower the stature of the human being. Not so long ago, he was ranked just a notch below the angels. Now, he is considered no higher than the apes.

Strange that science should make us human beings feel small, for haven't its technological marvels made us powerful, almost god-like? They have, but with much ambivalence, for it would seem that technological marvels can also diminish us in unforeseen ways. I am in an airplane that zips through space, but do I feel the speed, do I feel powerful? Not at all. Strapped in a cushy seat, I am as helpless and immobile as a baby. Has technology empowered my mind? There, too, a note of doubt is justified. Consider social networking. In a bustling market town, I am obliged to contend with all sorts of people—acquaintances and strangers, young and old, shoe cobblers and book sellers—in the process of which my understanding of the world is enriched and enlarged. Today, electronic gadgetry enables me to communicate with like-minded people all over the world and generate, in short order, new webs of connectivity. Are these new webs instances of "communitas"; that is to say, do they, in the quality of what is communicated, transcend social chitchat? I doubt it. Even if social networking transmits more information faster and the information so transmitted can be useful to fellow researchers and so promote science or to fellow activists and so promote a political stance, we should still bear in mind a general point: Information is not knowledge and flood tides of information, delivered in short surges, can choke the moments of silent reflection—the pregnant pauses—that are the source of deep understanding and sustained exchange.[8]

TRUTH

Another casualty of materialist secularism is Truth—Truth capitalized and in the singular. Truth used to carry great weight. It was believed to have the power to set us free. But, from Plato onward, it was also believed to lead us to death. T. S. Eliot famously wrote that "human kind cannot bear very much reality,"[9] a viewpoint endorsed by Bertrand Russell who said, "No one can view the world with complete impartiality; and if anyone could, he would hardly be able to remain alive."[10] Considered either way, truth has a different order of seriousness than truths in small letters and in the plural that are now prevalent.

Not so long ago, colleges and universities proudly engraved the word Truth or its Latin equivalent *Veritas* on their crests. Harvard's read *Veritas Christo et Ecclesiae* (Truth, Christ, and Church). In time, Harvard dropped *Christo et Ecclesiae*. Now only *Veritas* remains. Without religious and metaphysical underpinning, however, *Veritas* at American universities has come to mean truths about nature that are empirically verifiable, or truths that are socially constructed. The former kind retains its universalist character, the latter kind varies from people to people, which leads to the notion that truths are relative.

Truth's downgrading from something absolute, to which humans miraculously have access, to something relative and pragmatic, diminishes human dignity. But why would anyone want to downgrade

Truth and, in the process, diminish human dignity? One answer lies in the admirable desire, on the part of modern liberals, to extend the idea of human equality beyond the socioeconomic to culture and understanding. And this is where desire conflicts with harsh facts, for it would seem that a culture that has more than local significance and an understanding of reality that goes far beyond what good sense and experience offer requires an abstract notion of Truth, one that is distant and difficult of access. I would go a step further and say that such a notion of Truth acts as an inspiration and lure for achievements of the highest order. Unfortunately, only a few civilizations and only a small number of people in them embrace Truth so conceived. For most people, pragmatic truths are all that matter, since they are all that survival requires.

GLOBALISTS AND ETHNICS

As a man of my time, I share the desire for equality and abominate the inequalities inherited from the past. One form of inequality is, however, relatively new—that between what I call "globalists" and "ethnics." Globalists are the well-to-do and technically trained. They are connected via the Internet. They fall into two broad categories: sophisticated villagers whose primary interest is personal and social, and entrepreneurs whose primary interest is financial. Needless to say, the two overlap and may exist in the same individuals. Globalists of both categories may make political connections as well, but their purpose is rarely political in the classical sense of the word, which is the betterment of society at large.

Are there, then, groups that resist the globalist sweep? I would say yes: the "ethnics" are one such group. Oppressed or condescended to by their powerful white neighbors, ethnics seek to regain self-esteem and pride by reaffirming their heritage—their distinctive way of life, manifest in the way they cook, clothe, and house themselves, but especially in devotional artworks and ceremonials. Charismatic leaders periodically emerge from ethnic groups. Their task is to promote social and cultural cohesion. Such cohesion provides leaders with political power, which they can use to extract concessions from globalists. Although ethnics resist the globalist trend, globalists do not regard them as a threat. To the contrary, globalists patronize ethnics and see them and their cultures as one remaining source of diversity in an increasingly homogenized world. Where, after all, would globalists go for their vacation if the palette of ethnic colors turns monotone?

ORIGINAL COSMOPOLITES

To ethnics, their own culture is the royal road to self-esteem. I doubt that it is, for, as I see it, people cannot have enduring self-esteem unless they genuinely believe in their centrality in the world. Mere cultural difference from other groups—to be just one patch in a multi-hued mosaic—does not suffice. A comparison of modern ethnics with isolated tribes of a century ago is revealing. Ethnographers used to apply the label "primitive" to these isolated tribes, in part because they regarded their material culture as rudimentary. The label was a misnomer. More appropriate would have been "cosmopolite" or "original cosmopolite." Why? Because these peoples, for all the simplicity of their material culture, had a strong sense of self-importance, which they showed in various ways. One was that they lived at the world's geographical center.[11] Another, even more flattering, was that they were also located at the world's population and cultural center. Experience convinced them of their centrality. Thus, in regard to population, they knew through experience that as they moved away from their settlement, population diminished until only empty land remained. Moreover, only a few outsiders ever visited them, and they were often the same explorers and ethnographers. As for cultural superiority, visitors invariably probed them about their way of life, their beliefs and values. Why all these questions unless they came in search of superior knowledge and wisdom?

Last but not least, the cosmopolite label is justified in that primitive peoples lived in a cosmos rather than simply on the earth's surface.

Their world celebrated the heavenly bodies—the sun, the moon, and, for some, even the Milky Way, in comparison with which the world of today's "ethnics" can seem narrow and earthbound.[12] Even that of "globalists," ensconced in windowless rooms and glued to fleeting figures on the computer screen, suffers by comparison. Original cosmopolites needed a strong sense of centrality to cope confidently with nature's harshness. Sadly for them, their sense of being at the center proved to be delusory. In the course of the twentieth century, they were to discover that they did not occupy the geographical center, were not the most populous people, and had no claim to being the world's cultural capital. Once they recognized their marginality, they were no longer cosmopolites. They were ethnics.

IDENTITY, SELF-CONFIDENCE, SELF-ESTEEM

In social welfare and educational circles, there is much talk about self-esteem, the lack of it and the need for it. There is also the belief that if we only know our identity, we shall also have self-esteem. What is the basis of this belief? Have we forgotten that, not so long ago, identity was considered more a limitation, even a stigma, than a source of pride? Working-class people knew only too well who they were. One was a carpenter, wheelwright, tailor, ditch-digger, seamstress, and so on. Some of these occupations were so closely identified with manual workers and laborers that they became their proper names. In contrast, members of the upper class were named after places—geographic localities—rather than occupations. One was the Earl of Warwick, the duc de Guermantes. Place is less confining than occupation, and it goes without saying that the larger and better endowed the place the more choices it offers its owner. A tailor was born into a line of work and remained in it all his life. By contrast, to be born in Warwick, to be the Earl of Warwick, did not put him into a straitjacket; he could be what he chose: priest, warrior, courtier, scholar, or gentleman-farmer. Similarly, American citizens like to think of their identity as fluid, capable of changing as they move from one geographical location to another, or as they climb up the socioeconomic ladder. The closest thing Americans have to an identity card is their driver's license—a card that gives them license to drive into the blue yonder and there discover who they are and can be.

Occupation is one source of identity. Ethnicity is another. Both are too restrictive. To label me a teacher or a Chinese-American does not do me justice as a complex human individual. Are globalists better off in the matter of identity? Do they worry about who they are? Probably not. They can't risk wondering who they truly are when they change their place of employment, residence, possibly country, culture, language, and loyalty, from time to time. For lack of commitment to any one of these anchors, globalists may suffer from "a lightness of being." But is it unbearable, as the Czech writer Milan Kundera says, or does it give them a pleasing, light-headed sense of freedom?[13]

Identity's relevance is largely external, important to a society that wants to keep tabs on people. Self-esteem is important to the human individual, psychologically and emotionally. How to promote it? How to empower an individual so that he or she is justifiably at ease in the world? My answer is hardly original. It is education for the heights. Many barriers prevent the child from reaching the heights. The most common type, apart from poverty, is her confinement to the intellectual and moral resources of her group. Education both at home and in the school is all too often a narrowing rather than a broadening, an effort to fit a child into the group rather than developing her natural gifts so that she grows up to be a cosmopolite. For this to happen, each child is to be regarded as the heir to not only the best that her own people has achieved, but to the best that humankind has achieved.

EDUCATING THE COSMOPOLITE

Impossible? Difficult, certainly, but not impossible, for the grounding of such an outcome exists in the child's nature, which is one that predisposes her to be a cosmopolite. Until a child reaches a certain age, she is barely aware that she is female, much less that she is American

Indian or Chinese-American. Naturally curious and adventuresome, a child is more interested in space than in place, in things out there than in things at home. Parents may think otherwise, for they see their child playing in the safe places, and that if she strays, it is to the basement or the backyard. But what are the basement and the backyard to the child? To her, the basement is no ordinary place; rather it is a haunted underworld; and camping in the backyard has the same excitement for her as for an adult spending the night in howling wilderness. Another common adult misunderstanding is this: Parents and teachers think that the child should be taught the local geography first. From there they introduce her to ever larger units by graduated steps. The child is not, however, naturally disposed to learn by graduated steps. Her mind tends to leap from one spatial-temporal scale to another, such that, at seven or eight, she may well take a more lively interest in America than in Dane County, Wisconsin, in the dinosaur than in the dairy cow, in the Great Wall of China than in her hometown's water tower. Socially and morally, too, she is more drawn to issues of good and evil, fairness and unfairness, categories that affect her life, than to adult priorities of class, ethnicity, and nationality.[14] Unfortunately, adults have power, which they all too often use to steer the child to their own narrower concerns.

Mental and moral development requires, of course, cultural support. Permit me to use myself as one who was provided with such support. I went to a one-room elementary school in war-torn Chongqing, then the capital of China. What did I learn? Reading and writing from stories. These were drawn from both Chinese and Western sources. Chinese stories encouraged studiousness, filial piety, and patriotism. Seventy years later I can still remember a number of them. One tells of a boy who, having to work on the farm during the day, could study only at night. But the family couldn't afford even a candle, so the boy caught fireflies and read by the light they shed. The second story teaches filial piety. A woman was dying for lack of nourishment. Her son cut a slice of flesh from his arm and used it to make soup for his mother. The third story is a lesson in patriotism, appropriate enough when China was fighting for its life against Japanese invaders. A hero known to all Chinese is the general Yue Fei. In the twelfth century, he fought to prevent northern tribes from invading what remained of the Song empire.

As a child, I was steeped in Chinese lore. My teachers did not, however, want me to be a Chinese chauvinist; they wanted me to be a Chinese cosmopolite. So they supplemented my diet with stories of young Isaac Newton sitting under the apple tree and Benjamin Franklin trying to capture electricity in a storm, stories that led me and my schoolmates to direct our minds to nature writ large—the cosmos. The behavior of Newton and Franklin imparted other lessons as well, lessons that were non-Chinese and could even be considered anti-Chinese. To the traditional Chinese teacher, Newton might be seen as goofing off when he should be doing sums in school. As for Franklin, he should never have endangered his life in the interest of science, for his life belonged ultimately to his parents. Western stories implanted in us children the desire to reach for the intellectual heights. Our educators, however, were not content with the development of only our minds. They wanted us to have an inkling of the moral peaks, and this meant extending the obligation to help beyond family and kinsfolk to total strangers. They asked us to read Oscar Wilde's "The Happy Prince," a story of Buddhist/Christian inspiration that advocated a morality so elevated as to seem, by Confucian standard, not so much supernatural as unnatural.[15]

I read the Western stories in Chinese. Although I stumbled over the strange-sounding names, I never regarded Newton and Franklin, or, for that matter, Oscar Wilde's fictional hero, as foreign. To me they were simply admirable human beings whom I, also a human being, could emulate. Whatever confidence I have as an adult was built on this foundation—a confidence that I believe to be potentially available to every child.

Is the realization of this potential in every child wildly improbable?

Perhaps, for many forces—egregiously, poverty and its many ill effects—stand in the path. I have added two others—what I have called ethnicism and globalism. These two forces may seem opposed, yet, in certain respects, they work hand-in-glove. As I noted earlier, tourism, a major industry of globalism, depends on the continuing existence of exotic ethnics, who, for their part, extract money from tourists by putting their heritage on display. Ethnicism is, in addition, a political force, one that draws strength from the group's cultural icons. This strength can be weakened by a broad-based, disciplined yet critical education. Ethnic leaders are therefore unlikely to be wholehearted in its support. As for globalists, I reiterate their chief fault, which is shallowness, a consequence of the loss of a vertical dimension in their world picture. With this loss comes the rise of a strictly secularist point of view, which I have called materialist secularism. One good thing about it is that it has weakened superstition. On the other hand, by declaring all spiritual values uncool, materialist secularism has paved the way for the single-minded pursuit of wealth and its perks, and so helped bring about a pandemic of worldliness unparalleled in earlier ages.

Let me end with a mantra of our time—diversity. I take it that diversity is wholly desirable in the natural world. But in the human world, does it matter if cultures lose their distinctiveness and number? Such a world will certainly be duller than one in which the widest range of cultural practices are on display: say, foot binding and widow immolation next to tai chi and tea ceremony, genome mapping and radio astronomy next to animal vivisection and the castration of boys. But hardly anyone would now see such giddy diversity as desirable, or that sheer number counts. Most of us are only too glad that certain practices, once considered definitive of culture, are now relegated to the archives and resurrected, if at all, only in thrilling period movies. No doubt the cultural mosaic of our time will continue to lose its multitudinous hue as modernization and globalization continue. I can't say I am sorry. As a humanist of Christian proclivity, my concern is not that human groups and their cultures be preserved; that I leave to

ethnographers and museum directors keen to retain maximum variety in their collections. Rather it is with the life of the individual—a
boy in Burkina Faso, a girl in Afghanistan. Our sensibility must not
plunge so low that we can look at a child and think it quite all right for
him to grow up in ignorance of his *human* heritage, and hence never
savor, no matter how bright he is, the glory that is his birthright.

The Demand Side of Urbanism

WITOLD RYBCZYNSKI

No one has written more penetratingly about America's cities than Witold Rybczynski, and in this essay the distinguished urbanist brings his encyclopedic knowledge and sparkling prose to bear on a vital but often neglected prerequisite to place-making. Successful urban environments are places where people want *to be, where they* choose *to be, and it is the role of markets to facilitate those choices and make them as free and various as possible. Urban visionaries would do well to remember this fact. "Can we design or construct places that are better suited to deeper human needs and purposes?" Rybczynski asks. And then he answers his question with another. "We certainly can build such places, but will people want to live in them?" In other words, successful place-making must begin not with abstractions, but with the people that we already are, and the places we already inhabit. Places are made, but the best place-making is not done from scratch, since "adaptation," Rybczynski insists, "is always better than invention."*

IN A FAMOUS ESSAY titled "Urban Civilization & Its Discontents," Irving Kristol pointed out that in terms of the quality of people's lives, it no longer much matters where they live. "For the overwhelming fact of American life today," he wrote, "whether this life be lived in a central city or a suburb or a small city—or even in those rural areas where something like a third of our population still resides—is that it is *life in an urban civilization.*"[1] In the forty years since Kristol made this observation, its truth has become even more obvious. Encouraged by the Internet, mobile phones, videotapes and DVDs, e-shopping, and personal computing, the urban civilization that he described is firmly established. Incidentally, the spread of an urban civilization should not be confused with urbanization. Most countries around the world are urbanizing, but this does not necessarily mean that their civilizations are urban, far from it. Indeed, in many African and Asian countries, city life is distinctly rural and un-urban.

In the past, the term urban civilization implied the way of life and culture of *big* cities. Big cities had skyscrapers, nightclubs and excitement; small cities had sleepy Main Streets. In the United States, big cities predominated, both culturally and demographically. As late as 1961, when Jane Jacobs published *The Death and Life of Great American Cities*, more people lived in big cities than in small ones. Only a decade later, this was no longer true. In 1970, when Kristol wrote his essay, slightly more people lived in small cities (between 25,000 and 250,000 inhabitants) than in big cities (larger than 250,000). By 2006, the total urban population of the United States had increased by more than 60 percent since 1960, but the proportion of the urban population living in big cities had steadily declined, while the percentage living in small cities steadily increased; more than half again as many people lived in small cities as in big.[2] The preference for small cities is confirmed by a recent Pew poll that finds "not a single one of the 30 [largest] metropolitan areas was judged by a majority of respondents as a place where they'd like to live."[3]

The new small cities are in different places than the old big cities. They are predominantly in the south and west, rather than in the north and east. Climate has become an important urban amenity, whether it is the temperate Northwest, sunny Southern California, or air-conditioned Texas and New Mexico. The Pew poll finds that the major metropolitan areas that appeal most to people—Denver, San

Diego, Seattle, Orlando, and Tampa—all share "warmer weather, a casual lifestyle and rapid growth."[4] In fact, all of the highest ranked cities in the Pew poll are in mild climates, seven in the West and three in the South.

The new cities are, on the whole, less dense than the old. Simply put, they are horizontal rather than vertical. This form is the result of two factors: the prevalence of the private automobile as the chief means of mass transportation (compared to the railroads, streetcars, and subways that guided the growth of the old cities), and a preference for detached single-family houses (compared to the flats, apartments, and row houses that were the most common form of housing when cities first expanded). The notable exception is Los Angeles, which is a horizontal city that is also extremely dense, thanks to large households and the predominance of multi-family housing. Another characteristic of new cities is the proximity of recreation areas such as beaches, lakes, mountains, and deserts. As David Brooks puts it, "These [favorite cities] are places where you can imagine yourself with a stuffed garage—filled with skis, kayaks, soccer equipment, hiking boots and boating equipment. These are places you can imagine yourself leading an active outdoor lifestyle."[5] Industrial cities did not need beautiful settings; post-industrial cities do.

DEMAND-SIDE URBANISM

Cities have come into existence through many mechanisms: by royal edict, by centralized plan, by government regulation, even by the individual initiative of owner-builders, which is how large parts of the megacities of the Third World are built. In America, we have largely consigned community building to entrepreneurs. (It was thus from the beginning; most of the Founding Fathers dabbled in real estate.[6]) With rare exceptions, such as the construction of large city parks in the nineteenth century, and the Great Society urban renewal programs of the 1950s and 1960s, decisions about where and how to build have not been made by bureaucrats or planners but by market demand. A market economy in a large and varied country that spans a continent inevitably provides many choices. You don't like one neighborhood, you can always move to another; city schools don't suit you, move to the suburbs; want a bigger yard and are willing to tolerate a longer commute, move farther out to the exurbs. Hate winters, go south; love hiking and skiing, go west. That means that the answer to the question "Can we design or construct places that are better suited to deeper human needs and purposes?" is complicated. We certainly can build such places, but will people want to live in them?

It is easy to guess wrong about what people want. For example, in the 1950s, planners decided that cars and people were incompatible in city centers and experimented with various innovative solutions to separate pedestrians and vehicles: plazas, decks, skywalks, underground promenades, pedestrian malls. Time showed most of these solutions to be distinctly unsuccessful. Downtowns with skywalks and underground tunnels usually managed to kill what little street life remained; pedestrian malls became deserted as merchants migrated elsewhere. Most pedestrian malls have since been opened up to cars again, and the most successful downtowns—San Francisco, Chicago, Boston—have mixed pedestrians and cars in traditional streets-and-sidewalks (the exceptions are pedestrian malls in warm climates such as Florida and Southern California, and in college towns such as Ann Arbor and Boulder).

Entrepreneurs have made mistakes, too. In the 1980s, the combination of shopping and entertainment was touted as the formula to breathe new life into the venerable shopping mall, resulting in megamalls with amusement parks, water parks, and theme parks. But shopping-as-entertainment turned out to be a short-lived fad. Malls struggled with declining attendance as shoppers abandoned department stores for the convenience and low prices of big-box stores. Another failed developer experiment was the attempt to import the suburban mall into the city in the form of the multi-story urban shopping mall. It turned out that shoppers didn't like going up or down more than two floors, and they didn't much like parking garages either.

The latest stumble has involved what is popularly known as the Bilbao Effect, that is the perceived ability of distinctive and unusual architecture—so-called iconic buildings—to attract visitors and tourists to a city. The Frank Gehry-designed Guggenheim museum in Bilbao, Spain did manage to put that old industrial city on the tourist map, but the phenomenon has proved difficult to replicate. A series of startling-looking concert halls, museums, and public libraries, which have ended up with budgetary overruns and less than stellar attendance records, suggests that "Bilbao Anomaly" might be a better description.

So, what do people want? What are the ingredients of successful urban design?

WATERFRONTS

The most successful urban projects of recent years have one ingredient in common: waterfronts. Starting with such early developments as San Antonio's Paseo del Rio and San Francisco's Fisherman's Wharf, waterfront festival marketplaces such as Boston's Faneuil Hall, Baltimore's Inner Harbor, Chicago's lakefront Navy Pier, New York's riverside South Street Seaport, and Miami's Bayside Marketplace, have proliferated. Waterside residential developments have appeared in New York, Toronto, Vancouver, Seattle, Chicago, Philadelphia, and San Francisco.

As the citizens of London and Paris have known for a long time, nothing is as pleasant in the center of a city as a riverside promenade. Much like parkland, an urban waterway provides a spatial release from the density of the city. The 1.2-mile Esplanade alongside the Hudson River at Battery Park City in Lower Manhattan is a good modern example. The design includes all the necessary ingredients: comfortable benches, wide walkways, and shade trees. Although the river view is the main attraction, the details of lamps, balustrade, paving, enhance the experience.

Waterfront developments have taken three chief forms: retail and entertainment centers (Fisherman's Wharf in San Francisco, Navy Pier in Chicago), residential neighborhoods (Battery Park City in Lower

Manhattan), and parks. Mention urban parks, and most of us think of Frederick Law Olmsted's creations in New York, Brooklyn, Chicago, Montreal, Buffalo, Louisville, Atlanta and many smaller cities. Fifty years ago, these nineteenth-century parks, with their Victorian band-stands and wrought-iron benches, were considered a quaint throwback to the past. No longer. There has been a renaissance in large urban parks, especially waterside parks, with new parks built or planned in Seattle, Boston, San Francisco, Chicago, Toronto, Dallas, and Los Angeles. One of the most unusual examples is Brooklyn Bridge park, currently under construction. The park, which stretches over a mile beside the East River, is built on six disused piers that are being turned into meadowland, picnic areas, and playing fields.

Modern urban parks are more active than their Victorian counter-parts, and Brooklyn Bridge Park will contain tidal pools for wading and a still-water basin for kayaking, as well as jogging trails, bicycle paths, and courts for handball, tennis, and basketball. The park's 85 acres, planned by Michael Van Valkenburgh Associates, will also include non-recreational uses such as apartment buildings and a hotel, whose development will generate revenue that will be used to maintain the park. The juxtaposition of urban density with nature sounds odd but has been a feature of American urban parks since Olmsted and Calvert Vaux laid out Central Park.

Parks demonstrate another feature of recent city building. We have learned that while city administrations are good at building infra-structure, such as parks and bridges, they are not so effective at exe-cuting development projects, so the implementation of the commercial parts of the Brooklyn project will be left to private devel-opers. This combination of public and private participants is an important feature of contemporary urban design.

HISTORICAL LAYERING

The attractions of waterfronts are multiplied when, as in Brooklyn, they are combined with a sense of the past: the Brooklyn Bridge is a historical icon, of course, but the past is evident in the waterfront whose gritty industrial aesthetic is reflected in the design of the benches, park structures, and playgrounds, and in the recycled materials used in the park. A real city, as Jane Jacobs pointed out long ago, must consist of new and old buildings that provide opportunities for diverse experiences. It has taken architects and planners, who are understandably fascinated by what is new, far too long to appreciate this simple fact. The most successful urban places today (the High Line in New York being the most recent example) are a combination of new and old, recycled old buildings, adapted to new uses, preserving the many layers of the urban past.

The Yards in Washington, D.C. is another example of historical layering. The site is in a part of the city known as the Near Southeast, along the Anacostia River (water again!), on what was once a navy yard. This is a public-private partnership; the owner of the land is the General Services Administration, the agency responsible for managing the federal government's buildings and real estate, and the developer is Forest City Washington, which specializes in large urban projects. The 40-acre master plan, by Robert A. M. Stern Architects, Shalom Baranes Associates, and SMWM, reintroduces some streets and sidewalks that had been closed by the navy. The old industrial buildings are being preserved and converted into offices and condominiums; a machine shed will house shops. Although a single developer oversees the project, individual buildings are designed by different architects. New buildings, in an architectural style that could be called industrial chic, will be roughly ten stories high, in accordance with Washington's height restriction. The residential density of the Yards is about two hundred persons per acre, much denser than most residential neighborhoods outside Manhattan. Most of the blocks, whether they contain offices or apartments—or a mix of both—will have retail uses at sidewalk level, like a traditional main street. At the same time, the river's edge houses a six-acre park (which opened in 2010), a boardwalk, a boat dock, a large lawn for public events, as well as restaurants and a marketplace.

Immediately to the north of the Yards are seven hundred units of affordable housing, financed by a federal housing assistance program (HOPE VI) and built by private developers. An old public housing project has been replaced by a mix of social and workforce housing with nine hundred units of market housing, as well as commercial and retail uses. A new park provides recreation space.

MIXED-USE

The chief public space of projects such as the Yards is the traditional street, provided with wide sidewalks and shade trees. Stores open directly onto the sidewalk; cafés and restaurants spill out onto outdoor terraces. The rediscovery of the main street model owes a debt to a pioneering real estate development, Reston Town Center, located in the Virginia suburbs outside Washington, D.C.[7] Started in 1978, this development is almost complete today, and will have a daytime population of 80,000 workers and shoppers, as well as 6,000 residents. Reston, planned by RTKL, combines twenty-story office towers and tall apartment buildings with lower retail buildings, a large hotel, and a central square. It is all new, of course, but the mixture of building sizes and styles—this is not a themed development—creates the impression of a busy downtown. Not exactly what Jane Jacobs had in mind when she wrote *The Death and Life of Great American Cities*, perhaps, but close.

Smaller-scale versions of Reston Town Center, sometimes referred to as lifestyle centers, have sprung up around the country. Some are in built-up cities such as Dallas and West Palm Beach, others are part of entirely new communities. Stapleton, another Forest City project, is a seven-and-a-half-square-mile development on the site of what had been Denver's main airport. Some lifestyle centers look like Hollywood film sets from *It's a Wonderful Life*; the architecture of Stapleton's neighborhood center has a breezy modernity that could be Dutch or Scandinavian.

The common ingredients of successful lifestyle centers are vehicular streets that allow short-term parking, off-street parking in rear lots or garages, broad sidewalks that encourage uses such as café terraces, and sufficient population density. The latter is commonly achieved by introducing both offices and residential buildings above the retail spaces. Office workers populate the streets and restaurants during the day, while residents populate them in the evening and on weekends. Mixed-use has become a mantra for developers. The advantages are obvious but there are two chief disadvantages. Mixed-use buildings are more expensive to design and build than single-use buildings, so they work best in strong markets. Second, they require more management expertise since the owner must deal with a variety of tenants. This is why the most successful mixed-use developments have tended to be large, as the economies of scale in the design, construction, financing, marketing, and management of such complicated projects tend to favor large development organizations.

DENSIFICATION

Densification is the next great challenge for smaller American cities, not only the densification of downtowns, through urban infill projects such as the Yards, but also the densification of suburban neighborhoods. A heightened population density promotes walkability, allows more use of mass transit, supports a greater variety of amenities, and produces more active cities. But most newer American cities in the South and West were built to low densities (three to five persons per acre). Denser residential neighborhoods—fifty persons per acre would be the upper range—will include low-rise apartment buildings and townhouses, as well as detached single-family houses, which is still the first choice of most Americans. Detached houses don't have to be built on sprawling lots, however. Traditional neighborhood development, or New Urbanism, has shown how single-family houses can be placed on relatively small lots—one-tenth of an acre rather than one acre.[8] Houses facing pedestrian walks and a common green court, rather than sidewalks and streets, likewise increases density, at the same time reducing the surface of street paving.

If densification in large cities such as Washington, D.C. implies projects such as the Yards, what about small cities? In small cities in the Seattle region, the Cottage Company has pioneered developments consisting of clusters of cottage-like houses. In the Greenwood Avenue project in Shoreline (population 53,000), eight houses sit on a 0.8-acre parcel. The small (less than 1,000 square feet) houses are grouped around a common green space that gets rid of streets entirely—cars are parked in common lots or garages. According to developer Jim Soules, it is the sense of community as much as anything else that attracts buyers to his developments. And fostering community is what urban design is ultimately about. Cottage clusters, like green courts, lifestyle centers, walkable downtowns, urban redevelopment projects, and city parks are all strategies with that end in mind.

CONCLUSION

We have learned a lot about building urban places in the last three decades. Bright ideas are all very well, but in urban design it is the market that has the final say. It is best to harness private *and* public resources, since private developers are skilled at understanding the market and delivering built products, while public bodies are better placed to tie individual projects into the city at large and deal with large-scale infrastructure issues. Urban vitality can be assured by well-designed streets and sidewalks. Single-use zoning has its place, but vital downtowns require mixed uses: shops, offices, *and* residences. Density is important, and in most cities the key to successful urban development is densification. Waterfronts and parks are essential ingredients in creating an urban sense of place. So is history. The most vital urban places are those that provide a sense of the past, preserving and adapting old buildings to new uses. In city building, adaptation—of ideas as well as buildings—is always better than invention.

Metaphysical Realism, Modernity, and Traditional Cultures of Building

PHILIP BESS

Philip Bess is an architectural and urbanist visionary, with ambitions of impressive and inspiring scope. If Le Corbusier and other architectural modernists sought to adapt architecture to the machine age, Bess seeks to go in the other direction: to put forward ideas for urban design and reconstruction that adapt the machine to the human person—and not merely to modernity's impoverished understanding of the human person, but to the understanding put forward by the most penetrating philosophical critics of modernity, such as Alasdair MacIntyre, and by the longer philosophical traditions of metaphysical realism which they seek to recover. His essay makes an ideal companion piece, and debating partner, for Witold Rybczynski's reflections in the previous essay. While Rybczynski cautions against urbanist ideas that fail to take their bearings from people as they are, Bess insists that only by rethinking the built environment entirely, and grounding that rethinking in a deeper philosophical understanding of human nature, can the human prospect be improved and a sustainable future be created. They provide contrasting ways of understanding the centrality of place and place-making in urban design.

I TEACH TRADITIONAL architecture and urbanism at a school where my colleagues and I generally agree that good traditional architecture and good urbanism are genuine human goods, and that genuine human flourishing is a primary end of traditional architecture and urbanism. The previous assertions are meaningless unless human flourishing has substantive content, and one of my vocational mandates is to introduce students to a long Western cultural tradition most often associated with Aristotle that the best life for individual human beings is a life of moral and intellectual excellence lived in community with others, and most typically in a town or city neighborhood—that is, in a finite and generally bounded place with some degree of geographic character and specificity. I contend here that this understanding of both human well-being and the kinds of places that support human well-being has been and is undermined by modernity, in ways I will describe at greater length in what follows. And yet we are all moderns, and modernity does bring with it certain genuine human goods, most notably in the realms of health and wealth as measured even crudely by increases in life expectancy and per capita income of persons who live in modern societies. So although a worldview that supports the understanding of architecture, urbanism, and human well-being that my colleagues and I teach is in certain necessary respects a *counter-proposal* to modernity, what we teach ought not to entail or imply a complete rejection of modernity but rather should be a worldview that both embraces modernity's genuine goods and seeks when and where possible to ameliorate modernity's inherent errors—not least modernity's errors regarding both human habitat and human flourishing. Articulating such a worldview, and fighting for the kinds of places it engenders and the understanding of human flourishing it promotes, is a long-term cultural project. The agents of such a project have yet to fully reveal themselves, and have yet to fully emerge.

Let me hypothesize that modern human beings need a renewed *culture of building*, a communal enterprise that includes architects, skilled artisans, patrons, founders, developers, and financiers. And let me hypothesize further that we need a renewed culture of building for the sake of our individual and communal and trans-generational flourishing; and that for the sake of human flourishing human beings should make walkable mixed-use settlements of streets and squares and foreground buildings and background buildings; and should make buildings that are durable, comfortable, beautiful, and with a sense of decorum suited to the building task at hand.

How can this hypothesis possibly be true, when the contemporary culture of building, when modern culture itself, when so many prominent institutions and so many aspects of our own lives as individuals, all seem to deny it? When the way we live so often emphasizes motion rather than calm, mobility rather than place, the disposable over the durable, the temporal over the eternal, novelty over beauty? Consider dynamic fields of modern achievement for the pre-modern practices of which few of us do or should long: medicine, sanitation engineering, aeronautics, communication media, and information technology. All these fields are *apparently* modern in a way that traditional building and traditional urbanism *apparently* are not. Is this an intellectual and existential contradiction? Persons who on the one hand are modern, and who on the other hand seek to build traditional buildings and cities: are such persons living incoherent and contradictory lives, necessarily guilty of thoughtless and irrational nostalgia? This is what many critics of traditional architecture and urbanism would have us believe. But the critics are wrong, and their own criticisms are intellectually problematic. Because if we look closely, we can recognize that each of these apparently disparate modern practices I have cited has something in common. What unites them is that the respective practitioners of each have a more or less clear, shared, and reasonable understanding of the nature and purpose of what they practice, and of the end or good that the practice seeks—what the ancient Greeks called the practice's *telos*. Such, alas, is not the case in our contemporary culture of architecture and building, where there is no such clear, shared, and reasonable understanding of the *telos* of architecture and urbanism. Where once there was both theoretical and practical agreement that buildings should be durable, comfortable, beautiful, and related to each other in a proper hierarchical order, today we build everyday buildings for short-term economic gain, and monumental buildings as exercises in novelty, self-expression, and advertising. The cumulative result is our contemporary built environment of junk and bewilderment—though none responsible for it will admit that this junky bewildering environment is their intent, or argue that it represents a shared purpose, or contend that it is reasonable. But perhaps we have this built environment precisely because we *lack* a shared and reasonable understanding of the nature and purpose of architecture and building. And perhaps we lack a shared and reasonable understanding of architecture and building because we lack a shared and reasonable understanding of the nature of reality.

A SHARED VIEW OF REALITY

Grant me for the moment that traditional architecture and urbanism are more durable, more culturally and environmentally sustainable, more beautiful, and (in the long run) more economical than modern architecture and urbanism—in other words, that given certain premises there are rational reasons to make traditional architecture and urbanism. If this is true, why do we no longer make traditional architecture and urbanism? Let me suggest that we no longer make traditional architecture and urbanism because a precondition of making them is a shared metaphysical realist view of the world embodied and transmitted by institutions—and this is precisely what is lacking in modernity.

But what exactly do I mean by modernity? And what do I mean by metaphysical realism, and that we have lost it? To take the second question first—and at the risk of outraging professional philosophers—let me summarize the basic tenets of metaphysical realism as follows:

1. The world is real, and reality is what it is and is fundamentally sacred;

2. It is possible for human beings to have true knowledge of the world, with this qualification: that all true human knowledge is necessarily partial, individually and collectively perspectival, and mediated to us through narrative traditions; and

3. Human beings can only flourish by conforming ourselves to reality, but again with a qualification: that as artisans, human beings order found reality into a specific human reality that, so long as it accords with and participates in the larger reality of which human beings are part, enables us to flourish both individually and collectively.

These three tenets are fundamental to metaphysical realism; and I don't think it too much to say that all or virtually all pre-modern cultures have operated, if often only implicitly, with *at least* these three primary "common sense" metaphysical realist assumptions: that the world is real, that we can know the world truly, and that we flourish by conforming ourselves to reality truly understood.

From these three tenets a number of implications and associated intellectual challenges follow:

♦ One is the intellectual challenge of discerning and articulating how the many different parts of reality relate to the whole of reality. Addressing this question of the relationship of parts to the whole is a historic function of religion, science, and philosophy, and is also *the* classic enterprise of the university as a historical institution.

♦ A second implication is the challenge to understand the distinctive nature of things, both in terms of their *telos* and in terms of what they are and are not capable of being and doing. With respect to human flourishing and the relative importance or unimportance of good places toward that end, we need to understand the nature of human beings: as animals, as social beings, as artisans, as actors, and as thinkers who order, intend, and symbolize; we need to understand the nature of material things and their properties; and we need to understand the nature of architecture and of cities as artifacts made by embodied social beings who endow their artifacts with symbolic meaning.

- ◆ A third implication is the significance of saying that human beings flourish by conforming ourselves to reality—that is, human beings have a *telos*, which is to live well. As Alasdair MacIntyre noted in *After Virtue*, in pre-modern/metaphysical-realist cultures "living well" is the *telos* of a human being in the same way that farming well is the *telos* of a farmer, and keeping time well is the *telos* of a clock.[1]

So what do I mean by *modernity*? The modern world derives its distinctive characteristics from the transformation of traditional societies initiated by the rise of modern industrial capitalism in mid-eighteenth-century Protestant Europe and America, which was itself preceded by some 250 to 300 years of witting and unwitting cultural spadework in religion, art, science, commerce, and colonization. One consequence of the rise of industrial capitalism—epitomized by Adam Smith, Karl Marx, and Max Weber, and today *de rigueur*—has been an acute and increasingly sophisticated attention to economic behavior, indeed to economic interest seen as not only *a* determinant of human action but in many modern theories as *the* determinant of human action. More recently, particularly in modern societies that have been most economically successful, environmental concerns have come to be regarded as a necessary constraint upon human economic activity; but economics arguably remains the primary lens through which moderns continue to understand collective social behavior, not least with regard to how we make and inhabit the built environment.

There is a plausible and partially true narrative of modern industrial capitalism and the global economy—one of which globalists are especially fond—that identifies capitalism as an economic system proper to free beings, one that especially rewards certain kinds of entrepreneurial character virtues, and one that is to be admired not least for its unprecedented record of success in increasing both human life expectancy and per capita income in every corner of the globe in which it holds sway. And there is an opposing narrative of modern industrial capitalism, also plausible and partially true, perhaps presented with greatest rhetorical power in one of its earliest historical formulations, *The Communist Manifesto*, in thunderous words that reverberate to the present day:

> [S]ince the establishment of Modern Industry and of the world market, [the bourgeoisie has] conquered for itself . . . exclusive political sway. The executive of the modern State is but a committee for managing the common affairs of the whole bourgeoisie. . . . The bourgeoisie, wherever it has got the upper hand . . . has pitilessly torn asunder [all human] ties . . . and has left remaining no other nexus between man and man than naked self-interest. . . . The bourgeoisie has stripped of its halo every occupation hitherto honored and looked up to with reverent awe. It has converted the physician, the lawyer, the priest, the poet, the man of science, into its paid wage laborers. . . . The bourgeoisie cannot exist without constantly revolutionizing the instruments of production, and thereby the relations of production. . . . [U]ninterrupted disturbance of all social conditions, everlasting uncertainty and agitation distinguish the bourgeois epoch. . . . All [fixed relations] are swept away, all new-formed ones become antiquated before they can ossify. All that is solid melts into air, all that is holy is profaned. . . . The need of a constantly expanding market for its products chases the bourgeoisie over the entire surface of the globe. It must nestle everywhere, settle everywhere, establish connections everywhere. The bourgeoisie has through its exploitation of the

world market given a cosmopolitan character to production and consumption in every country. . . . [By] the rapid improvement of all instruments of production, by the immensely facilitated means of communication, [it] draws all, even the most barbarian, nations into civilization. The cheap prices of commodities are the heavy artillery with which it batters down all Chinese walls, with which it forces the barbarians' intensely obstinate hatred of foreigners to capitulate. It compels all nations, on pain of extinction, to adopt the bourgeois mode of production; it compels them to introduce what it calls civilization into their midst, i.e., to become bourgeois themselves. In one word, it creates a world after its own image.[2]

And as a kind of coda to this analysis come these words from American farmer and man of letters Wendell Berry:

If you are dependent on people who do not know you, who control the value of your necessities, you are not free, and you are not safe.[3]

These competing narratives about the merits of modernity notwithstanding, until about the last 130 years or so modern culture itself has operated with metaphysical-realist assumptions. Modern science for example, for I hope obvious reasons, is incoherent without the metaphysical-realist tenets that the world is real and can be known truly; and even more so is modern democratic political theory—"all men are created equal" and "endowed by their Creator with certain unalienable Rights"—incoherent without metaphysical-realist assumptions.

PUBLIC VS. PRIVATE

Nevertheless, modern culture has clearly ceased to be metaphysically realist. How has this happened? I raise the question because, however keen our intellectual insights, we are all moderns now, not least (indeed perhaps most especially) in our habits of thinking, living in a world shaped by modern institutions (most notably, technological production, bureaucracy, and modern communications media); and because I think the recovery of good human communities generally and good towns and neighborhoods in particular may prove much harder than many of us imagine. The answer to my question lies I think in a too-little-considered distinctive feature of modern life: In a way unprecedented in human history, modernity has sharply divided public life from private life. Personal identity and public roles were much more closely wed in pre-modern than in modern societies, with the result that pre-modern societies were more "simple" and less "alienating" than modern societies or, alternatively, more "restrictive" and less "free"—but in either account, less characterized by the anxiety or the pleasure of the multiple opportunities for individual choice afforded by modernity. The modern creation of a private realm is thus both a consequence and a further precipitating cause of the breakdown of religion as a shared teleological understanding of the cosmos encompassing both is and ought, facts and values; and the modern relegation of "values" to the private realm both engenders and reinforces pluralism, relativism, and individualism, especially in morals, religion, and the arts. Moreover, the rise of the so-called autonomous individual has affinities with the transformation of the university, once understood as a community exploring different facets of a universe commonly understood. The modern university, in contrast, is all about disciplinary specialty and expertise—"all trees and no forest," some wag has said—and to the extent that modern research universities dance to the piper of their modern commercial and governmental *padroni*, there is even less incentive and opportunity for persons in different academic disciplines to join together in disinterested explorations of how their respective disciplines may relate to each other and be understood as aspects of a larger shared pursuit of a true understanding of the universe. Nor in such a cultural milieu should it come as a surprise that what our elite architectural schools teach to young architects becomes increasingly incomprehensible to non-architects.

How did this division of public and private life come about? Since the middle of the eighteenth century—with antecedent influences—modern institutional life has been increasingly shaped by the instrumental rationality of technological production and bureaucratic organization. Institutions are artifacts shaped by persons who have themselves been shaped by institutions, *ad infinitum*; but successful institutions become so by producing the personality types they need, and the institutions of the modern economy have been so successful that the Scientist–Technician and the Bureaucrat–Manager have emerged as primary character types of modern institutional culture and, indeed, the modern world. Why? Because such characters represent in their person (but alas only within their narrow realm) efficiency, economy, accountability, predictability, and repeatability, character traits essential to the operation and management not only of modern business institutions such as factories but of any institution, commercial or governmental, seeking to efficiently organize a large scale operation. And it is this search for organizational efficiency that is what Max Weber was referring to when he wrote that the modern world is characterized by the triumph of rational authority—by which he meant instrumental rationality embodied in the persons of technicians and bureaucrats—over the authority of traditions.[4]

Modernity effectively separated economically productive work from the home. A primary consequence of this has been that at the same time life in the public realm has come to be organized according to an expanding bureaucratic rationality, it is (ironically) the organization of life *outside* the world of work that more and more has become a *laissez-faire* operation. Most strikingly, modernity has led to the rise of and belief in an allegedly autonomous individual self—a paradoxically modern superstition, because even apart from common sense, the idea of an autonomous self (articulated classically in seventeenth-century "social-contract" theory by, as Bertrand de Jouvenal put it, "childless men who must have forgotten their own childhood"[5]) is contrary to just about everything we know about human beings both from pre-modern societies *and* from modern anthropology and sociology. The modern world has developed a private arena of "freedom" celebrated as "choice"; but this is perhaps more aptly characterized as an arena that not only *allows* a variety of "lifestyle" choices but also *requires* such choices. So modern institutional life, on the one hand, is organized to serve most effectively the demands of the modern economy, in which control and predictability are paramount; and modern private life, on the other hand, is organized around the maximization of individual freedom under the rubric of consumerism, choice, and ultimately self-creation. Thus where the bureaucratically organized economic and governmental institutions of modern life and their rules are comparatively strong, the authority of institutions that in the past have organized human life in its non-economic aspects lived away from work are significantly weaker— three obvious examples being the Family for sexuality and child-rearing, and the University and the Church for knowledge and shared cosmic meaning. But just as the modern world developed the Scientist–Technician and the Bureaucrat–Manager as distinctive modern character types for the comparatively "hard" world of work, so likewise have the Artist and the Therapist emerged as distinctive modern character types for the creativity and the coping required, respectively, by modernity's creation of the autonomous individual in the comparatively "soft" realm of private life and choice.

The creation of these new modern character types registers itself in the material and spatial expressions of modernity. Where once Church and Town Hall and Courthouse and Public Square most prominently defined the cityscape, the modern era has produced a cityscape occupied most prominently by the Factory, the Office Building, the Museum, the Hospital and the Freeway—the habitats, respectively, of those distinctively modern character types the Technician, the Bureaucrat, the Artist and the Therapist, all mobilized to pursue as efficiently as possible their various lifestyle choices. And this brings us to Bess's Law of Architecture and Urbanism, and its Corollary. The Law is:

Architecture always symbolizes power, and aspires to symbolize legitimate authority.

and the Corollary is:

A widespread desire for and expectation of social predictability from everyone else—the culture of bureaucracy—combined with a widespread desire for and expectation of maximum freedom for oneself—the culture of personal autonomy—will never produce a beautiful, coherent, and intelligible public realm.

In tandem with the technological achievements that modernity has made possible, which have resulted in an almost infinitely complex global economy professedly oriented to individual consumer choice, I think this law and its corollary explain much of the character of modern architecture and urbanism, and how and why modern architecture and urbanism differ from traditional architecture and urbanism. What are some of these differences? Most succinctly, the essential differences are these: (a) in traditional buildings the *enclosure* of the building and the *structure* of the building are identical, and in modern architecture they are not; and (b) traditional urbanism is *spatial*, and modern cities and suburbs are not.

THE FORM OF THE CITY

To elaborate—and if only to contravene our own modern habit of viewing buildings as isolated objects—let me begin with urbanism and then move to architecture. Because of our common modern tendency to understand urbanism primarily in terms of economic exchanges and lifestyle choices, I want to begin with a characterization of urbanism that I contend is true of all cities, modern and pre-modern, large and small.

It goes like this: Whatever else a city is, it is constituted by five conceptually different orders that exist in dynamic and reciprocal relationship with each other. A city is always and everywhere and simultaneously an *environmental* order, a *demographic* order, an *economic* order, a *moral* order, and a physical/spatial *formal* order. These orders may be better or worse, and they may be more or less recognized and acknowledged; but they are always present, and always in play, in cities ancient and modern. But there are also differences between traditional cities and modern cities, and perhaps the most fundamental difference between them is that inhabitants of traditional cities generally understood themselves and their cities to be grounded in sacred order; whereas inhabitants of modern cities understand (correctly) their cities and suburbs to be expressions of corporate and individual will-to-power, though these are usually described as "market forces" and "individual choice." What are the physical and formal features that denote these two different understandings of cities?

Let me begin with traditional urbanism, by which I mean in the most general sense walkable settlements characterized by the pedestrian proximity of a variety of uses and activities accessible to human beings of virtually all ages. One elementary and recurring characteristic of traditional urbanism is the mix of uses that exist within a distance of a quarter-to-half-mile—a five-to-ten-minute walk for most human beings. Because of its relationship to the human body, the walkable mixed-use neighborhood is the fundamental unit of traditional towns and cities. A neighborhood or two standing alone constitutes a village or small town, while an accumulation of neighborhoods constitutes a larger or smaller city. In the latter case (in architect Léon Krier's memorable image[6]), a neighborhood is to a city as a slice of pizza is to the whole pie: a part that contains the same essential ingredients as the whole. In contrast, a post-1945 suburb separates all the "ingredients" of everyday life into allegedly functional zones, inaccessible to pedestrians. In addition, traditional urban settlements are hierarchical in form, characterized by a reciprocal relationship between public spaces and the more prominent religious and civic "foreground" buildings, and the less prominent domestic and commercial "background" buildings—which when assembled altogether become traditional urbanism in the form of both towns and cities.

I have been referring to public spaces, and the importance of space in traditional urban environments. The traditional city is above all a spatial environment, and the idea of urban space is not at all ethereal or "spiritual" or slippery. In traditional urban settlements, space is not a void without form, but rather its opposite. Traditional urban space is a void *with* definite form, something with breadth and depth, with limits, with figure. Moreover, space can be *con*figured. Space is an artifact, something that human beings can and do make. Shaped space is where much of what is most important in human social life takes place, whether in the intimate space of a private room or in the public space of a street or a plaza. The point I want to emphasize here is that, historically, space has been a product of and container for human communal sociability, and is the medium of traditional face-to-face urban culture and civil society.

As early as 1840 Alexis de Tocqueville saw and began to articulate that modern democracy has an inherent tendency to promote the phenomenon not of selfishness but of individualism.[7] What Tocqueville long ago recognized as American individualist culture in potential is today American individualist culture realized; and with respect to the built environment, modern individualism finds physical expression in at least two ways, one elite and one popular. Elite individualist expression can be seen in the buildings of the small but highly publicized world of avant-garde architecture, the domain of The Artist, the aspiring symbolic content of whose work is to legitimate freedom to live an experimental life as an authoritative cultural ideal. But the most popular and pervasive physical expression of contemporary individualist culture is the post-WWII American suburb, which manifests the ideal of a freestanding house in the natural landscape. There is nothing intrinsically wrong with this ideal, and it actually has a long history in Western culture; but until the eighteenth century it was pretty much an exclusively aristocratic ideal, valued typically as a temporary respite from urban life. However, when that ideal became democratized in the modern era *in opposition to* the Industrial City, it set off a series of historical events the result of which is not an agricultural landscape dotted with grand or modest villas, but rather a "middle landscape," neither rural nor urban, that practically everywhere looks like contemporary Long Island, New Jersey, and suburban Atlanta. Such automobile suburbs are what Americans since 1945 have been building almost exclusively, and exporting to the rest of the world—and are correctly understood as a physical embodiment of the inherent democratic cultural tendency toward individualism identified by Tocqueville, one made materially possible by government policies and the proliferation of the automobile. The post-1945 suburb is a world of unprecedented private luxury that is simultaneously and strikingly a world of unprecedented public spatial poverty, literally an *anti-spatial* environment, a world in which *the public realm doesn't matter*. In contrast, space is the medium of traditional urban life; it is where most of public life in traditional (pre-1930) cities takes place. And by "traditional urban life" I mean not only the dense historic urban center habitat happily consumed (but generally not produced) by today's postmodern cosmopolites, but also the traditional working-class city neighborhood and traditional small-town habitats of Front Porch Republicans. Space in these places is not a vague or amorphous concept: rather, urban space denotes a class of things possessing specific names that denote a variety of spatial types: public urban spaces such as the *park*, the *plaza*, the *square*, the *boulevard*, the *avenue*, the *street*, and the *alley*; and private and semi-private urban spaces such as the *courtyard* and the *cloister garden*, as well as the transitional *forecourt*—traditional urban spaces all.

If the most obvious formal difference between the traditional city and the modern city is the difference between a spatial environment and an anti-spatial environment, the fundamental difference between traditional buildings and modern buildings concerns their materials and methods of construction and their corresponding durability (or lack thereof). Buildings in pre-modern societies for the most part were made with materials locally available and locally produced. These were *low embodied energy* materials, in several ways: (1) in terms of their inherent properties as materials drawn from the earth and in need of relatively little refinement; (2) in terms of the relative ease with which they were acquired, prepared for use in buildings, and employed in the building construction process; (3) in terms of the energy required to transport them from their point of origin and manufacture to the building site; and (4) in terms of the energy required to repair and maintain them over time. In addition, as I noted earlier, traditional buildings more than modern buildings are characterized by an integral relationship between structure and enclosure. To put this most simply: in contrast to most modern construction, the walls of a traditional building also hold the building up. Prior to the modern era, admittedly under conditions of scarcity and lacking mechanized means of transportation, human beings typically made buildings characterized by the *identity* of structure and enclosure: the exterior walls of the building were also part of the structure of the building, typically mud, bricks, blocks or stones piled up on one another in compression. In contrast, standard practice in today's construction industry is for exterior walls to fill between and/or be attached to a building's steel or concrete structural frame (or its diaphragm of wood or steel studs), a practice generally not as durable as traditional construction because the building's component parts are not integral. This lack of integration makes buildings more vulnerable to water penetration and ultimate deterioration over time as their unintegrated components expand and contract during seasonal freeze-thaw cycles. (Such buildings are especially vulnerable if they have a flat roof anywhere but in arid climates.) Moreover, again in contrast to traditional construction, most modern construction employs comparatively *high-embodied energy* materials that are, for now, still relatively easy and inexpensive to manufacture and transport in an era of cheap energy. How long that can continue remains to be seen; but the facts are that traditional construction both employs lower embodied energy materials than modern construction and is generally more durable than modern construction. Stones artfully piled atop one another will stand a thousand years or more with minimal regular maintenance. Today's modern architectural *tours de force* are lasting a generation or less before requiring expensive maintenance and repair.

ARCHITECTURE, TRADITION, AND FREEDOM

I hope by this point I have made the case for how and why it is that traditional urbanism necessarily operates with metaphysical-realist assumptions, and how modern architecture, modern urbanism, and the modern suburb require a subjective, relativist, and individualist view of cities and human beings and a utilitarian and will-to-power view of both ethics and political authority. This suggests that we can maintain the modernist architectural and urban/suburban project so long as the economic and political forms of modernity themselves can be maintained. But can these forms of modernity in fact be maintained? There is much talk today about the environmental sustainability of modernity, but that is not the only question and type of sustainability with which moderns are confronted. Is modernity economically sustainable? Is modernity culturally sustainable?

If metaphysical realists are correct, *no* human culture is sustainable that does not acknowledge the constraints that reality imposes upon it. So another question that arguably needs to be asked is this: What living traditions of life and thought in the modern world presume and promote metaphysical realism? (The only alternative to this line of inquiry for would-be metaphysical realists seems to me to attempt to recover metaphysical realism on one's own, as an individual project—which strikes me as possible in theory, but much more difficult than recovering, adapting, and extending older traditions of thought and practice.) In the West, the oldest intellectual traditions of metaphysical realism are classical culture and Biblical religion (Jewish and Christian), worldviews that encompass facts (and *eo ipso* science), values, teleology, *and* a degree of sophistication about how cultures develop toward their *telos* over time. Biblical religion in the modern world has assuredly *not* been immune to transformation (and degradation) by modern culture. But to the extent that classical culture remains a living tradition in the modern world, it is mediated to us by Biblical religion; and Biblical religion remains a living intellectual tradition in which otherwise relativist moderns might discover a retrievable metaphysical realism.

Let me therefore conclude with a hypothesis: *If* traditional architecture and urbanism have a future, it will be for one or both of two reasons: (1) historical circumstances will force them upon us; or (2) communities of persons will choose them in acts of intentional self-limitation. So, are there examples of communities and institutions that, however haltingly and however imperfectly, are actually pursuing traditional architecture and urbanism? It so happens that at the moment there are several. Thomas Aquinas College dedicated its new campus chapel just a few years ago, a skillfully executed classical basilican church plan informed by Palladian and California Mission Style traditions. Notre Dame, Andrews University, Judson University, and the University of Miami all have schools of architecture that teach traditional urban design. In the United Kingdom, the Prince's Foundation for Building Community promotes traditional architecture and urbanism through a number of programs and ancillary institutions. And then there are classic Tocquevillian associations in the United States, such as the Congress for the New Urbanism, the Institute for Classical Architecture and Art, and the American College of the Building Arts, all of which do splendid educational and professional work promoting traditional urbanism and/or traditional architecture and construction. However, every one of these institutions has been created by persons who have been trained as modernists. Their leaders are autodidacts who have undertaken, voluntarily and mostly on their own, the recovery of their respective traditions, and who eventually found one another. And poignantly, every one of these institutions is facing the unavoidable modern challenge of how the traditions they have begun to recover can be sustained and handed over to the next generation.

One last consideration: where does human freedom as both a fact and a genuine good come into play in these scenarios for the future of traditional architecture and urbanism? I confess to a traditional American—indeed a Catholic Christian—regard for liberty as a great human good, and a respect for the freedom and moral necessity of individuals to choose the good. I therefore think we should teach our children by example the existential benefits of stability of life, of choosing to stay put in a place, but at the same time insist that we must allow and not disparage or obstruct the freedom of individuals to pursue their vocation—in the full theological sense of the term— wherever it leads them. I therefore continue to look to the paradigmatic characters to whom I have looked for many years: St. Benedict of Nursia, the founder of Western communal monasticism; and Alexis de Tocqueville, the chronicler and theorist of communities of virtue formed by free citizens. Traditional urbanism is a genuine good, but good governments provide incentives for free citizens to choose the good rather than forcing them to do so, except under the most dire circumstances when all are required to sacrifice. Such dire circumstances may well be approaching, but in the interim my sense is that the challenge for those of us who promote traditional architecture and urbanism as genuine goods is to persuade individuals and communities of the benefits of stability of life; to model it ourselves; to make it so attractive that it will draw others to it; and to once again build durable and beautiful environments in which persons born into or drawn to them can flourish over the course of their individual lives, and the community itself can flourish over the course of multiple generations.

A Plea for Beauty:
A Manifesto for a New Urbanism

ROGER SCRUTON

Our culture is a culture of cities, and without cities we could not conceivably have enjoyed the enormous scientific, economic, and political advances of the Enlightenment. Cities are also the heart of the modern nation state, and every country that modernizes does so by mass migration from country to city. We must therefore reflect on the factors that might prevent or reverse the decay of our cities. To what extent should we rely on urban planning? Although some successful examples of planned cities exist, such planning has often failed to produce city centers where people want to live or spend leisure time. To plan or not to plan is a false choice. Instead, argues the British philosopher Roger Scruton, civic leaders should think in terms of fostering beauty through the use of aesthetic constraints. These constraints may help reduce sprawl and make American city centers attractive homes—in the vein of great European cities such as Paris and Florence—rather than deserted eyesores.

IN A FREE MARKET, prices are reliable signals of the scarcity of products, goods flow from those who do not want them to those who do, and order arises by an "invisible hand" from the free dealings of the many participants. That these facts are all common knowledge does not detract from their truth. Not surprisingly, conservatives tend to look to markets as proof that effective social order can exist without the state and that freedom and order are not opposites but two sides of the same coin.

When it comes to the difficult problems faced by our ever-growing societies, conservatives tend to favor market solutions. This is especially true of conservatives in America, who have inherited the American spirit of enterprise and self-reliance and refuse to be dictated to by people who have not proven their right to take charge. Confronted by problems like environmental degradation, educational decline, health care inefficiencies, or crime, American conservatives' first response is to look to the free actions of individuals rather than to the state for a solution.

In one area in particular, neither market solutions nor bureaucratic controls have worked in a way that the ordinary citizen would wish: city planning and the built environment. Markets depend on cities, which are the principal places where people come together to exchange goods and services, as well as knowledge, aspirations, and ideals. "Civilization as we know it is inseparable from urban life," wrote Friedrich Hayek in *The Constitution of Liberty*.[1] However, our cities are in decline, becoming places where people will work or conduct business, but not live or play.

PLANNING: SOLUTION OR PROBLEM?

The first response of many Americans is that central planning is not the solution but part of the problem. The housing projects of the 1950s and 60s, in which attractive and settled neighborhoods were bulldozed and replaced by municipal housing that nobody wanted to live in, were the result of planning, as were the thruways and expressways that deprived city centers of their dignity and allure. Those projects had disastrous social consequences: a demoralized workforce frozen in places where jobs were no longer available, unvisited city centers, crime-ridden neighborhoods, and the vandalizing of public space. But the principal lesson was not learned: that plans have unintended consequences that accumulate over a far longer period, ultimately outweighing the short-term benefits.

In her celebrated book *The Death and Life of Great American Cities*, which first appeared in 1961, Jane Jacobs argued that zoning, the concept on which the entire American planning system is based, is misconceived. Zoning leads to a disaggregation of the many functions of the city so that people live in one part, work in another, spend leisure time in a third, and shop in a fourth.[2] Whole swaths of the city are thereby deserted for large parts of the day, and the fruitful interaction of work and leisure never occurs.

Zoning contributes to the dereliction of the city when its local industries die and ensures that the central areas are not places of renewal, but at best museums and at worst vandalized spaces no one can use. In successful cities like Paris, New York, and Rome, workshops, apartments, offices, schools, churches, and theaters all stand side by side, with houses borrowing walls from whatever building has a boundary to spare.

The complaint against zoning is surely right. But it is not a complaint against planning. The great planning disasters, some of which have been studied by Peter Hall, owe their negative impact at least in part to their scale.[3] When the layout of a town is conceived from a master plan, the possibilities for disaster are legion.

A telling example is the English new town of Milton Keynes, established in 1967 under a plan influenced by the centrifugal concept of the city developed in California by Melvin M. Webber. The resulting sprawl houses a population only two-thirds the size of Florence (a city you can walk across) spread over eighty-eight square miles of aesthetic pollution, absorbing and extinguishing villages, towns, and farms in a tangle of thruways and roundabouts, with the population trapped in little globules between the streams of fast-flowing automobiles. The center of Milton Keynes is recognizable as such only by its superlative ugliness, and it provides the residents with no place of social pilgrimage, no precinct for "hanging out" or being at ease with neighbors; it is simply a place you visit out of necessity when the food runs out.

The problem with Milton Keynes is less planning itself than using the wrong kind of plan. Washington, D.C., one of the most successful urban environments in America, was planned—admittedly by a Frenchman—but nevertheless in a way that enabled the city to grow in answer to its needs while retaining the dignity of a metropolitan capital. Large areas of the great European cities were laid out by plans, and in Venice even the crenellations of the palazzi on the Grand Canal have been governed since the fifteenth century by city ordinances. The enormous number of planning disasters should not blind us to the planning successes, though the disasters naturally raise the questions of what success amounts to and whether it can be measured, which I will explore later.

European examples do little to overcome another objection to planning. America is founded on a Constitution that guarantees the right to property and on a legal tradition that protects the right of owners to do what they wish with what is theirs. There are exceptions: notably, the use of eminent domain to confiscate property in the interests of the municipality or the state.

But these exceptions are controversial and unpopular, and any attempt to introduce planning controls of the kind familiar in Europe would be greeted by the ordinary American with cries of indignation. Landmarks and places of extraordinary historical and aesthetic interest, such as old Charleston, South Carolina, may be protected from destruction or alteration. But this is seen as a measure designed to preserve an existing heirloom, rather than as a guide to controlling how new things might be built or new settlements begun.

European planning controls do not merely conserve the past; they reach forward aggressively into the future. You cannot build a house in the Provençal countryside without obeying strict limitations on height and color and supplying the house with a roof of local pantiles—assuming you can get permission to build at all. In Brittany, walls must be white, and roofs must be pitched and made of slate. You cannot build a house in the English countryside unless you can make a case for it under the highly restrictive rules of the 1947 Town and Country Planning Act. In some Swiss cantons, existing residents must approve new construction; before they vote on a proposal, they may demand a wooden model of the final result to see whether they could stomach it.

Americans react negatively when bossed around in this way. But they are just as appalled by ostentatious eyesores as their European peers and do not object to measures to protect shared amenities, such as beautiful landscapes, precious habitats, or notable landmarks. They happily accept Virginia's scenic highway legislation even though it confiscates the right of landowners to place advertisements next to the road; they acknowledge that many good things in their environment— attractive roadsides, open spaces, subdued noise levels, the night sky—can be protected only as public goods, for which all must make a sacrifice. But the American homeowner believes that the right to property is a cornerstone of his way of life and that restrictions affecting the value and marketability of his house are unwarranted invasions of individual liberty.

This belief reflects the comparative mobility of American society. While Europeans move to new houses on average once or twice in their adult lives (depending on which country they reside in), Americans typically move every six years.[4] Hence they regard their houses, as they regard their cars and furniture, as goods to be exchanged and replaced, rather than as destinies to cling to. Anything that affects the market price of their property affects their plans for the future. This American mobility has facilitated the rapid transfer of workforces across the country, from places in decline to places of growth. This partly explains the rise and fall of American cities. Populations are as likely to move out of American cities as into them, and the cities themselves have some of the character of industrial sites, which die when the factories close (like Buffalo or Baltimore) or spring up overnight like mushrooms in the wake of innovation (like Silicon Valley). But this mobility comes with a price.

THE DECLINE OF THE CITY CENTER

A city may seem to be an industrial site when it is growing or dying. But at its zenith, it is a settlement with institutions, schools, hospitals, universities, and recreational facilities that cannot be easily moved and that serve to retain the population within their orbit. A city begins as a means but lives on as an end. The short-term economic purposes are then subsumed within the longer-term purpose of settlement, and even if the city's population is constantly changing, it owes its attraction and success to what is permanent. Cities are made by their long-term residents, by the institutions and facilities that grow within their boundaries, and by the public-spirited benefactors who care for them as a home, as the Cone family cared for Baltimore or J. P. Morgan for New York City.

Nothing is more important to a city than its center, and when the center decays, the result is an ecological disaster. Empty or vandalized lots, crime-ridden neighborhoods, declining schools, people who cannot move in search of work because their properties are unsellable: these are only some of the many problems that together defy our capacity to encompass and solve them.

Many causes have been assigned to the decline of city centers in America, and probably no single factor is preeminently to blame. Two factors, however, naturally stand out: the surrender of the downtown to business and the flight of residents to the suburbs. But which is cause, and which effect?

Businesses move downtown to enjoy the buzz of proximity and the infrastructure that makes business easy. People flee to the suburbs because the city center has become too costly, in terms of both taxes and crime. And of course, when the middle classes flee to the suburbs, the schools in the center go downhill, recreational facilities decay, and the city fathers are faced with the stark choice to be observed everywhere in America: museum or desert? Reflecting on this, many conservative-minded Americans tend to agree with the conclusion drawn forty years ago in a classic essay by Edward C. Banfield that the

downtown-plus-suburbs model of the city is the inevitable consequence of rising affluence and falling transportation costs.[5] Recent
writers like Joel Kotkin and Robert Bruegmann have agreed, arguing
forcefully that sprawl is the "market solution" to the problem of urban
growth, and although it leads to results that some people find alarm-
ing—for instance, the spread of the Chicago metro area over thousands of square miles—no solution exists that does not involve forcing
people to live where they do not want to live or in a way they would
not choose.[6]

The popular counterargument is that sprawl is unsustainable, and
in any case leads to the death of the city. Such is the contention of
James Howard Kunstler in his influential books *The Geography of
Nowhere* (1993) and *The Long Emergency* (2005), and it is a view with
a considerable history. The attack on sprawl originates with the nineteenth-century British protests against the industrial city, mounted by
John Ruskin, William Morris, and Philip Webb—which led to the
twentieth-century attack on ribbon development by Clough Williams-
Ellis and others, the defense of the bounded city by Lewis Mumford
in his 1961 classic *The City in History*, and the New Urbanism movement in Europe and America today.

Williams-Ellis was an architect who initiated the campaign that
led to the Town and Country Planning Act of 1947. This law allowed
and even encouraged the placement of "green belt" around British
cities to contain all development within a fixed boundary. Although it
has been challenged, the law has been in place for more than fifty years
and has proven popular with the electorate, who react adversely to any
suggestion that it might be relaxed. This does not contradict Kotkin and
Bruegmann's assertion that sprawl results from people getting what they
want. It merely affirms that, when many people individually get what
they want, the result may be something they collectively dislike.

Whatever side we take in this debate, it is surely true that many of
the most important cultural and social functions of the city cannot be
performed by a conurbation without a heart. Yet that is what a city
becomes when the people who frequent it have their homes else-

where. The suburbanized city is a city of absentees. Although people frequent it by day for the purpose of earning money, they vacate it at night, and therefore it cannot bring people together in activities of citizenship. Public lectures, clubs and colleges, theaters and concerts, festive meals and the ordinary mingling of strangers in bars and restaurants—all these are goods that a city provides and the true reason cities are needed. A city is a market not only for stocks and shares, but also for ideas and values and for crafts and skills. It is a place where strangers can spend leisure time and form networks of friendship and recreation that enhance the quality of life and renew commitment to the public realm.

Conservatives may say that such things will come to exist provided people want them and provided no system of rules and regulations gets in their way. But the fact is that these outcomes are killed by distance and gradually wither as the city expands. This is one major cause of the decline in the volunteer culture, which has been documented by Robert D. Putnam and others.[7] The local associations observed and praised by Alexis de Tocqueville came into being among people who could easily turn up to a meeting or join in a band.[8] But how can weekly meetings bring people together from both ends of Chicago? Equally, the volunteer culture declines when the locations where work takes place fall into disrepair or are "uglified" by the wrong kind of building. And the uglification of the downtown occurs as soon as no resident remains to protest against it.

The centrifugal city may seem sustainable in a time of cheap oil and easy transport. But even the office blocks are now beginning to move to the "edge city" described and in part endorsed by Joel Garreau.[9] Unfortunately, they leave a wasteland behind them. The abandoned city of empty glass towers is incapable of adapting to new forms of life and wholly without any social or cultural presence. The only way forward (other than costly demolition) is to shift the center of the city elsewhere, as London's center has shifted west or New York's has shifted north from Wall Street to Greenwich Village.

But suppose a city retains some kind of center. The real questions remain those Jane Jacobs and her followers posed: Can our cities be planned in such a way that people will want to move to the center? Is there an incentive that might be released by the right kind of plan and that is strong enough to overcome the flight to the suburbs, bringing the bourgeoisie back where they belong? It seems to me that this attraction to the center marks the success of planning, and the desire to escape its failure.

The problem is not particular to America. The new cities of China are being built on the American model; the Victorian cities of India are being bulldozed to make way for American-style downtown areas; American construction firms and architects are taking advantage of the developments springing up all over Asia and bringing with them the downtown-plus-suburbs concept because they know no other and can easily persuade the local municipalities to agree with them.

Many suggestions have been made as to how an attraction to the center might be generated. Building downtown convention centers, expensive museums, and concert halls; offering tax credits for city-center businesses; creating enterprise zones; and removing some of the regulations that make living, moving, and trading downtown so difficult have all been tried, and none has worked.[10] And the reason they do not work is because they are addressing symptoms instead of causes. People flee from city centers because they *do not like city centers*. And they do not like city centers because they are alienating, ugly, and without a human face. Or rather, they do not like city centers when they are alienating, ugly, and inhuman, the normal case in America.

But that is not always the case in America or elsewhere, nor does it need to be the case today. We are familiar with the "broken window" theory advanced by James Q. Wilson and George Kelling in *The Atlantic Monthly* in 1982, according to which neighborhoods that seem to be abandoned soon *are* abandoned.[11] Broken windows attract more broken windows, graffiti attract graffiti, neglect attracts neglect. The smallest amount of policing, sufficient to prevent that first broken window, might save a whole neighborhood from otherwise inexorable decay.

THE ROLE OF AESTHETICS

The broken window theory, in my view, is simply the first step toward a more comprehensive view of the city as an aesthetic creation. Cities degenerate when they are seen as mere instruments, temporary structures that are abandoned when their purpose is fulfilled. Already the downtown has the appearance of such a place at night, when its temporary occupants have fled to the suburbs; this is still more true when it is built so that appearances do not matter, when utility stares from every glass façade, and when the demands of the human eye are everywhere repulsed or ignored. A city becomes a settlement when it is treated not as a means but as an end in itself, and the sign of this is the attempt by residents, planners, and architects to fit things together, as you fit things together in your home or your room, to offer welcome vistas and a friendly patina.

The proof of this is easy to find in the old cities of Europe. People choose to live in the center of Paris, Rome, Prague, or London rather than the periphery. Others who do not live in those cities want to spend their vacations there to enjoy the culture, entertainment, and beauty of their surroundings. These are flourishing cities, in which people of every class and occupation live side by side in mutual dependency while maintaining the distance that is one of the great gifts of the urban way of life. And there is a simple explanation for this: People wish to live in the center of Paris because it is beautiful. It is also lively and rich in every kind of cultural and recreational opportunity. But it is rich because people of all walks of life live there—not just people engaged in specific occupations, but also the cultural elite—and this has made Paris a symbol of the urban experience, the *cité pleine de rêves* ("city full of dreams") of Baudelaire.[12]

Paris became beautiful over many centuries, through both the effect of top-down decrees of monarchs and ecclesiastics and the bottom-up consensus on how the residents should build. The city was radically altered by the plans of Baron Haussmann. But these plans were executed in a way that respected the prevailing aesthetic values: that is to say, they used materials, forms, and scales that derived from existing precedents and blended with the urban fabric. Many regretted the destruction of the medieval Paris invoked by Victor Hugo in *Notre-Dame de Paris*. But with the exception of a few blemishes, Paris has maintained its aesthetic identity, attracting culture, education, and social life to its center, where agreeable streets are maintained by committed residents.

Two kinds of planning laws exist: those that are applied by the municipal authorities and those that empower the residents to decide what may be built in their neighborhoods. The assumption in France is that the people are far too likely to make aesthetic mistakes or to be corrupted by local interests to be entrusted with a jewel like Paris. Hence, the planning decisions are imposed from above. Nevertheless, these laws have two important features that seem to be vital to the success of cities and that should also provide the model for American urbanization.

First, they are conceived as side constraints, rather than descriptions of some goal to be achieved. They do not tell us how the city should ultimately be, only what cannot be done during the course of its growth. Limits on height and scale, materials, and architectural details are laid down to ensure that whatever is built or renovated will conform to its surroundings. New buildings will fit in with the old, since they will share a language of form.

Secondly, the side constraints are aesthetic. They govern not what goes on inside a building, but how it looks from outside. In other words, they concern how the building fits into its surroundings. Of course, other constraints exist, not all of which would be acceptable to the freedom-loving conscience. But the lesson to learn is that aesthetic side constraints are enough to make a centripetal city: they are all that is needed to attract residents into the center.

When aesthetic constraints are obeyed, people come to hang out. When they are disobeyed, people flee. And where some people hang out, others come to hang out with them. The first aesthetic success is like the broken window, though working in the opposite direction:

just as failure breeds failure, success breeds success. This we have seen in Boston's Faneuil Hall Marketplace, which has brought people back to the city center, to some extent undoing the destructive work of the modernist Boston City Hall next door.

Other matters are relevant to the flourishing of a city: education; law enforcement; the circulation of traffic; lighting; public spaces; and the opening of the city to activities like worship, theatrical performance, and sports that require extensive cooperation if they are to emerge. But the lesson to be drawn from the centripetal cities of Europe is that all such matters are far less important than the side constraints that endow a city with its aesthetic identity. Those constraints are the *sine qua non* of successful urbanization, and their absence has caused the decline and fall of the American city.

THE CITY AS A HOME

The centripetal city is the city of the bourgeoisie, the city that attracts into its center the prosperous and adventurous middle classes who are not only the catalyst of economic life but also the ones who will invest in public order, rescue the schools from collapse, support the life of the theater and concert hall, fill and endow the universities, and even establish think tanks devoted to the perpetuation of shared ideas.

The principle I am advocating can be illustrated as well from American as from European instances. New York City owes its centripetal nature to the attractive areas that have retained their aesthetic identity despite changes in use and lifestyle through the twentieth century. Just ask yourself why people want to live in Greenwich Village or why the flamboyant neoclassical warehouses of Lower Manhattan have survived and adapted to every shift in the spirit of the city. Of course, the fabric of a city like New York is being constantly torn apart and renewed, and this means that few things are constant unless kept in place by some municipal edict. This makes conservatives nervous about aesthetic constraints: who conceives them, who applies them, and how do we protect the right of property against their abuse?

Rather than answering those questions in this brief essay, I shall leave them with the reader, because to me they define the real problem of planning. Our efforts should be directed to designing cities where residents are at home in surroundings that acquire the patina of home, and in which buildings happily meet us and adapt to our interests in just the way that people do.

Place and Poverty

WILLIAM A. SCHAMBRA

The cultivation of place is too often seen as a privilege of the well-heeled, the sort of people who have the leisure and affluence to worry about green spaces, tidy town squares, bike paths, and historic preservation. But as William A. Schambra shows, place is not only for the rich; indeed, the cultivation of a sense of place is a vital but neglected element in facilitating the overcoming of poverty. Schambra's story of Cordelia Taylor points us toward a more enlightened and effective approach to poverty alleviation and social policy, one that affirms and builds upon local knowledge instead of the more global and detached perspectives of social-scientific experts. The empowerment of local communities is only possible when the people of those communities have an intense commitment to them, as the places in which their lives and futures are rooted, and when their own self-understandings are accorded a primary importance in the formulation of public policy.

FOR THE PAST seven or eight years, I have made an annual pilgrimage to Georgetown University to speak to a class of graduate students in public policy—yes, for two full hours every year, they are pitilessly exposed to the unhinged ravings of a conservative.

I begin the account of my otherwise deeply perplexing political inclinations by noting that they are rooted in a sense of place. I grew up among the townships of mid-Michigan, I tell the students, where strong local communities created a solid, nurturing moral and religious climate for healthy families and children, and where the need to manage their own affairs provided the schools of citizenship so important in Tocqueville's account of the conditions of American democracy. That sense of local community, I maintain to them, is worth preserving against displacement by big government, as well as atomization by the marketplace.

In the discussion that follows, almost invariably the first objection is this: what you say may be fine for the well-off. (They have never seen the abandoned farms dotting the logged-off, inhospitably sandy soil of my youth.) But what about those who live in places of poverty, where none of these community institutions exist? Don't we need more encompassing, national solutions in such cases?

This is a fair question. If the perspective of place cannot speak to the needs of the poor and marginalized, it would have a significant moral and political blind spot. But in an age when formal, professionally run social service programs for the poor are prime candidates for the budget balancers' chopping block, the place perspective *does* offer a plausible alternative, and will have to become part of any future approach to the problems of poverty.

Let me explain by introducing you to one of the most courageous and effectively compassionate people I know, Mrs. Cordelia Taylor.

As a young person, Mrs. Taylor had prepared herself for a professional career in elder care management, with degrees in nursing and administration. But she was appalled by what she found in the large, institutional settings where she began work. The elderly were neglected and abused, treated with none of the dignity they possessed as, in her view, children of God. So she returned to her home on 11th Street in inner-city Milwaukee where she had reared her children, and launched her own senior-care facility, starting with just twelve residents.

With funds and volunteer labor from local churches, and ultimately with grants from the Lynde and Harry Bradley Foundation, she purchased and rehabbed the neighboring houses one by one, connecting them with wooden ramps. Her growing compound soon surrounded a pleasant lawn and several garden plots, raised so that her residents could still get their hands in the soil. Accented by a water fountain and bird feeders, this tranquil setting became the safest, kindest, most restful place her low-income African American residents had ever lived—a glimpse of the heaven in which Mrs. Taylor so fervently believed.

But Family House, as it was appropriately called, was more than just another community-based senior-care facility. It soon became the center of neighborhood life. Children started showing up on her porch, simply to hang out in a place where adults spoke to them with respect and love. Mrs. Taylor's son formed a homework club for them, and when a volunteer offered to teach them judo, the basement became their dojo. Family House was now a senior-care and martial-arts facility.

Mrs. Taylor noted that many of the children were asking for canned food to take home to their mothers toward the end of the month, as groceries ran low. So she began teaching them how to prepare and stretch out nutritious meals on small incomes. She also began hiring them to work as aides at Family House—now apparently a senior-care, martial-arts, home-economics, and job-training facility.

With Mrs. Taylor at its heart, this impoverished neighborhood began to take on some of the attributes of Tocqueville's township, becoming a safer place for families and children, a seedbed of personal responsibility and moral principle, and a venue for self-governance. The example of Family House speaks to the critical difference between fighting poverty with place, rather than with programs. Trained to run large, impersonal *programs*, Mrs. Taylor instead felt a call to exercise her vocation back in the *place* where she had reared her family and which she had come to love, no matter how unlovely its deterioration over the years may have rendered it to outsiders. But once Family House became securely *of* the neighborhood, not just *in* it, the local community began bringing other, unrelated problems to the feet of this wise elder.

She took them on, heedless of management-school doctrine that this constituted perilous "mission drift," because this was how her place, her community, spoke to her of its needs. No remote, rational program planner could have anticipated, much less designed, a coherent initiative for the peculiar constellation of strengths and weaknesses that Mrs. Taylor found on 11th Street. But her sense of place, her love of this neighborhood, demanded that she address those needs as they arose, one by seemingly disjointed one, rather than adhering to the narrow path dictated by her professional discipline.

Mrs. Taylor's attitude is, of course, anathema to the mainstream, program-based approach to poverty. That approach grew out of the American progressive movement, which assured us that the powerful new forces of the early twentieth century—industrialization, urbanization, immigration, and so forth—had forever doomed the notion of place in America, by sweeping away the boundaries of local communities.[1] Happily, the new century also brought with it new sciences of nature and society—modern medicine, public health, economics, sociology, psychology, and public administration—that taught us how to harness and control those forces. But only the intelligent few, well-versed in the emerging professional disciplines, would be qualified to deal with the problems of the twentieth century.

As Thomas Haskell argued, it was largely through the social scientist's "explanatory prowess that men might learn to understand their complex situation, and largely through his predictive ability that men might cooperatively control society's future."[2] And in the words of preeminent progressive Herbert Croly, "in the more complex, the more fluid, and the more highly energized, equipped, and differentiated society of today," the "cohesive element" would require "the completest possible social record," which could be assembled only by social-science experts "using social knowledge in the interest of valid social purposes."[3]

This would all be well beyond the ken of the vast majority of Americans, locked as they still were within the narrow horizons of their parochial worlds. Their views were hopelessly constricted by their rootedness in place—in the benighted ethnic, moral, and religious communities from which they continued to draw their beliefs, in spite of the fact that science had proven them baseless and that technology had breached their borders. To some extent a new kind of progressive education would weaken those beliefs among, and bring enlightenment to, the masses.

THE PROGRESSIVE PROGRAM

In the meantime, though, the new century's complexities demanded that political authority be transferred away from retrograde, place-hobbled everyday citizens into the hands of the more cosmopolitan, professional elites, and upward from smaller, local jurisdictions where tradition-bound opinions tended to predominate, to higher national levels of authority, where sophisticated expertise more easily held sway. The expert few, in turn, would design programs to service the needs of citizens—now better understood as clients—who had no appreciation of the complexity of the social forces shaping their lives, and were fortunate indeed to enjoy the ministrations of public servants who did.

The quintessential progressive sociologist Edward Alsworth Ross captured this approach in his early-twentieth-century, multi-edition textbook *Principles of Sociology*:

> [America suffers from] thousands of local groups sewed up in separatist dogmas and dead to most of the feelings which thrill the rest of society. . . . [The remedy is the] widest possible diffusion of secular knowledge . . . which narrows the power of the fanatic or the false prophet to gain a following, [plus] the public university, [which] rears up a type of leader who will draw men together with unifying thoughts, instead of dividing

them, as does the sect-founder, with his private imaginings and personal notions.[4]

This perspective is, of course, what my Georgetown interlocutors have imbibed. It prompts them to insist that a sense of place is of no use to poor neighborhoods, and indeed may hold them back. In this view, only national social programs designed by leaders with "unifying thoughts" can address problems of poverty. I have to remind the students, however, that we have now had a full century of experience with the elites' science-driven program approach to poverty. And it can hardly be said that poor communities are better off for it.

The irony, as Nathan Glazer pointed out in *The Limits of Social Policy* (1988), is that the very programs meant to alleviate social problems in fact only compounded them. The indigenous community institutions so contemptible to progressives were in fact a neighborhood's first line of defense against social ills, and their subversion unleashed far more misery than substitute social programs could contain. As Glazer put it, our social policies were "trying to deal with the breakdown of traditional ways of handling distress" located in "the family ... the ethnic group, the neighborhood, the church." But such policies were only weakening those structures further by snatching from them their function and authority, "making matters in some important respects worse."[5]

Recognizing this, beginning in the 1960s the social-policy experts adopted a new emphasis on the role of place in the war on poverty. But this hardly meant that the experts would now seek out the local wisdom of community elders in poor places, or bolster their native institutions. It simply meant that expert-designed programs would be reassembled at the local level in such a way that they vaguely resembled a naturally occurring community, only vastly more expensive and less effective. The professionals sought to displace genuine community with a "comprehensive, multidisciplinary, coordinated, interagency service system," with sporadic and ineffectual input from seldom-convened advisory boards of pliant community members.[6]

A dispute would arise later in the social-service industry between those who argued for such a "place-based" approach versus those believing in "people-based" approaches, which would enable the poor to vacate impoverished places altogether. But a so-called place-based approach still rooted in a reliance on professionalism is in truth no friendlier to genuine place than the alternative, which is outright hostile to it.

A PLACE-BASED APPROACH TO POVERTY

The example of Cordelia Taylor, however, suggests the possibility of a radically different kind of place-based approach to poverty.

My experience with her and scores of others like her whom I have met through the good offices of Robert Woodson, the founder of the National Center for Neighborhood Enterprise, has persuaded me that local communities, even the most poverty-stricken, have developed ways of dealing with their own problems their own way. Such undertakings are largely invisible to us because they bear no resemblance to the massive, bureaucratic nonprofit delivery systems our professionals have built, and which we too often mistake for "civil society."

Genuine community groups are typically very small and volunteer-driven, operating out of dilapidated storefronts with water stains on their ceiling tiles and duct tape on their industrial carpeting. They have none of the professional program staffs and trained fund-raisers that bring larger, more polished nonprofits to the attention of government and private funders. They typically explain their undertakings not with the language of social-science causality, but rather by resorting to hopelessly antiquated spiritual and moral categories like good and evil, God and Satan, sin and redemption. Although they may start out, as did Family House, with one mission in mind, they typically accrue other missions as the neighborhood comes to it with other needs.

And the neighborhood *will* come; for here, residents are treated as fellow *citizens* by leaders they know well, rather than as *clients* by professionals who drop into the community from nine to five.

The result may well be an apparently incoherent agglomeration of activities that no rational program planner would have designed, and that puts off potential funders, who are looking for concise mission statements and coherent theories of change. As Leon Watkins of Family Helpline in Los Angeles put it, "When someone comes in and tells me their house just burnt down, or they bring in a little girl with serious mental problems and she has no place to stay, what program do you put that under? . . . It's hard to explain to people that concept. People who pledge support want to see programs. But that's what life is like here—whatever comes up, that's the program."[7] Building around whatever comes up *from* the immediate community instead of what professionals design *for* the community—and will ultimately do *to* the community—that is what constitutes a genuinely place-based approach to poverty.

It's clear why my Georgetown interlocutors, as they train to become the designers of professional service programs, should balk at this approach. It suggests that they are being equipped with skills that have *not* proven effective, while donning blinders against approaches that *have*. Their profession will teach them to brush past the amateurish, unprofessional, uncoordinated, irrational efforts of neighborhood leaders like Mrs. Taylor, in search of the powerful but hidden social forces beneath the neighborhood that produce poverty in the first place—forces which their expertise will now uniquely equip them to understand and master.

A place-based perspective isn't so much hostile to their progressive ideological inclinations as it is to their choice of professional vocation, which they are pursuing with great effort and expense at a demanding and prestigious institution of higher learning.

Now, the dominance of American social policy by publicly funded professionals claiming mastery of social trends may be powerfully challenged over the next decade. Public budgets everywhere are in jeopardy, and it looks as if last on the list for cuts will be the primary culprits behind our mounting deficits—major entitlement programs like Medicare and Social Security. First on the list will be discretionary spending for social services—the dollars designated to create those expensive virtual communities in our neighborhoods. But skeptics of government spending will have to do more than criticize it and rejoice in its almost certain abeyance. They will have to reflect on ways to address the problems that the programs never seemed to touch.

Those who bring to social policy a particular sensitivity to the importance of place can perform a great service in these times. They are unencumbered by the framework of elite professionalism, with its reliance on social services. They can be attuned to and appreciative of the importance of local institutions and local wisdom, even in the poorest and seemingly most desolate of communities, which have been given up as barren wastelands by the professionals.

A strong place orientation should be able to identify as healthy self-governance a kind of neighborhood activity that may appear to some to be chaotic, disorganized, and amateurish. A place perspective understands and embraces the infinite variety of communities in America, each with different strengths and weaknesses, different needs and different answers to them. It does not try to shoulder aside those differences on the way to larger underlying truths, because it understands that to do so is to violate the integrity—and further diminish the capabilities—of the immediate and concrete communities before us.

In other words, a place perspective is important for the struggle against poverty not only because the most effective neighborhood leaders bring it to their efforts, but also because their efforts remain largely invisible or indecipherable unless observers come similarly equipped with that perspective. Understood in this way, a place perspective is indispensable to any future struggle against poverty.

The Rise of Localist Politics

BRIAN BROWN

*Like William Schambra, Brian Brown sees the potential for a transfor-
mation of political life and a revitalization of our democracy flowing
from newly revitalized local institutions. The failure of "rational planning" has, he believes, created the preconditions for such revitalization
to be not only desirable but necessary. Brown sees the widespread longing of young people for a sense of place as an indication that, even
when rational planning has been materially successful, it has failed to
address the psychological and spiritual needs of the whole person. Brown
sees the political Left as having pioneered such issues, though their
growth has ultimately been stymied by the Left's tendency to default to
centralized control. Interest in localism is now rising on the Right, though
as yet lacking political expression, and faced there with other kinds of
coalitional obstacles. Yet Brown holds out the possibility of a serious
reconfiguration of our politics, flowing from the recovery of the local.*

UNTIL VERY RECENTLY, the centralization of administrative power
under expert control—what we might call, for shorthand, *rational
planning*—was considered essential to public policy solutions. In the
industrial and post-industrial eras, advances in science and technology seemed to promise a future of unprecedented efficiency. Cen-

tralized programs could coordinate masses of people toward desired goals, in areas from government to business to philanthropy to city planning. Modern policy problems were considered to be, fundamentally, systemic issues too complex for local citizens and requiring expert professional attention. Technology and globalization would only increase the value of this approach.

Now, however, trends have begun to shift in a very different direction. Some of the preeminent projects of rational planning are foundering or altogether failing. The entitlement crisis, the housing bubble, and other prominent stories and scandals have made Americans more skeptical of distant experts. Advances in technology and business have created new possibilities for individual and local empowerment. The pressure is on for products, services, and organizational practices that will enable consumers and participants to solve problems themselves.

By contrast, rational planning viewed human beings mainly in the aggregate, essentially as a collection of data points that could be predicted and manipulated based on such categorical differences as race and gender. The messy web of mediating institutions—families, churches, nonprofits—could be sidestepped. Mass programs, which could operate on a scale impossible in the pre-industrial age, would be able to deal directly with the masses, matching problems with solutions and products with demand. Freed from the complex and sometimes onerous network of relationships formerly required for political life, Americans would interact directly with the powerhouses of finance and planning: the government, major corporations, big foundations, and so on.

This model, it was believed, could be applied across the board. Its most obvious value was in the mass production of goods and services. Top-down, command-and-control business models, replicated identically across the world, would bring ruthless efficiency to the private sector. Corporations would get bigger and bigger, driving material prosperity. And these concepts were applied not just to government and commerce but also to aspects of social life, including city design, which became specialized so that people would live in one place, work in another, shop in another, and play in still another (the invention of the suburb took this model to its logical end). What the French architect Le Corbusier famously said of houses—that they were "machines for living in"[1]—is how the rational planners tended to think of cities and of society at large.

But while rational planning allowed for success and efficiency on a greater scale than ever before, it also extended failure and inefficiency to the same scale—and nowhere has this been more obvious than in the political and social sphere. The impending fiscal collapse of the major entitlement programs of the twentieth century signals just what an enormous failure rational planning often proved to be. And "big philanthropy" ran into similar problems as "big government." Large private foundations like those of Rockefeller and Gates dedicated themselves to wiping out social problems with many millions of dollars and professional plans. These foundations have pursued technocratic solutions to such problems as school reform and AIDS in Africa—and they are baffled when, as so often happens, their multibillion-dollar efforts fail miserably. What these failures in government and philanthropy have in common is the idea that whole societies are just "machines for living in." Experts, the rational planners believed, could descend on a big problem, substitute their theoretical ("scientific") knowledge for the practical knowledge of the locals, and fix it.

Entire generations in the United States have now grown up in the society the rational planners envisioned, complete with established suburbs, schools, big businesses and foundations, and federal entitlement programs. They live in suburban socioeconomic segregation, and rarely participate in local politics (which has largely become professionalized). Some newer cities, like Houston, were designed by their planners around the car and the TV—not the citizen and the self-governing community. A parent today has good reason to take his family to the suburbs for cheaper housing and better schools, a low-income citizen has every incentive to collect a government welfare check, and neither has any clear reason to participate in politics except to lobby the bureaucracy to maintain his status quo. The experts will take care of the rest.

Yet over the course of a century, human experience has not validated the rational planning assumption—and a response is coming, if the rising generation is any indication. The people who grew up under the realized model of the rationally planned society are increasingly inclined to shrug it off. Rational planning seems to have created a demand for precisely the things it required people to give up. People who have grown up this way—particularly young people now in their teens, twenties, and early thirties—feel isolated and long for a sense of place. They want to make a difference, not in mass organizations or abstract causes, but in connections and relationships close to home. Where their parents protested, these young people volunteer. They often find their first taste of community life in college, where they live, work, and play in the same environment, and can participate in the community by choosing from among the hundreds of student groups and activities on offer. In 2010, a research project involving interviews with students at the University of Northern Colorado found that those who were involved with at least one campus organization considered the university to be a community; those who weren't involved did not.[2] In short, it seems that to feel connected to the big, they need to be active in the small.

Forward-thinking CEOs, looking to hire these young people, are structuring their companies accordingly. The cutting-edge companies of today still use metrics and scientific techniques of the sort that characterized the rational planning era, but they are also seeking to develop a more place-centered, organic approach. The simple reason: command-and-control can solve some problems, but often creates others—chief among them the corporate ignorance fostered by a lack of on-the-ground expertise. The Prelude Corporation, at one time the largest lobster producer in North America, tried rational planning—and discovered (too late to save itself) that lobster fishing relies heavily on local knowledge.[3] GM and Chrysler, bloated beyond the control of their centralized management, needed federal bailouts in 2009.

By contrast, Ford never received a bailout (although it did receive federal loans), and the company saw its performance improve after making aggressive changes to allow its teams the freedom to innovate. In 2008, the management of Starbucks realized it had started to obsess over mass production and growth, and gotten away from what made its company work—small teams dedicated to making good coffee.[4] Rather than the top-down hierarchical strategy of directed control, companies like these are developing organizational cultures manifested through smaller networks in which local knowledge matters; they emphasize getting the best out of a team rather than micromanaging and bossing it around. The organizations that have made these adjustments—or were founded based upon them, such as Apple, Amazon, and Google—are reporting higher job satisfaction, faster innovation, and greater profits than organizations still laboring under the old methods.[5]

CIVIC LIFE, POLITICS, AND PLACE

This "localist" trend is beginning to reshape American politics as well. Among its other flaws, the rational planning model was based on the mistaken notion that science could be substituted for the practical knowledge of ordinary citizens. But the social sciences have simply never come close to approaching the physical sciences in their explanatory or predictive power. They cannot grasp or manage some of the most basic variables in public policy, including the human need for ownership over our stake in society—that is, the needs for belonging and participation. As a 2009 report for the James Irvine Foundation puts it, people "want the opportunity to be more than passive audience members whose social activism is limited to writing a check."[6] And as Robert Putnam has documented, communities whose citizens feel a sense of local empowerment report (among other things) better local government, less crime, and faster economic growth.[7]

American cities are catching on to the change. Whether in city design or problem-solving, more and more municipalities are trying solutions that involve multifaceted participation, as documented in a

2009 report for Philanthropy for Active Civic Engagement.[8] Some, like Rochester, New York, have sought to improve their local governance by instituting neighborhood councils; this allows people to relate to the city from the vantage point of a smaller political unit they can see and understand firsthand.[9] Boston, with its "Complete Streets" project, is experimenting with "new urbanism," a mixed-use method of city design that makes neighborhoods more self-sufficient and friendly to social interaction.[10] And cities from Colorado Springs to St. Petersburg, Florida are making headway against social problems through public-private partnerships and a thriving nonprofit sector. For public policy at the national or state level to succeed, it increasingly appears that it must find ways to empower, rather than hinder, local self-government—and in doing so, it has to resist the temptation to micromanage from afar.

The move toward localism is driven by expediency more than ideology. Cities, businesses, and other organizations are instituting place-centered practices not because of identification with a movement or theory, but because they are finding that a more organic approach just plain works better. Doing things the "messy" way often proves more effective in the long run.

This shift makes electoral politics trickier, too: muddling through and finding messy local solutions is harder to sell to the public than a grand, oversimplified vision. Tougher still is encouraging localism while refraining from excessive intervention. But it is possible that the leader or party who embraces the localist approach, who articulates the ideas underlying it, who treats communities of engaged citizens as if they matter, may actually have the opportunity to sell it as a grand vision—to make it a movement.

LOCALIST POLITICS, LEFT AND RIGHT

Much of the recent rise of localism has come from the left, from foodie and environmental efforts on the cultural side, to the extensive use of social media to mobilize community activists on the political side.

Actually, localist rhetoric has existed on the "New Left" since the 1960s, when radicals like Saul Alinsky argued that rational planning left out the importance of community organization and local leadership. Fundamentally, however, even the New Left did not abandon the left's longstanding preference for rational planning with its emphasis on people in the aggregate—that is, in *masses*. "People are the stuff that makes up the dream of democracy," Alinsky argued in 1946.[11] He shared the old left's view of people as masses in categories and wanted to mobilize the groups for larger political goals. The modern new left has not departed from that mindset; only its preferred method is different.

The standard-bearer for the modern left is, of course, Alinsky's intellectual descendant Barack Obama, the community organizer whose 2008 presidential campaign is a useful case study in the irony of localism on the political left. His rallying cry was an appeal to ordinary citizens to get involved, to serve in our communities, to be the change that we'd been waiting for. This rhetoric may have been vague, but it was certainly not a call for big, centralized government. But localism and community service are not what the Obama administration has focused on or will likely be most remembered for.

It is hard, first of all, to find examples of Obama administration initiatives for community service that are significantly different from those of the Bush administration. More notably, President Obama has overseen an explosion in the size of the federal government, even beyond the controversial bailouts that at least had the (arguable) justification of averting a depression. Most significantly, his administration has delivered on another of his central campaign promises: the passage of his 2,700-page health care bill, which, along with Franklin D. Roosevelt's New Deal and Lyndon B. Johnson's Great Society, completes the great trifecta of the twentieth-century liberal vision of central administration. Despite the different packaging, the left and its leaders are still champions of rational planning, and they refuse to see the problems that arise from it as anything but evidence of need for further expert tweaking. It would be too difficult otherwise to admit the irredeemable failures that have arisen from a century of their governing philosophy.

But where do conservatives stand on questions of localism in American political life? While the rhetoric of the right has vehemently opposed the progressive faith in rational planning, the right has actually implicitly joined the left in its acceptance of the old paradigm: political life is characterized by individuals in the aggregate. The difference is that whereas the left emphasized the aggregate, the right has emphasized the individual. There were sound historical reasons for this orientation: conservative heroes such as Goldwater, Reagan, and their intellectual successors were fighting a battle against collectivism at home and abroad, protecting the individual against the heavy press of the group. But the resulting strong libertarian streak has led much of the right to blindly disdain all government, including the crucial institutions of local self-government. Likewise, the backlash against the Obama administration's big-government efforts—evident especially in the Tea Party movement—has come in the form of appeals to individual liberty rather than calls for local self-government, stronger communities, and responsible citizenship.

A nation's ability to have a "small" national government depends on its ability to foster strong civic life on the local level. For example, the federal government's direct role in fighting homelessness has noticeably decreased over the past decade, as public-private partnerships between city governments and local nonprofits have proven more effective than the federal failures of the Great Society.[12] The city of Denver, under a Democratic mayor (now governor of Colorado), reduced its chronically homeless population by over 60 percent in four years on the strength of strategic partnerships with faith-based nonprofits.[13] Although these efforts sound like they would appeal to conservatives, few have been promulgated or picked up by the GOP. While Republicans may be willing to challenge rational planning from time to time, they have largely been unable to recognize that they are arguing on the old paradigm's playing field—they are defending their own end zone, but not suggesting a different sport, responding to centralization and isolation by maintaining the individual's right to be isolated.

Meanwhile, a small "new right" has begun to emerge: more localist than nationalist, more Burke than Hayek, and fairly amicable with the New Left (many of its members are not Republicans). In Britain, a similar coterie has gained significant political influence with the ascendancy of Prime Minister David Cameron and his "Big Society," encouraging people to get involved in their communities instead of relying on the government for services.[14] In the United States, it is mainly comprised of offbeat academics, has few formal organizations, and has the Internet for its main intellectual outlet, on sites such as FrontPorchRepublic.com—an opinion source for so-called "crunchy cons," as Rod Dreher called them in his book of the same name.[15] "There are hopeful signs that people are beginning to think seriously about the importance of localism, human scale, limits, and stewardship, the very things woefully lacking in the current spending orgy," writes Mark T. Mitchell, a professor at Patrick Henry College and a regular contributor to FrontPorchRepublic.com. "While a return to these ideals is still only in its infancy, change is afoot. This represents a glimmer of sanity in a world succumbing to the apparent security promised by centralization."[16]

But overall, the new right is still at a theoretical stage: its adherents rarely offer specific policy proposals, and too frequently, its ideas are unspecific or unrealistic. This new right has little political influence and no organized strategy. But, like the right in general, it has devoted a great deal of thought to foundational ideas from which specific policies could be developed.

While localism has so far been a movement mostly on the left, it seems ripe for the right to take it up as its own. Indeed, it remains difficult to fully reconcile localism with the left's remaining adherence to centralized government and rational planning. Localism is philosophically more at home on the right: at the heart of conservatism is a belief in the value of relationships, self-government, and local institutions. It is high time for the right to put the policy together with the principles. We are, after all, the change that we've been waiting for.

The New Meaning of Mobility

CHRISTINE ROSEN

*Few people write with more flair and insight about the human impli-
cations of new information technologies—cell phones, social media,
"augmented reality," and the rest—than Christine Rosen, and here she
reflects on the ways in which the easy and unthinking mobility of our
lives both enhances and undermines the texture of those lives. Is mobility today the liberating force that it once was? Or has it destabilized too
much, and led to an undermining of family life and social harmony?
With the increasing prominence of "virtual" realities in individuals'
experience, the question, she asks, is "whether in exploring those virtual worlds, we lose sight of the importance of the real one." It is a
question well worth asking, with profound implications for the vitality
of our places, now and in the future. As in Gary Toth's essay, the question becomes whether the means take priority over the ends, and the
roads conquer the destinations.*

WHAT IS "mobility" and what is it for? The word has commonly been
used to describe upward movement on the socioeconomic scale, the
sort of classic American success story of which fiction and real life
have given us countless examples. This figurative meaning is related
to the more literal sense of mobility as freedom for movement across

physical space—which itself has an iconic role in the American tale, from the explorers through the pioneers and the Beats. Americans understood the two meanings of *mobility* as of a piece: moving out and moving up, both a means of striking out for new prospects. It was liberation, pursued in the spirit of self-reliance, exploration, and reinvention.

Today, when we speak of being "mobile," we refer to the myriad technologies that allow us to remain in constant contact with each other regardless of where we are. This kind of mobility isn't like that of immigrants struggling to break out of poverty, or of the pioneers heading west. That kind was engaged with places: escaping the confines of the old place, searching for opportunities in the new. For today's mobile citizens, place matters very little; it is an obstacle that technology painlessly overcomes, with our ever-present smartphones telling us always where we are, what's around us, and, thanks to GPS, how to get where we are going.

The cutting edge of mobility is "location awareness": smartphone content that automatically responds and reacts to your physical location. For instance, websites like Yelp allow you to see nearby restaurants and businesses. And Twitter, Facebook, and other social networking sites allow you to "geotag" your updates, so that friends and followers will know precisely where you are. Panasonic makes a camera with a built-in GPS that can automatically geotag every photograph you take, allowing picture-sharing sites to show where the photo was taken.

Although we rarely pause to consider whether this kind of mobility is good, we are beginning to see what it means for those who hope to profit from our use of it. In 2011, AT&T unveiled ShopAlerts, a "geo-fencing" service: as the *New York Times* Media Decoder blog reported, "marketers can create a geo-fence around an event, like a concert, a retail location or a geographic area," and when a person with a smartphone steps into the geofenced area, he is bombarded with offers of products to buy.[1] Other companies have since begun to offer similar services. This is but one example of how mobility has begun to deepen the commercialization of public space, moving it from mere ads and billboards to a point where every individual sojourn into public space becomes an opportunity for targeted commercial exploitation. In this sense, the digitization of public space seems to be following the path that the Internet took two decades ago, moving rapidly away from its initial status as a freewheeling, unencumbered realm and turning it into something that more closely resembles a shopping mall.

Consider an interview Eric Schmidt gave to the *Wall Street Journal* in August 2010 when he was still CEO of Google, in which he stated rather matter-of-factly, "We know roughly who you are, roughly what you care about, roughly who your friends are." This is true for millions of users of GPS-enabled smartphones—and, as users of Apple's iPhone and phones running Google's Android have learned, data on their locations and movements are stored and transmitted back to the parent companies, meaning that they know too *where* you are, and where you were.

Why do Google and Apple want to know where you are and where you've been? So that one day in the near future, when you are walking home from work, Google can remind you to get milk and urge you to stop into a nearby store to buy it. Schmidt foresees, in the *Journal* author's paraphrasing, that "a generation of powerful handheld devices is just around the corner that will be adept at surprising you with information that you didn't know you wanted to know." Schmidt calls this "serendipity," and promises that it "can be calculated now. We can actually produce it electronically."[2]

How desirable, really, is this "electronic serendipity"? It is no small historical irony that the technology that is meant to liberate us from place also allows such ubiquitous location tracking: You can go anywhere, but you can also be found anywhere. The possibility encapsulated in the old form of mobility—the freedom to escape one's past, the chance to start anew—is undermined by the technologies of the new mobility, which make it increasingly difficult for us, even from moment to moment in far-off places, to be free from society, from each other, and from ourselves.

Curiously, although we are ever more inextricably linked together in this way, human ties are not necessarily strengthening as a result. As many sociologists have documented, we frequently find ourselves "alone together," whether we are immersed in our individual cell-phone conversations in public or updating our Facebook pages at home while our family members engage in their own electronic entertainments. We are now available for communication with practically anyone at any time, yet large numbers of Americans report feelings of loneliness, fewer families sit down together to share meals, and the number of Americans living alone is the highest it has ever been. We have more hours of leisure time than any previous generation, and yet we spend most of them watching television. And while we are "connected" to large numbers of people via social networking, studies show we have fewer close friends than did previous generations.

As Sherry Turkle puts it in her 2011 book, which takes *Alone Together* as its title, "we expect more from technology and less from each other."[3] Perhaps we are justified in sensing something paradoxical at work in the progress of our technologies of mobility: their promise—to connect us to people and places—is belied by the reality that our connections to people and places seem only to be weakening.

MOBILE BUT TETHERED

"To be rooted is perhaps the most important and least recognized need of the human soul," Simone Weil argued in the mid-twentieth century.[4] Even our virtual playgrounds pay homage to the deeply felt need for place: MySpace was, until 2009, called "a place for friends"; Second Life mimics real-life places with its homes, offices, and restaurants. What is different about mobile playgrounds is that mobile devices force real life and virtual life (and real places and virtual places) to try to coexist in a way they never have before.

We want to see this as a good, enabling thing—I can fire off that e-mail to the office and then get back to relaxing on my vacation!—but it is instructive to go to a playground today: even on a weekend, you will see parents engrossed in their phones while their children make increasingly loud bids for their attention. The November 2, 2009 cover of *The New Yorker* sadly and beautifully satirized this trend: it shows an illustration of children out trick-or-treating, basked in the glow of houselights, while their parents bask in the glow of the smartphones in which *they* are rapt. Even our leisure time, it seems, has been colonized by our need to stay connected—and it is a constant struggle to set limits on our engagement with the virtual world so that we can attend to the real one in front of us.

And when we decide to leave home entirely, we find it difficult to leave the demands of work behind. Consider the cruise ship industry: every year, more than three million people board a Carnival Cruise ship to take a vacation. They spend a great deal of time eating—and gambling—and then eating some more. The perpetual buffets that have long been a staple of the cruise ship lifestyle cater to one kind of hunger; Carnival now caters to another—one that seems counterintuitive in vacationers eager to get away from it all: staying connected. With their twenty-four-hour Internet cafés, onboard WiFi, and an advertising campaign that features bikini-clad patrons lounging on deck chairs with laptop computers, Carnival Cruise Lines has enthusiastically responded to the demands of patrons who seek an ideal of maritime escape but still want to check their e-mail several times a day.

This, too, is the strange new world of leisure: never disconnected, and never really free from the demands of daily life. Notwithstanding all the talk of mobility, we find ourselves tethered in novel ways—not to a hometown, or to a particular social background, but to our devices themselves and the feeling of connection they provide, without which we seemingly cannot sit still.

This kind of ubiquitous connection transforms our sense of place. First, it brings the Outside in: it eliminates the boundary between work life and home life, and in the process disrupts many of the rituals of private life. Family members constantly checking in and out of virtual worlds exist in a state that has been dubbed "continuous partial attention," which is hardly conducive to healthy family life.[5] Neither is this erosion between work and home life at all like the days when the two were merged, with children tending to the family farm and family members producing goods out of home-based workshops, for this new shift does not bring with it the binding up of family members together in some shared activity or practice. Quite the opposite: what family members do around each other at home has less and less to do with each other.

Our new mobility also brings the Inside out by transforming public space. Every public space is now potentially a scene for the private if we can reach out to those we know via technology. The oft-told tales of being forced to listen to someone else's cell-phone conversation are but one example. More broadly, our new mobility brings the Inside out in the sense that we bring our personal connections with us wherever we go. We can talk to our neighbor when we're on the other side of the world, and update our Facebook page while climbing Mt. Kilimanjaro. This connectivity comes with a cost: the joy of being away from familiar places and discovering new ones unencumbered, the freedom of *dis*connection.

A related consequence of our increasing mobility is the homogenization of experience. We take our devices with us wherever we go, staying connected to our social networks and tapping into the same sources of news and entertainment that we would access at home. Even when visiting remote or exotic locales, we now need never go without the social chit-chat, political commentary, celebrity gossip, sports scores, and jokes that fill our everyday conversations. In the twentieth century, industrialization and mass culture, for all their blessings, greatly eroded local flavor and the particular character of places. Now, the 24/7 hum of electronic communication is having a similar effect, making our experience of every place like every other.

Mobility also continues to erode social institutions. As one writer for the Carnegie Council put it in summarizing the findings of a German research project, "Increased mobility goes hand in hand with increased economic uncertainty, especially among young professionals," which has led to delays in marriage and childrearing. "Not only are young people less economically able to start a family, but they also change locations more often than ever with the fluidity of labor markets. Spouses or couples are less likely to find appropriate work in the same place."[6] What was at first the *freedom* that mobility newly granted us to move about is increasingly becoming an economic *necessity*.

Seen in this light, mobility is less appealing. When mobility becomes transience, ennui often follows. In Keith Gessen's 2008 novel *All the Sad Young Literary Men*, one character remarks, "If you walked around America and looked properly, what you saw was a group of wandering disaggregated people, torn apart and carrying with them, in their hands, like supplicants, the pieces of flesh they'd won from others in their time."[7] They are probably also carrying their iPhones, thinking them a relief.

LOSING OUR PLACE

Perhaps it is time to reconsider "location awareness." Nearly forty million Americans change residences each year,[8] while the U.S. worker's average daily commute totals up to more than a full week out of each year spent traveling to and from work.[9] A genuine awareness of location or place might lead us to rethink mobility, to recognize that much of the ritual and happenstance of daily life—from the family meal to a passing conversation with a stranger on the bus—is necessarily tied to place. We outsource location awareness to mobile technology and exercise too little of it ourselves.

In a recent symposium about the Internet, architect Galia Solomonoff noted the way "our sense of orientation, space, and place has changed" because of the connectedness and mobility made possible by our new technologies. But she cautions: "The Internet at this point privileges what we can see and read over many other aspects of knowledge and sensation, such as how much something weighs, how it feels, how stable it is." And she wonders whether we are better able to navigate places now than we were before the advent of location awareness technology: "Do we have longer, better sojourns in faraway places or constant placelessness? How have image, space, place, and content been altered to give us a sense of here and now?"[10]

These are good questions to grapple with as we think about the future of mobility and membership in particular communities. Serendipity is not, *contra* Google's former CEO, something we can engineer; it is the ability to find something valuable when we are not even seeking it. Mobile technologies promise us access to just such a world whose vast riches we can explore, but in practice, Internet serendipity has come to resemble targeted advertising rather than exciting unexplored horizons.

The more fundamental question is whether, in inhabiting these virtual worlds, we lose sight of the importance of the real one—and our deeply felt human need for place, for community, and for the unpredictable pleasures of face-to-face interaction. Just as architects and urban planners can design buildings and city centers that encourage rather than discourage community, so technological designers and individual users can construct boundaries that make use of our tools without undermining the good life we originally devised them to better.

Making American Places:
Civic Engagement Rightly Understood

Ted V. McAllister

*The loss of place is, in part, a casualty of our culture's drive for libera-
tion from necessity—not only from the limitations of physical space,
but the limitations of any and all aspects of our given identity, including our pasts. This sense of liberation has long been a healthy element
of American life. But the health of both the individual and society
depends on the existence of certain democratic dispositions that need
exercise and expression in acts of civic engagement. This requires local
institutions in which citizens can deliberate on questions of public
good. Without such institutions, our democratic dispositions will
wither and die, and democratic self-rule with them. The "liberation"
from place, argues Ted V. McAllister, is no liberation at all, while the
commitment to place is the path to self-reliant freedom.*

PLACE, THE STORY usually goes, is about limits, and defending the
importance of place is really a species of repression. There is much
truth in this line of reasoning. For so many people in history, place
was either such a basic fact of their lives that they never came to see it
conceptually or, if they did, saw it as a sort of prison. In villages or

neighborhoods all over the world and throughout history—as diverse as fifteenth-century France and early twentieth-century Tennessee (or, for that matter, contemporary Afghanistan)—the experience of place has often been oppressive. It is an experience of prying eyes, leaving no privacy, no relief from the tedium of small expectations, no meaningful escape to a larger world of possibility—not even a reasonable hope of a liberated imagination to dream of other possibilities. For so many of our ancestors, place was just another word for hopelessness.

Do we really need a place in the world today? Isn't the world itself our "place"—our global community? Perhaps for previous generations, the world was too large to be a place and so they were forced to find or carve out a little space to call their own, a provincial home for protection against unruly nature and lawless strangers. We moderns are liberated from the unchosen restraints of our ancestors, for we have largely mastered space with transportation and communication technologies. Who needs the walls of their fortress cities against the barbarians? Certainly for many, portable wealth and countless "connected" locations around the globe liberate them from any meaningful dependence on one place, one society, one polis. We have escaped the limits of geography.

This presumed liberation from physical space (or at least from connection to specific physical spaces) also suggests deeper forms of liberation, including giving ourselves to the creative urge to re-form and reinvent our identities. In this sense, the very idea of place is restrictive. Whereas we might once have said that someone should know his place (which, beyond the racist overtones this language has taken, suggests that we ought to play roles that are given to us, that we did not choose), we now assert that a person should find space in the world for his particular experiment in living. Because we are no longer bound by inherited roles or even strong familial or social pressures to fulfill the expectations that often come from a strong sense of place, we prefer to think of the world as a space big enough for us to find our true selves or create new selves. By mastering physical space we turn the world into metaphorical space for individual expression. Liberation from specific places also means release from bonds of social institutions like family or church. The expansiveness of this world allows us to create or join whatever social networks we choose, designing a social, political, artistic, and sexual life that reaches from Little Rock to Timbuktu, from our laptop to the ether.

Perhaps the most overlooked form of liberation promised by the gurus of modern emancipation comes in the form of historylessness. Human beings have usually had a "place" in history, the felt presence of ancestors, of inherited culture, a sense that as individuals and groups they played an appointed role in a story not of their making. But as the pace of technological, social, and cultural change accelerates, we increasingly experience our environment in a way that exposes no clear dependence on the distant or middle past. The ways of our grandparents are so hopelessly ill-suited to the contemporary environment that one might well consider knowledge of history a useless form of antiquarianism. The conquest of space is also the conquest of history, if not of time. No longer bound to our places of birth, we can more easily ignore the history attending any temporary places we might later inhabit. We have not only turned place into space but we have abandoned history for the ever-present now. As I will argue, to the degree that we live free from the constraints of the cultural and political spaces that we call communities and from the grounding role of history, we sever ourselves from the creative energies of richly encumbered lives. This form of liberation leads to a form of powerlessness.

AMERICAN SPACE AND PLACE

Like most of the contributors to this volume, I believe that the modern liberation of the individual from the constraints of place constitutes as much a limitation as an emancipation. To put the claim bluntly, place constrains but it also empowers, and a radical emancipation from place does not lead to creative freedom but to boredom, emotional and spiritual fragmentation, and tyranny. Thus, it is important to create, preserve, and improve real places for real people (not abstract individuals of indeterminate identity) to find attachments, to empower them to engage meaningfully and well with neighbors toward collective purposes, and to help them understand their particular role in the larger story of humanity. The task must be a constructive one, active rather than passive. It is not a matter of simply not getting in the way of communities but rather of thinking more positively about policies that can cultivate or protect healthy places as lively habitats for citizens, families, businesses, and civil society. To affirm that America needs healthy places requires a theoretical defense of the importance of place to human flourishing but also demands a serious reflection on policies to fit that philosophical and anthropological vision.

But, is it possible that Americans love space more than place? Our cultural mythology is particularly rich with the liberating power of wide-open spaces, the awesome beauty of trackless wilderness, the adventure of the frontiersman untethered to place, the romance and fresh possibilities of the open road, the power of placeless space to inspire self-discovery and creativity. We are often in need of "space" to clear our heads—space to breathe when obligations make us claustrophobic. Many of us need to put space between ourselves and our loved ones, lest we lose our identity in the tight bonds of familial or communal affection. We talk about real and metaphorical space in terms of freedom, creativity, opportunity, and a profound individualism—emotionally connecting "space" with our very identities, our sense of self. It seems that without "space" we cannot find ourselves or create ourselves.

Space can also be forbidding, mysterious, dark—the source for experiences of ennui, loss, and fear. Driving through the vast open spaces of the Great Plains or the western deserts produces, in many a sensitive soul, a sense of spiritual nausea. The horizon is vast, the terrain appears unchanging, time slows down as miles go by without detectable landmarks. One can easily feel insignificant, small, meaningless in such a space—a space that bears little trace of human contact and evokes no sense whatsoever of history. With little effort the sojourner through such spaces meditates on the formless, the timeless, on the infinite—that is, on the terror of boundlessness.

However much we need space for adventure and growth, we need, perhaps even more, boundaries that give structure to our lives, that turn space into something knowable and that help form the architecture that preserves memory. What is needed is an art of place-making, for we can say with G. K. Chesterton that "Art consists of limitation. . . . The most beautiful part of every picture is the frame."[1] The art of turning space into place is the art of limiting in order to create. Indeed, American history is as much the tale of place-making as of seeking space. We Americans are peerless in the practice of this art and we have made America itself into a "place," a huge but not boundless place that incorporates both a built environment and open spaces into a meaningful whole. America is bound by shared history, language, cultural affinities, and collective purposes that emerge from democratic participation—from civic engagement rightly understood. And yet it is reasonable to argue that America is a place only because of the rich and robust nature of its many different and distinct places. Loyalty and attachment to "America" requires, in most cases, complex and almost invisible cords of affection to particular people, local institutions, and places.

In American lore, devotion to these particular places, or to the insistence of building such places, is almost as great as our myth of intrepid individuals bound for virgin land. We celebrate foundings, which, among other things, are acts of turning space into place. The Separatists (so-called Pilgrims) established order in the wilds of America with the Mayflower Compact. At nearly the same time, the Puritans created a robust social and political order on their "errand into the wilderness." What was the Northwest Ordinance of 1787 but the imposition of order on space—the mechanism by which space can be turned into social and political places favorable to human needs? The United States Constitution was the product of a deliberate and deliberative effort to create a new political structure to help solidify a

single, multifarious, coherent place. Every story of the lone frontiersman unfolds against the backdrop of one of the greatest place-making
adventures in human history—the constant settling and organizing
of towns that brought order and stability to previously lawless spaces.
Devotion to place was an important part of the story of the Civil War
and how it was fought. And in the twentieth century, fascination with
what kinds of places we could build and what those places could do to
and for us pushed urban development to new heights, governed the
development of the post-1945 "crabgrass frontier" of suburbia, and
led to the creation of a national transportation infrastructure. Say
what you will about the American love for space and freedom, but
few peoples have shown the same genius for creating places and order.

CIVIC ENGAGEMENT RIGHTLY UNDERSTOOD

Edmund Burke famously argued that "to be attached to the subdivi-
sion, to love the little platoon we belong to in society, is the first principle (the germ as it were) of all public affections. It is the first link in
the series by which we proceed towards a love to our country and to
mankind."[2] Much is at stake in Burke's claim, and what he claims goes
against the trajectory of modern liberalism and the most current tendencies of American society. Burke would have us believe that a
healthy patriotism is rooted in deep attachment to particular and
flawed people rather than devotion to abstract principles. We must
belong to something that we can experience directly, to people and
institutions (and ideas or beliefs that are embodied in people and
institutions) that require daily small acts of loyalty and reciprocity, in
order to prepare us to love well and moderately something too large
to experience directly.

Despite being among the most mobile peoples in history and
despite the great expanse of space that shaped our imagination, culture, and politics, the American people have largely lived true to
Burke's dictum "to love the little platoon"—even if in America that
required us to create continuously these platoons. In the abstract, one

has good reason to doubt that robust localism can coexist with high levels of mobility. In this sense, Americans created something that defies expectations and perhaps is not repeatable for other cultures. The cultural reasons for this success are debatable and beyond the scope of this essay, but it is enough to marvel at the accomplishment, particularly at a time when many suspect that contrary trends pose new and grave threats to this form of ordered liberty, this species of moderated patriotism, and this kind of devotion to place that overcomes the tendencies toward dangerous and narrow provincialism.

If the ability to create, preserve, and improve "place" is necessary to the health of a people, then serious reflection on what we might call "the problem of place" is appropriate for citizens and policymakers. The natural tendency of modern democracy is toward despotism. Modern democracy does not, on its own, encourage a political life and therefore does not encourage people to think of themselves as citizens. If those who advocate civic engagement mean by that phrase a deep investment by citizens in the deliberations of the community about shared purposes and ends—about the kind of place they want to create together—then they will have to develop strategies that check the natural tendencies of modern democracy.

In her excellent book *Democracy on Trial*, Jean Bethke Elshtain stresses the need for what she calls "democratic dispositions," which include a willingness or perhaps even eagerness to act with others toward shared purposes, to compromise, to converse, and to understand one's unique life as entangled in a skein of relationships that help constitute one's distinctive personhood. The maintenance of these dispositions is a necessary condition to preserving the civic virtues of "sobriety, rectitude, hard work, and familial and community obligations."[3]

What Elshtain calls democratic dispositions are, by my way of thinking, really habits that begin by "doing" and then venerating that way of doing. In other words, these are not virtues that one necessarily expects in a democracy, but rather habits that make possible the rare combination of democracy and self-reliance. These habits modify and moderate democracy, rather than express its inherent nature. The "savage instincts" of democracy, to use Tocqueville's phrase, encourage people to withdraw into an intensely private world and to see the world from the narrow perspective of their own self-interest, crudely understood. Disconnected from public obligations, having come to think of individualism as a virtue, the democrat sees only his own small world of family and close associates and then the abstractions of nation or humanity; the rich world of political and civil associations in between are invisible to him.[4]

For Tocqueville, the logical end of democracy left to its savage instincts is an administrative regime that oversees infantilized individuals. In his chapter on democratic poetry, Tocqueville emphasizes that equality reorients human consciousness by destroying the middle ground between the individual and the broadest abstractions, leaving the person with something very small to contemplate—the self—and something too vast to comprehend—humankind.[5] He tends to understand the latter in relation to what he knows about the former, but in order for this to work he must assume an abstract idea of the human; thus, being a human whose nature is universally applicable to the species, he can look inside to his own nature to understand the whole of which he is a part.[6]

Thus the unmoderated democrat—the one who lacks the democratic dispositions that Elshtain so cherishes—makes a virtue out of indifference. Typically, he will say "who am I to say" how some other person should live, thus implying that he operates with an expansive openness to his fellow citizen while more truthfully he is undermining any real relationship—antagonistic or otherwise—that might require meaningful social and political engagement. So long as most "public" matters are really administrative matters, which require the individual to appeal to the government directly for redress, then there is no context for robust political and civic life. Democracy, at this point, is about administration rather than self-rule, about individualism rather than self-reliance.

This unmoderated democrat will recognize few obligations to

people or institutions. Confining his life to those most like himself—often in lifestyle enclaves—he has no reason to care about those who aren't like him. Meanwhile, this democrat will love humanity and will traffic in self-evident abstractions; this both establishes his command of universal truths (and therefore his standing as a citizen) and provides him with the vocabulary by which to engage in political speech that requires no particular, concrete political knowledge.

The point is that democratic instincts destroy the middle ground between the individual and humanity, and the democratic dispositions about which Elshtain writes are the primary means by which individuals enter into public life. If voluntary associations, mediating institutions, and robust local politics help form citizens who are capable of civic virtues—who can at a minimum operate with self-interest rightly understood—then we must pay attention to how Americans form the habits of self-rule, of gregariousness, and most importantly, of serious conversation and compromise.

Most discussion of this problem focuses on the decline of civil society, the decline in voluntary associations, the retreat of certain forms of religious engagement, and the relative decline of local and state politics at the expense of the administrative state. But there is a very complex relationship between the institutional arrangements that allow or even foster these democratic dispositions and the deeper social and cultural forces that give us the desire to participate meaningfully in our self-governance. To design our political world so as to encourage the growth and development of both localist politics and mediating institutions requires that people want such arrangements and that they prefer the messy adventure of self-rule to the comfortable slavery of the administrative state.

At least in the past, Americans have wanted these arrangements and have accepted self-rule as something noble. As a result, we have cultivated the democratic virtues that people like Jean Elshtain and Christopher Lasch have cheered even as they worried that democratic virtues are, in our day, waning. What exempted Americans, for a time at least, from the logic of modern democracy, and what has changed to make citizens less enthralled with the ideals of self-rule? Part of the answer is the decline of place, or what Tocqueville called the "native country."

Tocqueville's first real discussion of "native country" in *Democracy in America* comes in the context of his examination of township freedom. He argues that freedom didn't emerge in America in the abstract, as expressed, for instance, in the Declaration of Independence (a document that he never mentions in his two-volume analysis of American democracy). Nor did American freedom spring from the freedom of an individual in a state of nature. The most important freedom to appear in the American wilderness was political freedom—the power and latitude of citizens to govern themselves without any real interference from outside and more distant authorities. This political freedom, resting on the authority of a historically expansive franchise, allowed each township to define its own laws.[7]

American devotion to freedom emerged from social and political life, not from solitary individuals seeking protection of what is theirs by nature. Because democracy serves as a solvent to relationships that bind individuals together through mutual forms of obligation, it tends to reduce society to a loose association of individuals whose connections are products of affection, desire, and mutually agreed-upon contract. The origins of American freedom are essential to explaining how democratic instincts were altered by circumstance.

The township, Tocqueville argued (following Aristotle), is a natural form of association, found throughout history. But, however natural the township, history knows very few cases where township freedom (the freedom to govern themselves without interference) lasted long enough for citizens to establish deep habits of self-rule and emotional attachments to their own town. Because American townships (or at least New England townships), during a long period of salutary neglect, produced countless and distinct varieties of these self-governing communities, they also produced a patriotism attached to each town wrought by these ongoing habits of self-rule. By investing as many citizens as possible in the regular acts of government, these townships foster a distinct sense of ownership or meaningful participation—for their citizens it was truly "our town."

The constellation of choices, laws, traditions, and habits that emerge from this robust form of self-rule produces something akin to the "native country." "In this manner," wrote Tocqueville of the multiplication of civic duties, "life in a township makes itself felt in a way at each instant; it manifests itself each day by the accomplishment of a duty or by the exercise of a right."[8] The constant and regular action of political life gives a very specific character, look, even feel to each town. "The Americans are attached to the city by a reason analogous to the one that makes inhabitants of the mountains love their country. Among them, the native country has *marked and characteristic features*; it has more of a *physiognomy* than elsewhere."[9] The shape of a town, its features, its laws, its history, its way of doing things, gives rise to attachments, to the love of the particular, the eccentric, the known in ways that no generic expression of a town can produce. Most important of all, Tocqueville claims that the very particularistic character of each town, and therefore the means of producing loyalty, a sense of duty, and love of what is one's own, is the product of what we might call civic engagement rightly understood.

Civic engagement does not mean organized appeals to a distant government, nor does it include any conception in which the citizens construe their relationship to the government, local or distant, in a manner similar to a client or a customer. Civic engagement rightly understood, in whatever particular form it takes, requires that citizens engage as citizens in a deliberative process in which they understand themselves to be partners in governance. Governance, in this use of the word, is not limited to, nor must it be primarily, an expression of an organized government that supplies services. Indeed, the more centralized the administrative functions of the town, the fewer the opportunities for self-government. A large administrative apparatus leaves individuals free to live largely unconnected from social and political arrangements, free to live and let live, free to cultivate a lifestyle. Individualists, thus produced, see no need to rely on their fellow citizens or their closest neighbors or their fellow congregants or their lodge members. The well-functioning administration (local, state, and federal) liberates them from mutual dependence and thereby robs them of township freedom.

Civic engagement, therefore, must incorporate a sense of self-reliance rather than individualism. Habituated to solving problems with their neighbors as those problems emerge, citizens do not reflexively turn to the administrative state when a bridge washes out, when the little league needs a place to play, when a family loses its income. Civic engagement surely includes citizens working through the political process to make changes (often to get that bridge or baseball diamond built) but it must also open up social space for other groups, clusters of volunteers, and nongovernmental institutions to solve problems. The common denominator of all such civic engagement is the investing of citizens in the task of governing with some or all their neighbors and the fostering of a sense of ownership that can only come from each town developing its distinctive physiognomy.

By contrast, Tocqueville's admiration for the way American democracy produced countless native countries and for the salutary effect of this prodigious expression of self-rule also meant that he saw the risks of tyranny as great to the extent that America lost this habit of local self-rule. Freedom depends on local self-rule. At the end of his second volume, as Tocqueville anticipated what would happen if democracy were to be abandoned to its savage instinct and thereby stripped of its virtues, he placed the loss of native country as the very expression of despotism:

> I want to imagine with what new features despotism could be produced in the world: I see an innumerable crowd of like and equal men who revolve on themselves without repose, procuring the small and vulgar pleasures with which they fill their souls. Each of them, withdrawn and apart, is like a stranger to the destiny of all the others: his children and his particular friends form the whole human species for him; as for dwelling

with his fellow citizens, he is beside them, but he does not see them; he touches them and does not feel them; he exists only in himself and for himself alone, and if a family still remains for him, one can at least say that he no longer has a native country.[10]

Understood this way, strong places that are distinct, that have a purchase on the attention and affection of their citizens, that engage at least a large minority in robust self-rule (civic engagement rightly understood), are the necessary condition for the protection of American freedom. The problem we face today, as I noted earlier, is that people must want this kind of freedom, this political and civic involvement that requires them to give up individualism for communal self-reliance. Healthy freedom, at least in the American story, require places that move citizens to love where they live, to find themselves part of a local story (history), and to invest their time and energy in the evolution of a place strange, distinct, and perhaps even a little weird. To paraphrase Edmund Burke, to make us love our native country, our native country ought to be lovely.[11]

Place as Pragmatic Policy

PETE PETERSON

Pete Peterson approaches the issue of place from the standpoint of practical politics—particularly at a time of the "new normal," in which fiscal and operational constraints on the ability of public agencies to act effectively in the public interest appear to be greater than ever. He tells several illuminating stories about how local civic engagement, far from being a misty romantic ideal, can be the most feasible approach to reform. In Kauai, Hawaii, a strong sense of place and an engaged citizenry were key to doing things that government seemed incapable of doing. A contrasting example is provided by the city of Bell, California, which became a byword for predatory urban mismanagement because the citizenry ceded political control to an astonishingly corrupt leadership class, with predictable results. Bell's near-death experience underscores the importance of place, and a sense of place, to the sheer survival of our cities and towns.

> *Modern public administration has been too generally dominated by the nineteenth-century rationalist's conception of society as a vast aggregate of unconnected political particles.*
> ROBERT NISBET, The Quest for Community[1]

WE FIND OURSELVES in a happy place when a concept fraught with such philosophical and theoretical connotations as "place" is recognized as at least a partial solution to the very real challenges confronting leaders in our local and state governments. For reasons ranging from a historically difficult fiscal environment frequently described as the "new normal," to a general distrust in our governing institutions, to the challenges of leading an increasingly diverse citizenry, connecting citizens to one another through a sense of place is developing into an important leadership skill for an array of our local officials—from mayors to city planners.

Though he never researched the influence of place explicitly, the death in 2012 of America's eminent pragmatic social scientist James Q. Wilson offers an opportunity to look at the significance of place in the formation of public policy. I did not know Wilson well, but had the honor to meet him on several occasions through his deep and significant relationship with the Pepperdine University School of Public Policy.

Several years ago, he was kind enough to be a guest speaker in a class I was teaching on California policy issues. The topic that night, coincidentally, was the relationship between this state's incredible ethnic diversity and its reported low levels of civic participation. Wilson had just responded in the pages of *Commentary* magazine to a controversial study on this subject by his friend and former Harvard colleague Robert Putnam.

Putnam is best known for *Bowling Alone,* his groundbreaking book on the decline of national civic engagement, and more recently for his study on American religious habits, *American Grace.*[2] In his study on civic participation, which he titled "*E Pluribus Unum*: Diversity and Community in the Twenty-First Century," Putnam examined the public participation habits in forty-one communities across America—from Los Angeles, California to Winston-Salem, North Carolina. What he found, even qualifying for factors like household income, education, and race, was an inverse relationship between civic participation and ethnic diversity.[3]

In other words, to quote Putnam, "inhabitants of diverse communities tend to withdraw from collective life, to distrust their neighbors, regardless of the color of their skin ... to expect the worst of their community and its leaders, to volunteer less, give less to charity and work on community projects less often, to register to vote less, to agitate for social reform *more*, but have less faith they can make a difference, and to huddle unhappily in front of the television."[4] Of the forty-one metro and rural areas he studied, the places with the most ethnic diversity—places like Oakland/East Bay, North Minneapolis, San Francisco, Los Angeles, and Houston—tended to be the places where the fewest people trusted their neighbors and people of other races, or even of their own race.[5] Then, going above and beyond his task as a researcher, Putnam concluded his article with a set of recommendations to address the problems presented by ethnic diversity. Some of these are policy-focused, including one recommendation for the federal government: to consider national aid to localities affected by the costs of diversity.[6]

Wilson's response in the pages *Commentary* was titled "Bowling with Others."[7] He did not take issue with Putnam's results—he, in fact, buttressed them, quoting supportive research.[8] What Wilson did tackle, however, were Putnam's prescriptions, which he largely criticized as either unlikely to work or unworkable. Wilson also noted the inherent tension in a democratic republic between "rights" claimed by individuals, and broader community-focused commitments. In this latter sphere of allegiances, where Putnam uses the word "tolerance" to describe obligations beyond the self, Wilson uses a more disconcerting word—"morality":

> Much as we might value both heterogeneity and social capital, assuming that one will or should encourage the other may be a form of wishful thinking. That is because morality and rights arise from different sources. As I tried to show in *The Moral Sense* (1993), morality arises from *sympathy among like-minded persons*: first the family, then friends and colleagues. Rights on

the other hand, grow from convictions about how we ought to manage relations with people not like us, convictions that are nourished by education, religion, and experience.[9]

This passage is a lovely example of Wilson's genius: to see what policy can and can't do, to be humble, to have a sense of irony. And it also offers us a new lens through which to view place. Specifically, while policymakers use terms like "civic engagement" and "democratic participation," really what we seek to do is encourage "moral behavior"—which includes both sympathy and participation in the lives of others. Discussions of place are really about finding another platform upon which we—this increasingly diverse people—can become, in Wilson's term, "like-minded."

As director of Pepperdine University's Davenport Institute for Public Engagement and Civic Leadership, my work focuses on supporting legitimate and productive public processes at the city and county levels—first in California, and, more and more, throughout the country. When I first started in this work about five years ago, I'd talk to local government officials about public engagement. In the days before the economic collapse, I'd get a nice pat on the head from these folks saying, "good luck with that good government and democracy stuff, but we're fine here."

Times have changed. Cash-strapped municipal governments and a diverse and distrusting citizenry necessitate the intentional involvement of citizens in both decision-making and service provision. The pathway to this participation is to create a sense of "like-mindedness" through an appreciation of place.

So what does this look like in practice, and what can happen if a sense of place is not inculcated? For the remainder of this essay, I will look at three case studies highlighting the centrality of place in local policy formation.

BEACH AS PLACE

We begin by going about as far west as one can in the habitable United States—to Polihale State Park on the southwestern edge of Kauai.[10] Just after the national economic crisis hit, the island was savaged by a natural crisis in the form of a tropical storm that severely damaged facilities and the entry road to this area. It is here that we not only witness one of the greater feats of self-governance in recent years, but also catch a glimpse of the changing relationship between citizens and their governing institutions.

Set just below the Na Pali cliffs, this wild eighteen-mile stretch of sand, with dangerous undertows and no lifeguards, draws locals and visitors from around the world, so local businesses—from kayak companies to restaurants—have sprung up around the park entrance. Without access to the park, these businesses would have no customers.

Within a month of the washout in late 2008, personnel from the state's Department of Land and Natural Resources (DLNR) came to scope out the damage and devise a solution. Returning to Honolulu after their visit, they contacted local officials back in Kauai to schedule a public "information meeting" in February 2009 to discuss next steps.

Officials from the DLNR announced their findings to those gathered: reconstruction would cost $4 million and take at least a year to complete. Even this dire estimate seemed optimistic, given Hawaii's fiscal condition. As local resident and surfer Bruce Pleas remarked, "The way they are cutting funds, we felt like they'd never get the money to fix it."[11]

DLNR representatives did suggest that local residents could help the situation if they would petition their state legislators to support a "Recreational Renaissance Fund" bill that would generate more monies for the department. The DLNR's chairperson, Laura Thielen, implored: "We are asking for the public's patience and cooperation to help protect the park's resources during this closure, and for their support of the 'Recreational Renaissance' so we can better serve them and better care for these important places."[12] Essentially residents were being told by the DLNR, "Stay out of *our* park until you can send *us* enough money to fix it."

The government's response was typical of that of many large institutions—public and private—facing a crisis: to look *in* (at internal resources), or to look *up* (to higher levels within the organization for financial or logistical support). Citizens become a mass to be lobbied (at times for good reason) to pass spending measures. Missing was a reaction that we are starting to see more frequently as cash-strapped governments seek to deliver consistent levels of service: looking *out* for support (to citizens and civic organizations).

The DLNR's approach did not sit well with local residents, to put it mildly. "If the park is not open, it would be extreme for us to say the least," said Ivan Slack, co-owner of Na Pali Kayaks, which promotes tours on the coastline. "Bankruptcy would be imminent."[13] A group of local residents organized to develop a plan for opening the park earlier. Slack said what was on the minds of many: "We can wait around for the state or federal government to make this move, or we can go out and do our part."[14]

As Alexis de Tocqueville might have described it, this was truly a case of self-interest rightly understood, but it is also obvious from reading quotations from the area's residents that much of their engagement was inspired from a love of this beautiful natural place. The DLNR's initial review suggested that this was no simple "beach cleanup" but a significant construction project that included bridge building, road grading, and bathroom construction. Area restaurants supplied food, and nearby Martin Steel donated about $100,000 in steel and hundreds of volunteered work hours.

As a result, the project the state had forecast to take at least a year and cost $4 million was completed in less than two weeks. Following inspection by the state, the park was reopened in April. Interestingly described as the result of "collaborative efforts" between the DLNR and Kauai residents in a state-government press release, the DLNR's

Thielen spoke in glowing terms of the effort: "Due to their love for this beach park, community members devoted themselves to accomplish those repair tasks necessary to allow us to safely reopen as much of the park as possible."[15]

Given the facts as we know them, it appears that Troy Martin, president of the aforementioned Martin Steel, has a more accurate reading of the affair: "We shouldn't have to do this, but when it gets to a state level, it just gets so bureaucratic, something that took us eight days would have taken them years. So we got together—the community—and we got it done."[16]

It would be easy to dismiss this story as anomalous, but those of us working with local governments know that what happened in Kauai was more than a Norman Rockwell portrait to be admired; it is a window through which one can see a new relationship being mediated between stressed local governments and citizens, a relationship built on a love for place.

LEGISLATING PLACE?

In a time of pervasive state budget deficits, few states are dealing with the structural persistence of California's budget crisis. Year after year, legislators in the state capital of Sacramento wrestle over how to close shortfalls measured in the billions of dollars. Out of these efforts, long-treasured government programs—from public universities to state parks—endure funding cutbacks at historic levels.

In response to Governor Brown's decision to close 70 of nearly 280 state parks, Jared Huffman, then a Marin County assemblyman, wrote Assembly Bill (AB) 42. The bill, signed into law by the governor in late 2011, cuts the red tape involved in the transfer of park management from the state to a local civic organization or municipal agency.[17] As in Kauai, the law has sparked dozens of efforts by local nonprofits, which, out of desire to protect and care for beloved public places, are assuming responsibility for tasks ranging from marketing to ticket-taking and maintenance.

As Huffman described the purpose behind his legislation, "Particularly in these tough economic times, creative public/private partnerships are an essential tool in providing ongoing protection of, and continued access to, these treasured public assets."[18]

In early 2012 the Valley of the Moon Natural History Association signed the first AB-42-enabled agreement, keeping open the Jack London Historical Park in Sonoma County after it was initially on the governor's closure list. The Association now assumes responsibility for the park's $500,000 annual budget,[19] and is responding creatively with greater volunteer participation and plans for open-air theater-event fundraisers, as well as collaborations with local wineries.

On the importance of keeping the park open with public participation, the park's executive director, Tjiska Van Wyk, borrowed words and inspiration from the park's namesake: "Just like the famous author, we are aiming at creating a new model, a sustainable one that will echo his words: 'Try to dream with me my dreams of fruitful acres . . . watch my dream come true.' The message of this famous writer-become-farmer was: 'If we redeem the land, it will redeem us!'"[20]

It is somehow appropriate that the first California state park saved through civic involvement should be the retreat of a writer, who, among other things, wrote so compellingly about the wild beauty of nature. But communities around the state are now working with government officials in order to take over these places from what can only be loosely described as the "public sector."

WHAT'S THE WORST THAT COULD HAPPEN?

Geographically it is one of America's ten smallest cities, but after the story of its official malfeasance was revealed on the front page of the *Los Angeles Times* in the spring of 2010, much of America heard about Bell, California. The tale of incredible misconduct by the city's administrative and elected leaders continued to unfold over the next year.[21]

From the city manager's reported salary of nearly $1 million (five times the average salary for the position in California) to elected city council members receiving six-figure pay packages (twenty times the average salary for small city council members in the state[22]), comparisons to America's most corrupt municipal "machines" were plenty and justified.

While the stunning compensation figures and shady revenue-raising practices received most of the coverage, precious little attention was paid to the origins of the fraud. For as much as Bell is a study in official misconduct, it is also a lesson in the perils of civic disengagement. The problems in the tiny South Los Angeles municipality (population 36,000[23]) began not in the city manager's office, but in the ballot box.

It sounded like a perfectly Tocquevillian idea back in 2005 when Bell's city council, along with city manager Robert Rizzo, placed a measure on the local ballot to change the city's bylaws—making it a "charter city" rather than "general law." The alteration would effectively disconnect the city from the State of California, devolving power back down to the city, including the ability to set council salaries. Former city councilman Victor Bello was convinced by Rizzo to support the ballot, recounting, "The way I understood it, we would have better control of governing ourselves."[24] Then-mayor George Mirabel added, "It enabled us to create our own vision for the future. That was the way I look at it then and now."[25]

Bellians passed the "local control" measure overwhelmingly: 336 to 54. That is not a typo. In a city over 35,000 residents with at least a third eligible to vote, fewer than 400 people voted on whether to effectively remove state oversight from Rizzo and the council—a costly election to say the least.[26] Within months of the election, council and staff salaries began to balloon.

It is this 2005 election that makes the current prosecutions of Bell's officials far from open-and-shut cases. As the head of the L.A. district attorney's Public Integrity Division, David Demerjian, told the *Los Angeles Times* after the events were uncovered: "We deal with the crime.

What people consider corruption may not be a crime. I tell them, 'Any dysfunction within the government has to be handled by you.' The residents have a lot of power.'"[27]

So what are the costs to the residents of Bell for their civic malpractice? Possibly the loss of the eight-decade-old city itself. Even with its exploitative leadership gone, the city is still in a massive fiscal hole. More than a few local-government experts have advocated consolidating Bell with neighboring cities to form some sort of larger "South Los Angeles" municipality. Former Ventura city manager Rick Cole, in a much-read *Los Angeles Times* editorial, opined that "such a solution would not be a panacea. . . . But the dysfunctional and easily plundered fiefdoms would be swept away. There would be a substantial population of homeowning, taxpaying voters that neither politicians nor the larger media would be able to ignore."[28]

But Bellians are not going quietly into that good-government solution.

Beginning with the appointment of interim city manager Ken Hampian in 2011, the city began a turnaround based on greater civic engagement and transparency in municipal decision-making. In early 2012, the city hosted its first "Goal-Setting Community Forum"—a facilitated public discussion about the city's upcoming annual budget (full disclosure: the Davenport Institute consulted with city leaders on this process).[29]

At the foundation of this civic reawakening is the evident desire on the part of Bellians to preserve this 2.6-square-mile piece of real estate in the southern shadows of Downtown Los Angeles. Speaking with many residents and local leaders during the Forum process and since, it is obvious that residents know what's at stake. Bell is not neighboring Maywood or Cudahy or Huntington Park. It has its own history and culture that its residents love and want to preserve. As Hampian told me, "If Bell is to survive, it will be up to its residents. There are some good signs—there is a solid group of residents who love this city, and they're the only reason Bell is still intact today—but there are massive challenges too."

PLACE, LEADERSHIP, AND POLICYMAKING

Even though Robert Nisbet penned the words that introduce this essay back in 1953, the field of public administration still approaches the masses it serves from the high and detached perch of technocratic expertise. These divergent but related stories, with backdrops ranging from the sunbaked beaches of Kauai to the sunbaked asphalt of Los Angeles, demonstrate that this is changing, and for reasons that will not be temporary.

As these stories illustrate, the connection to place has become more important in light of the ongoing fiscal crisis. This is particularly true for local governments. And this resource-depleted environment is not likely to change anytime soon. It has been dubbed the "new normal" by Harvard professor and former New York City Deputy Mayor Stephen Goldsmith. "The current fiscal crisis isn't a passing phase; it's a new, enduring reality that must be confronted," Goldsmith has written. "Crisis is now the norm. Intuitively, Americans understand the need for fundamental, transformational change in their public institutions."[30]

The public is becoming more involved not only in decision-making but in actual service delivery, as local governments around the country are forced to pull back on their standard service offerings. Creating and sustaining a sense of place is a pragmatic leadership response to this situation, as effective local leaders will have to find ways to engage their residents in these historically difficult decisions.

Implicit in this response are three related municipal-leadership skills that will be necessary to practice in this "new normal" era. First, leaders—both elected and administrative—are going to have to act more as *behavioral economists* than rational ones when it comes to how they regard their residents. From the rational social scientists we have the term "rational ignorance" to describe the civic behavior of citizens who, understanding that their individual participation (in the voting booth for example) makes little difference in policymaking, deliberately choose to disengage from engagement in the civic sphere.

In the wake of the challenges noted here, leaders must overcome this rational ignorance by appealing to what might be called "softer incentives"—things ranging from citizenship to participation in the preservation of services and places.

The words of Tocqueville once again resonate. At the conclusion of his famous chapter on "self-interest rightly understood," the young Frenchman writes, "One must therefore expect that individual interest will become more than ever the principal if not the unique motive of men's actions; but it remains to know how each man will understand his individual interest."[31] Indeed, how will a local resident "understand his individual interest"? In purely economic terms, in terms of what it means to his pocketbook, or in other terms framed in questions about what is worth preserving about our places in light of significant fiscal trade-off decisions?

Second, public officials must become *historians*. They should possess a keen historical knowledge of the communities in which they serve, and be able to communicate that unique history within the decisions they make and plans they propose. In an era of tremendous change and movement, the importance of knowing what is distinctive about the places in which we live has never been greater. History can be both an attracting and binding agent for residents who desire a reason to participate in local decision-making while at the same time they wonder why certain policies are under consideration.

Finally, like no other time in our history, the power of technology to organize factionalized opposition to local policies, combined, somewhat ironically, with a generally disengaged public, has forced local leaders to be more *conveners* than pure hierarchical decision-makers. At a recent conference at Pepperdine on land use planning, the planning director for a major metropolitan area acknowledged, "we often put people [planning staff] in front of the public who are the least prepared to be there." What she meant by this was not that the city's planners were not experts in their craft—understanding the intricacies of "build outs," "setbacks," and "floating zones"—but that they often lacked experience and local knowledge relevant to the public that would be affected by planning decisions.

While it would be logical to view these proficiencies—to be a behavioral economist, a historian, and a convener—as helpful in addressing tough local fiscal issues, the challenges described earlier by Robert Putnam in addressing any problem with an ethnically diverse populace can also be resolved through leaders valuing place. Towards the end of Putnam's "*E Pluribus Unum*" article, he offers a suggestion for how best to lead ethnically varied populations: "my hunch is that at the end we shall see that the challenge is best met not by making 'them' like 'us,' but rather by creating a new, more capacious sense of 'we,' a reconstruction of diversity that . . . creates overarching identities that ensure that those specificities do not trigger the allergic, 'hunker down' reaction."[32]

I posit that these "overarching identities" can best be formed at the local (as opposed to national) level, where citizens are invited to share in a place-based public enterprise in which all are immediately touched, in decisions from parks to schools to public safety. It may be a stretch to demand new citizens fully comprehend what it means to be an American, but knowing what is unique about being a New Yorker or Chicagoan or Bellian is more approachable, and a good starting place towards realizing broader commitments.

There are certainly challenges to these new leadership skills based on an appreciation of place. From within governing institutions, it is the nature of our bureaucracies to expand—a process that exemplifies the theory of collective action defined by the social scientist Mancur Olson over half a century ago as the dynamic where concentrated benefits are supported by diffuse obligations.[33] Elected and administrative officials along with their contractors receive immediate benefits (from employment to prestige), while taxpayers pay a relatively small amount each to support this system. Given this, internal defense of the bureaucratic status quo is understandable, with institutional agents often promoting the complexity and necessity of their roles, while exaggerating the costs of retrenchment.

To counter this institutional inertia, political and policy leaders have to trust a citizenry they may have distanced in the past. This demands not only the skills of the behavioral economist, the historian, and the convener, but also an outlook, described most directly by Northwestern University professor John McKnight: "Modern heretics are those professional practitioners who support citizen competence and convert their profession into an understandable trade under the comprehensible command of citizens."[34] Part of making policies "understandable" is to identify them most closely with the people, places, and history of the area to be affected.

McKnight is partly right in blaming our governing institutions, and I've had many of the public officials we work with accept part of this responsibility. But we as citizens can be just as culpable. Every time we blame government for our public problems without contemplating our own role in their solution—from public safety to public works—we view ourselves as "customers" rather than citizens. This is the difference between selfishness and self-interest rightly understood. As Stephen Goldsmith put it, "Intuitively, Americans understand the need for fundamental transformational change in their public institutions."[35] We have seen citizens from around the country respond accordingly. A sense of place—a sense of what makes our community unique and what is uniquely worth working together to preserve—may be the only genuinely American response to this "new normal" environment.

Local History:
A Way to Place and Home

JOSEPH A. AMATO

The historian Joseph A. Amato is a powerful advocate for the dignity and importance of local history. Local history is often disparaged as the province of mere antiquarians and historical societies. That prejudice may or may not be justified. But when the practice of local history is in the hands of a master like Amato, the microcosmic tale of place and locale and region is as dazzling and compelling as the story of the fall of the Roman Empire or the drama of the Battle of Britain, and made doubly so because the tale is an exploration in self-knowledge and self-consciousness for those who do the writing and reading. Amato is both a profound theorist of local history, and thereby of place, and a gifted practitioner of such writing. Like the poet William Blake, he has learned how to see the universe in a grain of sand. His essay gives us a glimpse of how we can go about doing it, and why we should want to, for the sake of our souls.

LIFE IS LIVED out in a place. Any given place has a natural geography and belongs to a shaped landscape and a built environment of structures, buildings, homes, organized spaces, and a multitude of objects, tools, and machines. Also, a place, which can be defined as a discrete locality or as an expanded region or state, embodies a type of commerce and industry, as well as a stage of an economy. A place is also a society—a set of institutions, a collection of groups, and a mixture of communities and cultures. A set of unities, similarities, contrasts, juxtapositions, polarities, and contradictions, a place exists also as a combination of differing states of change, development, maturation, decay, and decline.

Natural and made environments combine to make a place a shell of life. A combination of nature, woods, fields, walls, civil structures, and buildings form the outer surface, the boundaries, and the confines of experience. At the same time, this outer cover outlines the perimeters and horizons of social action and understanding. In a place there are common phenomena and unique manifestations of movement, motion, and growth and of forms, colors, and stimulants of primary perceptions. The latter give rise to and yet define emotions and senses, and they are inextricably entangled with passions, loves, and hates. All this stuff of first experiences becomes the signs, signals, and metaphors by which we think, form images and express dreams and hopes.

More concretely, we can say structures, spaces, homes, neighborhoods, villages, and inhabitants define and distinguish a place. In singular, unique, and kaleidoscopic combinations, a place in turn forms young minds and the veins and roots of engrained habits in older citizens. Sidewalks, storefronts, alleys, fields, churches, and schools host the rituals, ceremonies, and celebrations by which individuals and generations experience and know, make and represent their lives. A temporally distinct group of people joins and synthesizes an extraordinary sum of things, objects, images and associated feelings, ideas, and values in a single place. Literally or metaphorically, within the walls of a place small worlds come into existence and perish.

As much as a place is rendered real by its geography, environment, demography, social and built structures, organized spaces, made things, and social forms and ways, a place also belongs to a time: a period and its happenings, events, memories, and dreams. A place forever belongs to real and imagined temporalities. It belongs to a mix of conditions, idealizations, expectations, and occurrences. On this count, I plead guilty to singing the historian's song: when philosophers, artists, geographers, and sociologists have recited their lyrics of place as home, family, neighborhood, town, village, and region, so the historian offers the music—the rhythm and the beat—of a linking narrative. Narrative alone affords an understanding through stories and tales of what a place was, where it stood in the process of becoming, and how it exists in the folds of memory and the unfolding layers of interpretation.

As I show in my book *Rethinking Home*, local historians can interpret, research, and write their narratives as unique stories.[1] They can borrow their points of view and establish the frames of their narratives from recent works in social, economic, and cultural history. They can adapt environmental and ecological history, including studies of climate, flora, and fauna, and tell the stories of their regions around their geological structures or the possession and control of a place's water and land. Exceeding older local histories, which at one extreme make place an autonomous entity or, at the other, a mere reflective microcosm of national history, local historians can enrich their narratives of a singular and unique place by joining them to larger regional, national, and even global histories. (In the study of places in the Upper Midwest, where *Rethinking Home* has its focus, useful themes are the transformation of nature, the eviction of native peoples, the building of the railroad system, the immigration of new peoples, and the integration of people and place into the institutions and values of the encompassing and developing nation.) Borrowing from contemporary cultural history (something I frequently do for the sake of fresh approaches to local history), the local historian can expand a narrative of a place to local stories of machines, technology, civil engineering, the building of new structures, and the use of new techniques and materials. It can be about a changing landscape and the forming of a new microcosm of distinct senses, smells, sounds, sights, and touch. It can seek to account for changing emotions and altered definitions and treatments of insanity or address altered sensibilities in matters of the beautiful, the criminal, and the clandestine. In this way the local historian can find fresh perspectives and invigorating themes for reconstructing and enlivening a community's understanding of its own history.

First, to underline other premises of *Rethinking Home,* which underpin this essay and give it a paradoxical if not contradictory spirit, I implicitly advocate the unlikely marriage of the professional and the amateur as most likely to give birth to an invigorated genre of local history. Second, I inventory the counterbalancing and nonreducible burdens, pains, and rewards of writing local history. I see the revitalization of the history of place as dependent on largely uncelebrated and solitary work that seeks to reconstruct and preserve, against all likelihood, the unique experiences and conditions of a place in an age of ever-increasing specialization, centralization, and homogenization.

The rewards of local history for its practitioners, whether or not their goals are achieved, are pearls of inestimable value. They are first and foremost the recognition that human life turns on small, individual places and that in them one finds the genesis and formation of selves and individual families. In other words, place is home. Place is where self first lives, imagines, dreams, and remembers—joins senses, concepts, myths, and metaphors into a sense of reality.

Furthermore, opening the door to one place called home opens doors to studying many places called home. At least, that was the case for me. Writing the history of a microregion near the northern tip of the tall grass prairie, where waters run north to Hudson Bay, west and south to the Missouri River, and down off the Coteau du Prairie east to the Minnesota River and south through Iowa to join the Mississippi, I discovered, as paradoxical as this sounds, how much I belonged to my youthful neighborhood on the east side of urban Detroit in the 1940s and 1950s. There I belonged to a neighborhood, a set of streets, a distinct family, a set of shops, a school, a church, a park, and a bus that ran downtown to where my father worked, my mother occasionally shopped, and I caught an annual Detroit Tigers game. So it is that distinct places make distinct biographies, memoirs, poems, and the best, most human, and yet universal literature.

Only by becoming a local historian did I realize the informative powers of place. Without this sense I could not have taken my family history into myself or entered myself into it. In addition to genealogy and stories, family history depends on a history of places and a migration from one to another. To provide a family with a context and a narrative, one must trace its installation in and migration from a place. At least, I tried to establish this in a companion book to *Rethinking Home*, a volume titled *Jacob's Well: A Case for Rethinking Family History*.[2] In it I trace my multiple-ethnic family from its places of origin across Europe to different sets of immigrations and migrations across North America, reaching from seventeenth-century French Acadia to nineteenth-century rural New England to mill-town Wisconsin to twentieth-century Detroit. In this way, I came to know self and family as equally rooted in places and migration, and in terms of their roots and routes; I came to understand part of the greater junctures between local and national, family and universal history. So with a narrative moving between place and home, farm and village, town and industrial city, I unlocked hidden meanings of self and world. I take this to be a great gift of local history.

ORIGINS AND CHANGE

People of every place and time deserve a history. Local history can help satisfy the elemental need to remember the first and lasting things of childhood. Local history carries with it the potential to reconstruct our own and our ancestors' everyday lives—the machines and tools with which they worked, the goods and objects among which they lived, and the faces and groups in which they were raised, matured, had ambitions, and lived out distinct fates. Local history, in adroit hands, recaptures how peoples of a place and time experienced the world through their senses and the emotions and the gestalts that formed their perceptions. It reconstructs what they thought, how they felt, and what formed their passions and follies; it explains why they formed friendships, fell in love, knew their enemies, and learned compassion; it recounts what they prayed for and, finally, how they died and were buried. None of this argues that people and places did not belong in measure to a nation, a period, an age, or worldwide events.

Every community has a vault of stories. Cherished but misunderstood, encompassing wholes reduced to fragments, local stories are worthy of reconstructing and telling. Few communities have historians worthy of their understanding and perpetuation. Match the finite number of skilled storytellers and historians against the infinite number of local stories and one easily grasps why oblivion yawns wide in a world of increasing change. Indeed, on every front of their inquiry, local historians of modern and contemporary places encounter accelerated alteration and metamorphosis. Changes characterize materials, technologies, institutions, whole environments, and the very depths of family and individual minds.

Contemporary local historians cannot resist asking whether their subjects constitute a new order of society, even a species of being. Long ago, French critic Paul Valéry characterized modern culture by its "*interchangeability, interdependence,* and *uniformity,* in customs, manners, and even in dreams."[3] Over the past 150 years or more, Western civilization, from its center to the most distant outposts of its influence, has been measured by multiplying desires, consumption and production, laws, and government agencies. Specializations outrun local populations and their assets. The past ways of thinking and doing are displaced at dizzying rates. Traditions and mentalities are superseded; manners and crafts are extinguished. Places and locales are overrun as suburbs, subdivisions, and malls bring increasing homogenization. Peasants and villages—respectively the dominant form and the crucible of human life since the agricultural revolution of twelve to ten thousand years ago—have been commercialized and nationalized, diminished and forgotten.

Local history, no static practice, focuses on the laboratory of change.

It must acknowledge that its subject, humanity, is multidimensional, plastic, and ever self-defining. Knowledge of distinct places is required by the abstract reaches and theoretical improvisations of contemporary social sciences and history. Historian Constance McLaughlin Green points out that "for any true understanding of American cultural development, the writing and study of American local history is of primary importance. There lie the grass roots of American civilization.... [There one finds] our varied population stocks and their sharply differentiated cultural inheritances, the widely differing environments ... and the rapidity of changes in our economic life."[4]

Nevertheless, beyond providing the foundation for science's sophisticated generalizations and hypotheses, local history satisfies an innate human desire to be connected to a place and one's own childhood. More than any belief in a distant utopia, remembrance of our childhood (its formative images, words, persons, and particular faces and places) feeds our emotional hunger to re-experience life when it stood immediate, fresh, and unveiled before us. First places satisfy our desire for a simpler time and a more authentic being. They meet our need to have the world when reality was first given to us. All serves nostalgia. Even when one concedes nostalgia's political and literary cultivation and exploitation, it remains far more compelling as a cultural force than the idealization and quest for progress.[5]

We each have a primal attraction to our own youth. There is only one per individual and generation in the unique, irreversible, and ultimately nonduplicable succession of life. In the words of turn-of-the-century French Catholic poet and essayist Charles Péguy, "One never makes friends except of the same age and time." Our only friends are contemporaries "of the same fellowship, of the same formation, of the same society, of the same world. . . . Friends of an only time are only friends." This singular friendship is a good without equivalent. It is "of the cradle of a family, a people, a homeland—of a time, a date, an entire temporal order which, unique and of irreplaceable importance, transpires only once and forever."[6]

Local history serves even more than personal nostalgia, however.

It meets the living's duty to honor, pay back, and not forget the dead. Groups' collective yearning to bring back to life people, places, and times that lay behind—or somehow to preserve and keep them alive—aims at remembrance, on which every place and time and particular constellation of people set a claim. Of course, far beyond the exploitation of heritage by commerce and politics with pageants, theme parks, and real estate ventures, remembrance is a living and active force in us. It is fed or we starve. As American cultural critic and enemy of mass cities Lewis Mumford points out:

> Every old part of the country is filled with memorials of our past; tombstones and cottages and churches, names and legends, old roads and trails and abandoned mines, as well as the things we built and used yesterday. All these memorials bring us closer to the past, and, so doing, bring us closer to our own present; for we are living history as well as recording it; and our memories are as necessary as our anticipations.[7]

History in general is self-defining, self-vivifying, and self-authenticating. Local history, with its particular allegiance to place—as I, along with my original colleagues in the History Department at Southwest Minnesota State University, have discovered in a decade of teaching required rural and regional courses—provides the natural link between immediate experience and history. It confirms the idea that one's own home—thus, one's youth—is worthy of study and, again in the words of Mumford, promotes "a decent self-respect," and it is that "form of self-knowledge which is the beginning of sound knowledge about anyone else."[8] Of course, it is assumed that one will attribute to the other what one claims for the self.

RENOVATING LOCAL HISTORY

Local history's topics are innumerable. Reasons for its study can be multiple, including the desire to know, to preserve, to understand,

and to commemorate, as well as curiosity about a person, an event, a legend, an institution, a situation, or a time. Its fruits are its variety and heterogeneity. Thomas Jefferson holds sway over Charlottesville and the University of Virginia. Nearby, at Petersburg, a single Civil War battle commands the landscape itself. Alternating stretches of the seaside as one moves north along the Mid-Atlantic coast direct local historians to a changing ecology, the rise and fall of the fishing industry, or the conditions of pre-Civil War agriculture and slavery. At Cape May, New Jersey, local historians not occupied with town walks devote their time to gathering information and maintaining homes from the town's early golden age of leisure for the sake of tourism and community.

Amateurs in the main, local historians' interest in the past is not joined to the desire to write critical history. They don't even take up analytical questions about the changing borders and dimensions of a place. They don't share the professional historian's commitment to a structured narrative, a consistent causality, or a scientific explanation. Although local historians' interests in the full sweep of the physical and the mental landscapes of a place can resemble those of the material anthropologist, folklorist, or ethnographer, they commonly eschew theory. Their fidelity is not to methodology and professional discourse but to details, anecdotes, and eccentricities.

Their emphasis on the particular can make them tenaciously parochial. They overlook entire epochs and whole nations because of the value they attribute to a singular place and time. Their love of a select past can even lead them to negate the present and to treat change as an aberration of an idealized past. They often find no reason in the revelations and manifestations of today to rethink their views of yesterday. The treasure of their hearts has its embodiment in local museums, which are chock-full of redundant collections. One museum like another amasses nearly identical coin collections, boxes of arrowheads, endless sheets of music, hats sufficient in number for a dozen Easter parades, uniforms from all branches of the service, band instruments, dental chairs, and old Coke signs. Crammed basements and stuffed attics materially document that mass-produced goods, national causes, and widely shared images and icons defined a single place. In the Upper Midwest, museums give a material face to stereotypic and sentimentalized depictions of sod houses, one-room schools, early settlement days, the coming of the railroad, the good times of the 1920s, the dust of the 1930s, and a nation going to war in the 1940s.

Such standard depictions and official commemorations of a locality's past leave many other realities great and small unnoticed. Local historians do not take into account such manifest topics as existing and changing local building materials and techniques and environmental transformations. They leave unexamined mechanisms for the propagation of national ideologies and the perpetuation of established cultures. They disregard such subtle matters as the role and alteration of emotions, sensations, sensibilities, and the mind in general, and they do not grasp even the possibility of studying traditional gathering, hunting, and fishing cultures or the inner cultures of churches, schools, town governments, and laws, nor yet dare to take up, other than bootleggers and whiskey runners, pervasive but clandestine places and types such as local gamblers, pornographers, pedophiles, prostitutes, members of strange sects, and practitioners of occult magic. Likewise, often overlooked as imagined and even invented are those who came and passed through their proverbial River City as short-term workers, itinerant salesman, and scam artists, as well as the parade of characters who came with the unforgettable summer carnival and circus.

If local history is to be renovated, it will depend on the commitment of keen-eyed, witty, and candid amateurs seeking to uncover the unstated truths of home. They most likely will be solitary and eclectic and find pleasure standing home on its head. They will not fit a pattern and certainly cannot be created by a prosaic college curriculum. They may be community college teachers, rise out from the ranks of the retired, or come forth out of a collection of stray individuals who (perhaps once trained in literature, anthropology, or even history) find themselves curious to grasp where destiny has delivered them. They may even find it their passion to fathom the singular place that has imprinted the childhood minds and formed the lives of others. They may believe that fostering and cultivating memories points toward rethinking home and conclude that the variety of past places and peoples far exceeds what the government, the law, and ideology have deemed cultural diversity.

Surely, local history will not come from the ranks of those who insist on repeating established forms of collection, research, and representation. It will not come from those who harness their work to national and international ideologies. Proving the old saw that historiographers rarely write good history, theory will not produce local history. Place does not exist in sweeping and moralizing views of humanity.

Yet again, I teeter on contradiction when I discount theory. If local history is to be renewed, as it constantly must be to preserve its vitality, historians must scrutinize and reject the premises of past writing about the place they call home. They must doubt the reasoning that locks place to nation. On another front, they must draw fresh inspiration from professional history, especially from the emerging field of environmental history, whose insights contribute grounds for considerations of all places, rural and urban.[9] Also, they might fruitfully draw on fresh work in cultural history, both European and American, that offers novel themes for historical composition.[10] Above all, they cannot isolate themselves from the present or the ongoing metamorphosis of environments, things, groups, minds, and individuals that irreversibly and at an accelerating pace come with contemporary times. Both to reinvigorate their own understanding and to secure fresh audiences, they must dramatize their subject around the theme of places caught up in great transmutations. Standing in Heraclitus' stream, their work must bear witness to the omnipotence of change. Their language, depending on place, must speak of—even if ultimately to nuance and contradict—revolution, innovation, decline, fragmentation, turnover, and turbulence. They must confess as part of their witness the growing penetration and dominance of outside powers over local places and people.

REGIONAL HISTORY

As vigilant as local historians must be in not sacrificing their home to bountiful clichés and vacuous generalities, they must stand equally ready to incorporate their place into surrounding areas that since the beginning have defined and characterized it and played a role in its loss of autonomy and its interconnections with the world. This obligation, which can only be outlined here, requires local historians to master the use of the accordion-like notion of *region*—and its subsets, zones, belts, and sectors—in order to define primary and appropriated contexts of the interconnected life of a place.

In my own work on Marshall, Minnesota—a lead town and regional center of 13,700 with a university—I often treat it as part of southwest Minnesota, which shares a common history by virtue of being an agricultural zone within the state. Depending on the context of my study, I conceive it as a region encompassed by other, larger regions, like the tall grass or northern prairie or the prairie lakes region. I place it at the northwestern corner of the Midwest. A borderland between prairie and plain, wet and dry lands, I suggest it is a gateway to the Great Plains. Yet as a region comprising approximately twenty counties, roughly 10,000 square miles, and only three other towns within seventy miles that are approximately Marshall's size, it is too large in any sense to be a locale, especially insofar as a locale implies a concrete place that one experiences and knows directly.[11] Furthermore, southwest Minnesota's geography, ecology, towns, and ethnic settlements are diverse. Economic, political, and cultural developments furnish it with a changing historical definition, which we admittedly create by the very act of writing about it.

On the basis of my training in European history, I grasp that the concept of region has been adjustable and omnipresent for more than the past thousand years, for it was medieval Europe that witnessed the birth of regions. Regions took form in distinct environments: mountains, woods, plains, and lowlands. They were shaped by climate, vegetation, and oceans and rivers, and defined by agriculture, forestry, and mining. Culture, religion, economics, and politics also drew odd, intersecting, and capricious borders of regions. In Europe, even fiefdoms, duchies, principalities, islands, centralizing city-republics, and empires defined regions. In early-modern European history, regions existed by virtue of membership in Mediterranean or Atlantic economies or, to show the crisscross definition of a region, Catholic or Protestant faiths. The Atlantic community settled the New World. The people of northern France—especially Normandy and Brittany—settled the St. Lawrence River valley, traveled the rivers of the Midwest and northern prairie, and explored the Minnesota River system. Names like Coteau des Prairies and Lac qui Parle testify to the early presence of French explorers and traders in southwest Minnesota.

Historians can use multiple definitions of a region. They can base their usage on that of anthropologists, who traditionally employ the notion to identify the space of tribes and customs or, more recently, to stake out spatial and material realms of "peoples without history."[12] Linguists use similarities and differences in language to stake out regions, whereas demographers characterize regions by types and numbers of people. As geographers use spatial boundaries around a region to describe its topography, resources, and economic development, so historians conceive regions in terms of political and cultural borders.

The history of European names suggests that in the Middle Ages particular and modest features of a landscape—a stream, a church on a stream, a marsh, or a single tree—afforded places names. In contrast, testifying to the tremendous transformative powers of contemporary civilization, whole regions are identified by the nation that colonized them. Of great importance is that the physical geography and the history of a place are not the same. A place belongs similarly but never equally to the course of nature and human events. Topography, soils, and climate define conditions and set limits to human settlements. The degree to and manner in which nature and humans seem in harmony or stand at odds with each other form the histories of macroregions. Maps themselves record the encounter of Old World conceptions and New World realities.[13]

Historians do not escape these testing problems. Regions also rise out of contested events—and vast claims about civilization. French Canada belongs to the history of French colonization, the British victory in North America, the plight of a single Canadian province, Quebec, and the preponderance of the French language. Ukraine— where local history presently thrives as fresh potentials are perceived and novel identities are required—was recently born as an independent nation out of the ashes of the Soviet Empire. All regions are subject to reinterpretation as events and politics mutate and elite groups foster fresh ideologies. All historians to a degree both record and invent pasts and presents for peoples, places, regions, and nations. They are makers of place and home.

In the hands of its definers, a region—again acknowledging its accordion-like nature—can be micro- or macrocosmically defined. Those with environmental commitments may conflate a region's distinct ecology with the fate of its first people or one of its physical attributes, such as a chain of mountains, a body of waters, or the distinct mixture of them.[14] Historians of the West like Donald Worster, Richard White, and Patricia Limerick create narratives of entire macroregions and their interaction to match vast historical processes.[15] They invent moral narratives and agents to express nation building, the expansion of democracy, and the establishment of new economic and industrial orders. The aim of their regional histories is to reflect critically the transformations of society and nature. Localities and microregions become forgotten stars in the movement of such immense heavens.

Local historians turn the concept of region to a different use. They use it as context for the general conditions, actions, and stories of select places. They articulate smaller, even miniscule, regions—microregions where two rivers join or divide, where one or two crops controlled the economy for a century, or where a particular industry such as extracting iron ore commanded life and settlement. Microregions provide a kind of mediating identity among a collection of places and localities that have contact and share a common experience, are mutually shaped or fall into the orbit of an expanding metropolis, or belong to the fate of a nation.

The need to separate and define place as an intimate, if not autonomous and independent, terrain intensifies in direct relation to the growth of impinging nations; mass, abstract, and specialized society; global and technical capitalism; and encompassing ideologies and mass culture.[16] In the past three to four decades, regionalism, despite moves toward unification in the West, has exploded in Europe. Microregionalism does more than criticize centralization and excess taxes. It ignites passions, warms souls, and pedals politics. (It also sells wine and cheese.) Tourism often adds a picturesque distant past to a failed present. It sells stories of yesteryear's bandits in the mountains of Sardinia and offers train trips across the North American plains. Frequently, local and regional historians, with the goading of the chamber of commerce, conspire to provide local color and culture to freshly created places. (We have yet to deliberate on the possibilities of creating electronic regions out of interactive websites.) History has not begun a fully critical discussion of how much home, tradition, and place are recent creations.[17]

Wise local historians will grasp all of this. They will not sacrifice locale to region or region to locale. In fact, this conceptual complexity will lead them to timely and even strategic reformulations of home and place. It will above all else enhance their sense as makers of places—as creators who must toggle between the immediate givens of place and experience and the profound influence of state, nation, and world. They will learn to use the notion of region—so important to contemporary environmental and economic history—to write their histories of individual places.

Yet as much as complex issues stand outside their door, they, unlike their academic counterparts, will not allow methodical argument and moral disputation to devour home and its stories. Even when perplexing theory, contradictions, and ambiguity nip at their heels, they must pursue their own pathways of detail and particularity. They must feed themselves and their audiences on the far more humble fare of getting right the names, places, deeds, motives, associations, circumstances, and events of a chosen place, even if many profound worlds fraught with universal meaning reside therein and beyond. This is the labor and reward of rethinking home.

Inescapably, if local historians are to establish their place in a full and dramatic context of time and world (and prevent their portraits from being eccentric or idyllic), then they must define the microcosm of home in the macrocosm of region. They must learn from the best of such generalizing regional books, which in the case of the American Midwest includes historian William Cronon's *Nature's Metropolis*, geographer John Hudson's *Making the Cornbelt*, and John Borchert's *America's Northern Heartland*. They must engage, however adverse they are to abstractions, with analytical history, as in the regional discussions offered by Andrew Cayton and Peter Onuf in *The Midwest and the Nation*.[18]

As much as local historians must learn, however, from the power of comprehensive explanations and narratives of new regionalism, they must not surrender to an inherent global determinism and the scientism of ironclad laws and fixed causalities. To save the very dignity of their subjects, local historians must honor human existence, past and present, as turning on particular places, individual peoples, and freedom.

REWARDS AND BURDENS

In less theoretical terms, local historians can be viewed as the agents and servants of concrete community. They can instruct local leaders on who inhabits their home, what has happened to it over decades and even centuries, and what trends are clearly underway. When for example, I announced the pervasive reality of decline in southwest

Minnesota at the major conference for the League of Minnesota Cities in 1988 and developed the idea into a book—*The Decline of Rural Minnesota*—I spurred influential conversations in diverse political and economic quarters of the region.

A subsequent book on the region's new immigrants, *To Call It Home*, also helped shape the region's dialogue over present and future conditions. When I, with colleagues, identified the meat-packing industry and its turnover rate as the principal sources of immigrants in the region and a range of social problems initially associated with them, we provided a basis for clear conversation of who was now among us. This information proved crucial for education, housing, police, and language training.

From the experience of doing contemporary research—which I passionately exhort local historians to do—comes the exaltation of discovering that historical knowledge can create communities of understanding and help set vital agendas. Different from those who promote economic development, establish policy centers, or coordinate rural coalitions, local historians can create scarce but indispensable self-knowledge. And this type of knowledge (which is, among other things, empirical and developed by continuous retrospective and projective inquiry) serves the intelligence that frees the energy of local people to work in the dimensions of the possible.

Not incidental to the local historian's own energy, local history can even impart its practitioners with a certain level of regional recognition, and at some point, local historians can become an important voice of a place and a region. In time, historians may have the good fortune to appear in educational television documentaries and even have select writings turned into documentaries, which happened with my book *Servants of the Land* when it was made into the award-winning Flemish/Belgian television production *Ghent, USA*. Along with all this comes an array of friends, acquaintances, and experiences and an occasional ecstatic thought that one's work actually revivifies a place and connects it to future generations and the world at large.

What local historians win for themselves they gain to a degree for their respective institutions—and the institutions might reciprocate. I experienced this with the formation of our university's Center for Rural and Regional Studies—which in its now-past heyday brought together three faculty (around geography and rural and regional studies), an environmental educator, a journalist, a handful of graduate students, a rural and regional studies curriculum, a history center, a geographic information studies laboratory, a small press publisher, and an independent local and regional history society.

Teaching also brings practitioners of local knowledge—be it in history, rural studies, geography, or environmental studies—their fair share of bliss. Teaching means showing students how to create things out of their own background and place in society. One's materials can serve as texts and illustrations of local inquiry. Students' own work can be transformed into publications and conferences. In the process they learn that their own region is worthy of study and that learning depends on getting one's own feet muddy. Beyond that, they discover that knowledge is made, and they learn pride in making it. Their work—be it a history of a flood, an environmental study of a county, or documentation of Civil War veterans' or women's role in the early years of a town—gives student and teacher an immediate laboratory and community and provides them with a voice in defining home.

Yet the screw also turns the other way. Local historians can grow hardened and even embittered, and a lifetime's investment in telling the local story can foster a surly attitude. Practitioners of local history may even develop a defiant streak and a contrarian attitude, as allies of the small and out of the way commonly do. Local historians almost instinctively cheer for the remnants of our once-populous peasant ancestors and the traditional countryside—and all those local teams who play without uniforms. Even if they know full well that they survive and thrive by the privileges and goods that city, nation, and market bring—the organizations of the modern order—they applaud any sign of independence and autonomy.

Adding to their sense of being on the side of outcasts and even bandits, local historians' subjects are often classified by the world as insignificant and not worthy of attention. Their places, localities, and even regions are seldom at the epicenter of earth-shaking events, as southwest Minnesota was during the Dakota War of 1862. Even though worldwide forces are continually at work reshaping communities, lives, and landscapes, local historians' primary subjects are modest. They often focus on a neighborhood, a township, a collection of families, a church, a company, a bay of sailors, or a valley of farms.

Local historians, accordingly, do not play to mass audiences, although an occasional film or book may make everyday life in a place a stage for a universal study, often under the rubric that the common is the universal. Aside from producing for small and even vanishing audiences, local historians are ever short of time, money, skills, and collaborators. Even when supported by a rare university appointment, they find few allies among circulating and cosmopolitan administrators and fellow faculty, who are sequestered in disciplines that are in the main devoid of historical understanding of and affection for the place they reside. The local historian may be tempted to travel the dead-end road to fame, which in traditional academic terms leads to presenting at conferences and publishing in journals and with academic presses—which, themselves increasingly impoverished, accept manuscripts based on projected sales and the fads, fancies, and insecurities of their editors. Local historians must, however, find their roads and recognitions on other grounds. They must travel far less elevated terrain and continue in a sublime way studying the familiar and the anecdotal. They must persist in shaping their work around the particularities and details of things, situations, personalities, ethnic groups, and institutions. Like a type of anthropologist, they must find their medium studies, and like their close cousin the genealogist, they must aim at telling unique stories that hinge on specific places, situations, and periods of time.

Nevertheless, local historians do not follow this trail without substantial if less material rewards. They know that their contribution to a place is singular and irreplaceable. They accept the fact that their

234 · WHY PLACE MATTERS

reputation is grafted to a place. Although their works rarely gain national or even regional recognition, they find consolation in knowing that they will usually outlast popular nonfiction and standard academic tomes, which run the cruel and fickle gauntlet of fashion and popularity. Far beyond that, their keenest pride is in knowing that their work gives birth and continuity to a place. It awakens and recollects what was and is home for some. Local historians do what French local-regional historian Guy Thuillier considers so important: they define the tissue and memory of every sort of endangered local community.[19] And this is a powerful antidote to worlds helplessly enmeshed and encapsulated in global change.[20]

With the labor of any long historical projects comes the pain of solitude, though. As much as it might form a community over seasons, its everyday work can be experienced as stern and lonely. Beyond material and social reasons, the historian might experience indifference and not find support. The subject and the craft of local and microhistory does not offer established traditions and pathways. Local history requires its practitioners to forge their own discipline at every juncture. Even when drawing from the past through great wells of documentation, historians must fashion links between present and past and establish new models. The abiding burden of the historian's craft remains: striking a balance between story and explanation, finding the meeting ground between force and freedom, and, testing the quality of spirit, judging what perishes over time and what emerges within time. They must do this with a mixture of technical sophistication and popular appeal.

Their solitude, at points, is not unlike the romantic in the graveyard in conversations with a skull and stones. Like the town booster who has seen Main Street go from antique shops to thrift and second-hand stores to abandoned buildings to Halloween haunted houses to teardowns, the local historian of vanishing places tangibly knows the ravages of time. Time dries up old fishing holes, witnesses the tearing down of dance halls and roller rinks, and destroys the details of a childhood bedroom, the back-breaking labor that went with putting up first hay, and all the sounds, sensations, fears, and madness of the countryside of old. Industries—mining, lumbering, fishing, and agriculture—disappear. Fields and groves of rusting machines and abandoned sheds bear witness. Local places vanish in the countryside, at the heart of the city, and even in the malls and neighborhoods of first-ring suburbs. Their solitude turns into a boundless and swelling meditation on mortality and a hope that God shares their passion to remember and revive the singular and particular, lest all be lost.

Their melancholic reflections include the feeling that the past is being forgotten and the present disappears in the changes it fosters. Everything is being lost—even everyday images, gestures, objects, and impulses—and there isn't enough time or means to observe or preserve the impermanence of place. Historical imagination, conscience, and passion are limited, and historians themselves are finite and mortal.[21] And, for that matter (to draw again on Paul Valéry), whole civilizations—Elam, Nineveh, and Babylon—fell into oblivion and remain but dry stones and "beautiful vague names."[22] In the highest mountains of Sicily and the deepest recesses of Brazilian jungles and on this prairie, under its staggering sky, change prevails. All local places are but peripheries registering the churning centers and idle chatter of Chicago, Los Angeles, New York, Washington, London, Paris, Rome, Tokyo, and other world-shaping cities.

Temporality does not, however, weaken local historians' fidelity, at least as I idealize it. On the contrary, it salts and intensifies it. Mortality does not disinvest hearts from earthly passions but rather stimulates their wish to preserve particular objects and temporal connections, knowing full well that redemption and immortality is for God to bestow. They know that they have a singular duty to a singular place. They know that their work uniquely counts. They know themselves to be blessed in a protean age and amorphous world to have the duty of offering a specific testimony that must be given and that they alone, perhaps with the help of a few friends, can make a difference, however small it may be. On this count local history is a mission that belongs to committed amateurs.

On out-of-the-way shores, local historians ply their craft. Their burden is giving form to little places in an era of massive forces and generalizations. Like folklorists or ethnographers, they strive to keep alive in memory ways of life and habits of mind that civilization no longer countenances. And their reward for doing so is carrying out the duty of their affection. Their passion for the meanings of small things forces them to deliberate not just on the fate of their beloved places but on all things human. Their faithfulness to home is a compass in a great and shifting sea.

Although it forever moves between the ragged edge of contemporary change and the cutting blade of time, local history compensates its practitioners with the blessing of preserving and creating other lives, places, and times. Surely, to offer a consolation tinged with melancholy, there are less-worthy callings than giving fresh forms, however transitory they be, to the work and complex ways of human beings.

Local history can also bless one with a passion and a mission. How can one measure the gift of being joined to a conversation one can't truly quit? How wonderful it is to be caught up with a hundred topics that need exploration and exposition! One day, I imagine what a regional history of insects would look like; the following day, I wish to consider the different types of aging that now characterize the region; and the day after that, I try to encourage a local specialist in soils to try to write a history of bacteria. At my university's Center for Rural and Regional Studies, we plotted developing regional river maps, bicycle tours, and a travel guide organized around ecological, geological, and ethnic themes. The local historian's driving ambition is to record the manifold realities of the place one calls home.

Ecstasy cries out that all history is local. Every place is a universe unto itself. Yet home remains the microcosm in which we learn and know all we will ever learn and know of our fellow human beings and the world at large. And when joy subsides, there remains a puzzling delight to be caught somewhere between the exceptions we cherish and the determining sciences we cannot ignore.

There is no complete history, yet local historians provide a passionate attachment to concrete places in an age when home and place, locale and landscape are in a state of great mutation, transformation, and metamorphosis. This tension provides the basis for an ever-deepening conversation. It provides fresh ways of researching, thinking, writing, and disseminating knowledge. It offers a substance, integrity, and individuality offered by neither contemporary academic nor ideological discourse. One hundred good historians committed to one hundred contemporary local subjects would be a wonderful thing; indeed, a renaissance of trustworthy diversity and a true rethinking of home.

The Space Was Ours
Before We Were the Place's

WILFRED M. McCLAY

This final essay draws together many of the strands of the essays that precede it, but shows a particular interest in how to balance the need for planning against the need for spontaneity in place-making. A vibrant sense of place is neither entirely created nor entirely given, neither self-consciously planned for nor spontaneously generated, but relies on both, along with an engaged and involved citizenry willing to enter into an "urban conversation," at the end of which they can see with fresh eyes the place where they already find themselves and the possibilities that beckon to them. Drawing on the work of Jane Jacobs and Lewis Mumford, as well as the poet Robert Frost, Wilfred M. McClay argues that we build our spaces into places, and then, if we are wise and fortunate, we allow the places to build us in return.

VIEWED FROM THE SKY, the city of Mesa is "an irregular splotch sprawling east from Tempe—133 square miles, roughly in the form of a hook." So reported Scott Carlson in the *Chronicle of Higher Education*, at the beginning of a lengthy and thoughtful examination of the Arizona city's woes and prospects.[1] Viewed from ground level, Mesa doesn't look much better to him: its concatenation of "strip malls and developments of one- and two-story buildings flow as if they had

238

been accidentally spilled out of a bottle," and even the presence of the lavish new Mesa Arts Center, an architecturally distinguished complex that includes four theaters and five galleries, does not prevent the downtown from being the sort of social desert where they might as well roll up the sidewalks when night falls, even on weekends.

Mesa is no Podunk. It is the third-largest city in Arizona, behind Phoenix and Tucson, and its population of just under 450,000 exceeds that of Atlanta, Miami, Minneapolis, Cincinnati, Greensboro, Pittsburgh, Fort Wayne, St. Louis, Tulsa, Wichita, and Cleveland.[2] But Carlson found Mesa to be a conurbation in severe cultural limbo— and found that many of its inhabitants feel the same way. "The city is still trying to find a sense of place," he wrote, "and a reason for its burgeoning population of young people to stick around."[3] Like Phoenix itself, and like so many other cities and towns in the Southwest, it has grown with breathless rapidity in the past three decades, but in ways that took little regard for the shape and texture of the community to which that growth was giving rise. The space has been filled, but that act of inhabitation has not yet given rise to a sense of place. The latest thinking from Scott Smith, the mayor of Mesa, and other local officials is that drawing one or more smaller colleges to the downtown could change the situation for the better, enlivening downtown businesses and street life, and supplying focal points for some part of the city's missing sense of place. Hence the *Chronicle*'s interest in the subject, as the trade organ of higher education.

There is much to be said for the resourceful spirit of the Mesans' thinking in this regard, but it also raises some questions. Does one best establish a sense of place by importing a new institution designed to draw in a cohort of young people who are, by definition, only passing through, living out a finite and temporary phase of their lives? Is not such thinking being driven largely by economic considerations, in which the institution is being valued not for its intrinsic mission but chiefly as an economic multiplier, a magnet for customers with disposable incomes, rather than a sustaining source for permanent and deeply rooted residents? Might such thinking be an example of what might be called the silver-bullet syndrome, the belief that the key to effective place-making lies in the ingenuity of planners making one big catalyzing change?

Of course, such a belief is not completely without foundation. There are locales in which one big change has indeed been a successful source of catalyzing force, with effects rippling outward into many forms of unforced organic change. The city of Chattanooga, Tennessee, for example, has emerged spectacularly from a grimy post-industrial torpor partly through the building of the country's largest fresh-water aquarium, a boldly counterintuitive but highly successful move that anchored the revitalization of the city's formerly decayed downtown area, as well as its northern and southern flanks. But Chattanooga's renaissance had many other sources too, not the least of these being a cohesive and bipartisan group of leaders who were stung by the city's reputation for air pollution, and were determined to do something about it. They embraced an imaginative community-wide planning process that created a broad consensus for change by seeking systematic and sustained input from a varied and inclusive sampling of the city's citizenry about what they wanted to see their city become.[4] Chattanooga did not seek to start from zero and reinvent itself, but sought to build on the existing sensibility of its people, and its existing strengths as a river city with great natural beauty, an abundance of historic antecedents, and a sense of its own past—in short, to become the place it *could* be by more fully being the place it already *was*. Hence the city of Chattanooga's successes illustrate the central paradox of place-making: a vibrant sense of place is neither created nor given, neither self-consciously planned for nor spontaneously generated, but relies on both, and on a fruitful dialectical relationship between the two.

The title of this essay is meant to invoke this dialectical tension by drawing on Yi-Fu Tuan's important distinction between "space" and "place," as well as Robert Frost's great poem "The Gift Outright."[5] Frost's poem is mainly concerned with the historical emergence of the American nation at the time of the American Revolution, and the emergence of a distinctively American form of national self-consciousness after the long formative experience of British colonization and the great galvanizing act of political separation. But the poem's argument also traces uncannily well, and perhaps not coincidentally so, the dialectical path of place-making. The poem begins thus:

> The land was ours before we were the land's.
> She was our land more than a hundred years
> Before we were her people.[6]

Here Frost describes the European settlement of the continent, in which the settlers (who are the "we" of the poem) are taking hold of the land, take dominion over the *space*. But the land itself is devoid for them of the elements of memory, the deep and rich investment of time and labor and history and particularity and shared suffering that make for a sense of belonging, of peoplehood, of *place*. At first the land was for them something malleable, but also something empty, inert, unenchanted, lacking in feedback effects, not to mention being devoid of supervisory gods or ghosts or geniuses.[7] What supervisory spirits there were had come strictly from elsewhere, imports from the mother country, which had succeeded in projecting their cultural influence across the ocean, but had become a barrier to full cultural maturity, overriding and limiting the imaginations of the colonial settlers:

> But we were England's, still colonials,
> Possessing what we still were unpossessed by,
> Possessed by what we now no more possessed.

The colonists suffered from what T. S. Eliot might have called a dissociation of sensibility, or so Frost posited; and overcoming this split-mindedness was precisely what the American Revolution in all its fullness would mean for him. But such a move as he described is also a key move in the making of a sense of place. It involves learning to be fully present in one's setting, to give oneself over to being fully and self-consciously accepting of the place in which one already finds oneself and is already rooted, and to claim it consciously for one's own.

> Something we were withholding made us weak
> Until we found out that it was ourselves
> We were withholding from our land of living,
> And forthwith found salvation in surrender.

Yes, this Revolution was an act of independence and self-determination. But Frost wants to insist that this self-determination was dependent upon a prior acceptance by the revolutionaries of what they already *were*—indeed a "surrender" to these facts, in all their particularity, which is precisely what is entailed in accepting that a place is one's own, one's "land of living." To fail to make that surrender, to withhold one's sense of belonging to a place, is to leave oneself weakened and uprooted, trapped in a virtual reality, possessed by phantoms and abstractions that have lost touch with their referents, forced to struggle on without possessing the nourishment of the memories and concrete associations to be derived from the very soil on which one is standing.

There are no silver bullets to be had, then, when it comes to the act of making or reconstituting place. This caveat includes the propositions and projects generated by any and all theories, which must be viewed with skepticism unless they begin by deferring to the existential reality of place as something that begins and ends with the particularities of human consciousness, memory, experience, and therefore cannot be—and should not be—engineered. The making of place is both participatory and collaborative, both conscious and unconscious, and ultimately reliant upon the vagaries of human consciousness, individual and collective.

But there is another meaning to be taken away from Frost's text. It matters what we do with our land when it is still a space, when it is still unformed potential awaiting a structuring influence from us in order to begin *becoming* a place. In other words, there is no escape from the responsibilities of planning, for the same reason that even an anti-theoretical theory is still a theory. What is needed is a special kind of planning, one built around respect for the element of contingency, whose chief goal is the support and enabling of human spontaneity and creative possibility, rather than the inhibition or oversteering or overriding of them. The solution to oppressive and ineffective planning is not the elimination of all planning altogether, but a recognition that the best plans are those that renounce the aspiration toward comprehensive solutions and benevolent paternalism at the outset, and are modest and tentative in their claim to understand final causes; but instead move with caution and respect, leaving many matters tentative and many corners undeveloped, showing concern for the flourishing of the citizens as they actually exist, not as they can be imagined to be, and showing solicitude for the energies of generations yet to come—above all, building a sense of place on the foundation of present realities, on the "land of living" that is already here.

THE SOUL OF THE CITY

What might such planning look like? One could usefully begin the inquiry by looking back at Jane Jacobs's *The Death and Life of Great American Cities* (1961), a book mentioned several times in these pages that still enjoys a large and devoted following after more than fifty years precisely because its readers find it just as rich and stimulating as when it was published.[8] A full-scale, relentless assault on what then passed for advanced wisdom regarding urban design and development, Jacobs stuck an audacious thumb in the eyes of arrogant top-down planners, clueless modern architects, and ignorant bureaucrats, and offered a vote of confidence in the superior power of spontaneous order, which for Jacobs meant the ability of ordinary people to fashion a satisfying form of urban life without the "help" of the accredited experts. Her book was refreshingly un-abstract and densely empirical, built upon an accumulation of lovingly rendered details about what works and doesn't work in the context of modern city life. Despite the withering contempt of experts and allies alike—even the distinguished architectural critic and polymath Lewis Mumford could not resist dismissing *Death and Life* as a "preposterous mass of historic misinformation and contemporary misinterpretation"[9] assembled by "a sloppy novice"[10]—this unaccredited journalist-mother, with no college education, no training in planning, and no institutional support, wrote a book that would change the way the world thinks about cities.

The author of *Death and Life* was also an astonishingly acute observer. Where others saw in a bustling lower-Manhattan street only a welter of uncontrolled, uncoordinated, and therefore wasteful activity, Jacobs paid homage instead to a miraculous "sidewalk ballet,"[11] a complex and dynamic system of diverse and interacting human actions, wants, and needs being enacted and reenacted on a daily basis, without any help from officious expert choreographers. Even the humblest matters—the placement of sidewalks, the uses of front stoops, the virtues of old buildings and mixed uses, the presence of children, the need for short blocks and neighborhood parks, the protections of constant "eyes upon the street"[12]—attracted her attention, and *Death and Life* is a compilation of odes to such things, and a persuasively detailed argument that their presence makes all the difference between a successful and an unsuccessful urban setting. The density of the modern city, which urban visionaries such as Mumford and Le Corbusier saw as a problem to be solved through dispersion, Jacobs saw as an asset to be jealously guarded, one of the necessary conditions for urban flourishing. The celebration of "diversity," now a shopworn trope of American political correctness, was, for Jacobs, something vibrant and genuine, an endless source of economic and social vitality, and she offered it as a counter to the dehumanizing modernism that had come to dominate both architecture and the field of urban planning.

By now, her insights have become commonplace wisdom, particularly her disdain for the urban-renewal movement of the postwar era, a well-intentioned but disastrous effort undertaken with all the arrogant blindness of which high-minded social engineers and visionaries are capable. Men like New York's Robert Moses and Boston's Edward J. Logue "knew" what was best for cities, including the urban poor, and in forcing it upon them, demolished countless acres of existing historically rooted neighborhoods in favor of ugly superhighways and grim, soulless housing projects surrounded by vacant, moonscape-like plazas, settings which ably reflected modernist design principles but showed absolutely no understanding of the human preconditions for the urban ballet that Jacobs had described. They committed the cardinal sin of failing to take seriously the "land of living" of those whom they would save, and see it as something to be worked with and built upon, rather than razed.

One does not romanticize the conditions of such poor and marginal areas to acknowledge that they still sustained many faint elements of the ballet, and thereby the potential for eventual renewal, and did not deserve to be bulldozed in the name of something brutishly called "slum clearance." Such wanton erasure of memory wrought by such "renewal" was arguably even worse than poverty, since it robbed the inhabitants of their sense of relationship to their own past, and robbed the city of a piece of its very soul. But what made the displacement even worse was the abject failure of the very megaprojects themselves that were to provide a more habitable substitute for the slums that had been bulldozed. It is not for nothing that the famous demolition of the Pruitt-Igoe housing project in St. Louis in the early 1970s has been put forward as a potent symbol of the hopeless bankruptcy of modernist architecture and urban-renewal expertise.

As it happens, Jacobs's convictions were put to the test on her home turf soon after the book's publication, when a series of urban-renewal projects, culminating in the construction of the Moses-designed Lower Manhattan Expressway (LOMEX), threatened to alter forever the face of her own beloved Greenwich Village. Journalist Anthony Flint relates the story of these clashes in an informative if somewhat breathless book, *Wrestling with Moses* (2009), which shows what a fierce and effective activist Jacobs could be, and how seriously she took the tasks of citizenship.[13]

But Flint's book also, perhaps without meaning to, shows some of the limits of Jacobs's vision. For not only was it her own neighborhood, the block of Hudson Street between Perry and West 11th Streets, that she was defending in these struggles. It was also this same neighborhood that she had been describing in her book's presentation of the urban ballet. *Death and Life* was thus a kind of love poem to the Village, offering it as the exemplar for modern urban life. But whatever its virtues, Jacobs's neighborhood was hardly a typical American urban neighborhood whose origins and inhabitants could easily be duplicated elsewhere. Indeed, the history of that neighborhood could not have been more unique.

To begin with, the Village had long enjoyed the peculiar good fortune of being cut off from the rest of the city by its physiognomy, as a motley but charming collection of narrow, winding, diagonally oriented streets that resisted assimilation into the north-south grid dominating the rest of Manhattan. This fact made it easier for the Village to maintain a settled and residential character and a balance of ethnic and economic groups that other neighborhoods, such as the Lower East Side, could not sustain. Then in the 1890s the balance began to change: immigrants began to arrive, rents began to decline, properties began to become shabby, and at that moment, the Village became a magnet for artists, musicians, writers, and all manner of ambitious people who migrated to New York from all over America and the world in search of a free and high-powered life.[14] The Village soon became the stuff of literary lore: "We are free who live in Washington Square," enthused the pseudo-revolutionary John Reed in his rambling, goofy, self-celebrating 1913 poem "The Day in Bohemia":

> We dare to think as Uptown wouldn't dare,
> Blazing our nights with arguments uproarious;
> What care we for a dull old world censorious
> When each is sure he'll fashion something glorious?[15]

The neighborhood had lost none of this ebullient and artsy quality five decades later, in Jacobs's time: in fighting LOMEX, she had the benefit of a protest song composed for the occasion by a fellow Villager, singer-songwriter Bob Dylan. One might just as easily claim that this is a typical neighborhood as one might claim that the membership of the Metropolitan Club represents a typical cross-section of New Yorkers.

Nor is it possible to freeze optimal circumstances in their moment of perfection. For time and chance happeneth to them all. Jane Jacobs's neighborhood today is a very different place from the hospitable but inexpensive retreat from morally pinched middle America that beckoned to John Reed and other Greenwich Village intellectuals and free spirits and glorious wannabes a hundred years ago. In 2009, Jane Jacobs's beloved home at 555 Hudson Street went on the market for $3.5 million, prompting the following headline in the *New York Observer*: "Jane Jacobs' Old Hudson Street Townhouse for Sale in West Village Jane Jacobs Probably Wouldn't Have Wanted to Live In." The accompanying article went on to quote residents who tell sad tales of displacement, failed businesses, and astronomically high rents. "Bleecker Street is a mall now," sighed one of the few remaining independent businessmen, an antiques-shop owner. "They've ruined the Village, as far as I'm concerned."[16]

Today's Village is often held up as a poster child for the dreaded ravages of "gentrification"; but truth be told, it is largely a victim of its own success, meaning its own lore and notoriety, and the unique desirability of the very features Jane Jacobs worked so hard to preserve. Indeed, even the notion of the Village as an asylum from a middle-American morality seems downright quaint today, when the culturally ascendant figure in the land is not the Puritan zealot or Victorian prude, but the genially tolerant bourgeois bohemian as described by David Brooks.[17] The mainstreaming of bohemianism has, ironically, made for a much less colorful or diverse neighborhood than Jacobs's. Fifty years ago, as historian Christopher Klemek has observed, the neighborhood included "old working-class tenants from old immigrant stock, new immigrant groups, particularly Puerto Ricans who were just coming into New York in large numbers, middle-class families like [Jacobs's] own, some affluent residents, as well as bohemian counter-cultural figures." Not so today. The neighborhood can no longer support such diversity. "There are a few people grandfathered in there with rent control," Klemek remarks, "but not new arrivals."[18]

In addition, one must insist that the appeal of the Village as a place to live, even in Jacobs's time, is far from universal. Not everyone wants to live that way, or ever did. The suburbs, for all of the relentlessly bad press they have received for the past half-century or more, seem to have lost none of their appeal for the great majority of Americans, particularly those trying to raise families on middle-class incomes.[19] On the other hand, the New Urbanist advocates of density, such as Andrés Duany and Peter Calthorpe, and others who have been directly inspired by Jacobs's work, have enjoyed little success so far in creating urban environments that meet their demanding aesthetic standards while remaining affordable for ordinary people.

That does not mean that the task is inherently impossible. But the value of Jacobs's larger vision regarding the importance of freedom and choice in the making of decent human habitations should not be lost in the insistence that this vision can only be realized in a particular configuration of narrow streets, short blocks, and high density— or any other collection of desiderata. The good life can be lived in a variety of settings, because it depends more than anything else on the health of the moral imagination, and a balance between the persistence of shared memory and an openness to the dynamic energies of the present, as well as the prospects of the rising generations. The larger lesson to be taken from Jacobs is that the trick of intelligent and effective planning is not in prescribing and regulating everything in sight, and trying to use cleverly devised structures to remake human desires and aspirations, or to "nudge" them in the "right" direction.[20] Instead, it is in the far more modest goal of creating sturdy basic structures that respect, and enable, the free and spontaneous exercise of our human endowment. It doesn't necessarily take a Village to do that. Indeed, there is reason to think that the Village's day of being exceptionally well equipped to do so has passed, at least for now, and perhaps for good.

LIVING PLACES

But the problem posed by the loss of a sense of place in so much of modern life, the problem experienced by countless cities and towns like Mesa, remains before us, and it is real. We need to find ways to foster a sense of place, even in challenging and unpromising situations, in order to have happy, healthy, cohesive neighborhoods full of flourishing families and engaged, public-spirited citizens motivated to decency, generosity, hard work, and mutual respect. Jacobs's work reminds us that this task is not for accredited experts alone (if at all). But we may need to be reminded not to treat Jacobs herself as an expert either, or as the final word on anything.

It is a complex task, not only because there are so many different kinds of places, but because "place" is not just a physical quality obtained by mechanical means. You can spell out every one of the objective and structural aspects of place, and never get to the heart of the matter. It is at bottom a quality of spirit, existing more in the eyes and hearts of the beholders than in the permanence of glass and stone and asphalt. This is why the humblest of places, even notably ugly places, or places others dismiss as slums, may yet be places nonetheless, places radiant with distinction and dignity and integrity that sites far grander may lack.

The centrality of human psychology makes it clear that, for us to recover the knowledge of place, we have also to recover an accurate view of human nature. As Lewis Mumford warned in 1952, at the height of the worst urban-renewal atrocities in American cities:

> The architectural embodiment of the modern city is in fact impossible until biological, social, and personal needs have been canvassed, until the cultural and educational purposes of the city have been outlined, and until all of man's activities

have been integrated into a balanced whole. One cannot base an adequate architectural conception on such a crude sociology as that which led a group of modern architects and planners to examine the modern city with reference to only four functions: work, transportation, dwelling, and recreation. The city, if it is anything, is an expression and symbolization of man's wholeness.[21]

As this expansive description implies, the optimal urban place is both a nexus of memory and a generator of activity, an enabler of personal aspiration. Place draws us back to the past, but it also serves us as a launching pad from which we are made capable of thrusting forward and upward, exploring new territories and creating new things. It can ground us, and root us in itself—but also lift and inspire us, pointing us beyond and above what we otherwise could be.

As Winston Churchill famously declared during the Second World War, as an intervention in the debate over whether Britain should rebuild the bombed House of Commons just as it had been before, "We shape our buildings, and afterwards our buildings shape us."[22] Churchill favored the complete restoration of the initial design, but for reasons that were as much functional as traditional—albeit a kind of mystical functionalism. He believed that the institutions of British parliamentary self-government had been made possible in crucial ways, ways that defied enumeration, by the specific *physical* structures within which Parliament grew and matured into its present role—even down to the shape and size and seating arrangements of chambers. The space is ours to shape initially, but once we have filled and shaped it, it begins to take on a life of its own, as a *place* that molds us in turn. One tinkers with such places only at one's great peril, particularly when the shaping has been done by many hands over many years. Not only does it rattle the bones of the dead, but it may undermine the prospects of those yet unborn, and weaken us by burying memories that deserve to live.

PLANNING AND ITS LIMITS

Churchill's example, and his interpretation of the vital but unplanned role of architecture in the evolution of parliamentary democracy, brings us to an important paradox. Planning and spontaneity seem, on the face of it, to be opposites. But they are not necessarily so, particularly not in the American tradition. As historian Robert Fishman has argued, the American approach to planning has often succeeded by failing; or as Fishman puts it, the best effects of planning have generally been those that emerge out of an "urban conversation," a wide-ranging, wide-open, and sometimes messy and unruly collision between and among various factions, often entirely self-interested in their motivations, operating sometimes inside the political process, and sometimes outside of it, in which the voice of government and its planning authority is either absent altogether, or comparatively weak and rarely dispositive.[23] In this view, planners must take a back seat; or, as the familiar saying goes, experts should be on tap but not on top. Alexis de Tocqueville captured the virtues of this approach exceedingly well:

> Under [democracy's] empire, what is great is above all not what public administration executes but what is executed without it and outside it. Democracy does not give the most skillful government to the people, but it does what the most skillful government is often powerless to create; it spreads a restive activity through the whole social body, a superabundant force, an energy that never exists without it, and which, however little circumstances may be favorable, can bring forth marvels. Those are its true advantages.[24]

Or as Fishman dryly but aptly summarizes the matter, "the absence of a controlling central power invites collective action outside a bureaucratic hierarchy."[25] The area of greatest strength in the American planning tradition, he argued, was "coalition-building at the local and regional levels."[26] And those are precisely the areas in which the revitalization of the American tradition of civic engagement is most vitally needed today.

The visionaries of the Progressive movement in America had something very different in mind. Contemplating the disorder of an industrializing, urbanizing, stratifying, and increasingly polyglot country, they had no faith in spontaneity, and little use for the political process, with its corruptions and inefficiencies. Instead they embraced the "science" of administration, which for them meant the application of "social intelligence" generated by accredited experts in research universities, and administered by civil servants accountable only to the "public interest," which government alone had the capacity to discover, express, embody, and advance. Although the Progressive movement drew heavily on the nation's deep reservoirs of Protestant moral passion, it sought to blend such passions with an essentially technocratic ideal. The application of disinterested social research generated by scholars trained in the sciences of government and administration, and applied by disinterested and uncorrupted public officials—including "city managers" who would be appointed rather than elected, and therefore rendered immune to political pressures—would lead to ever-improving governance.

Such a view had obvious applications in the regulation of giant corporations, one of the chief objects of Progressive concern. But it also applied on state and municipal levels. No place was this ideal more fully realized than in Wisconsin, where the state university was consciously envisioned as an embodiment of the social intelligence of the state; its president in 1905, Charles Van Hise, stated that he would "never be content until the beneficent influence of the university reaches every family in the state."[27] One also sees the same idea reflected in the growing influence of "scientific management" as exemplified by the work of Frederick Winslow Taylor.[28]

In the wake of the Second World War, the so-called "liberal consensus" seemed to be a triumphant iteration of the same idea, although in a more self-consciously value-neutral key, drained of any taint of Progressive moralism. It was in a sense a purer realization of the ideal, offering a dispassionate, pragmatic, experimental, flexible, and non-ideological approach to governance, envisioning the American society and economy as a system of countervailing forces that could be kept in balance by intelligent, problem-solving experts. Daniel Bell limned the scene in 1960 with a not-entirely-approving description of the "end of ideology" and "exhaustion of political ideas."[29] A similar view was laid out in a more upbeat way by President John F. Kennedy in his 1962 Yale commencement speech, where he declared:

> What is at stake in our economic decisions today is not some grand warfare of rival ideologies which will sweep the country with passion but the practical management of a modern economy. What we need is not labels and clichés but more basic discussion of the sophisticated and technical questions involved in keeping a great economic machinery moving ahead.[30]

Kennedy concluded not with the usual inspirational uplift, but by advising the graduates to take their part "in the solution of the problems that pour upon us, requiring the most sophisticated and technical judgment."[31] He was coolly ushering them into the ranks of the governing experts.

Small wonder that the large-scale urban-renewal efforts of those same years reflected a similar deference to experts and technicians. Robert Fishman, like Jane Jacobs, is severely critical of this move in the world of planning, chiefly because it required that "the urban conversation" be pushed aside in favor of "the technical discourse of the academy and the bureaucracy," a mode of discourse that "abandoned the strategy of public persuasion for a delusive centralization that sought to bypass the need for public support."[32] Such an approach has now brought us to a dead end and left us operating in a theoretical vacuum, without a new orthodoxy to replace the discredited one. But Fishman speculates that this theoretical impasse may not be such a bad thing, since it is precisely under such circumstances that a vigorous "urban conversation" would be most likely to return, and flourish.

He sees signs that this is precisely what is happening, and the example of Chattanooga, which managed to institutionalize a lively urban conversation as the central feature of its revival, would suggest that he may be right.

So, what might it mean to pursue the goal of creating sturdy basic structures that respect, and enable, the free and spontaneous exercise of our human endowment? One highly successful example to offer is the familiar American urban grid, the geometrically regular cross-hatching pattern of streets epitomized by Manhattan above 14th Street, and found in the downtowns of most major American cities. There is nothing romantic about a grid; indeed it is, considered by itself, the least evocative form imaginable. But when a grid is laid down as the foundation and template for urban development, it becomes an instrument of freedom. It opens the way to a highly vibrant street life, with maximum permeability and ease of energy flow and navigation, the optimal efficiency in the utilization of space, a cornucopia of architectural variety and diversity of uses—in short, a combination of orderliness and energy exceptionally conducive to human creativity, including such achievements as the New York skyline, a more or less spontaneously arrived-at beauty built up by the largely uncoordinated but near-symphonic collocation of great buildings on a great urban grid.[33]

It is useful here to think, as the American Studies pioneer John Kouwenhoven did, about parallels between the urban grid and the structure of jazz, two of the dozen items he regarded as "distinctively American."[34] Both are expressive forms in which a relatively rigid plan governing *some* fundamental elements makes possible variety and spontaneity in *other* ways. A substructure of strong uniformity is what produces the preconditions for a wild and intoxicating freedom. Or to put it another way, firm procedural regularity makes for wide substantive liberty. Jazz considered in its most characteristic forms is a remarkably free and highly improvisational musical form; but what makes that improvisation possible, and fully intelligible to the listener, is the fact that it rests upon a structure of predictable harmonies and predictable rhythms. In addition, the classic jazz performances are "covers" of familiar and predictable songs (mostly "standards" drawn from the productions of Tin Pan Alley and Broadway) that follow a very uniform but supple 32-bar structure immediately graspable by listeners, but susceptible to all manner of melodic and harmonic innovation.[35] Jazz is made free by its self-imposed limits.

I am not arguing that there is something sacrosanct about the grid form. Far from it. The point here is a more general one, that the best kind of planning does not seek to rule all things, dictate all details, or spell out all phases of activity, or seek to prescribe or proscribe, as the case demands. It merely seeks to establish the rules within which diverse creative energies can flourish. The grid is only one example of that, providing a simple organizing structure within which individual initiative and choice can be encouraged and made meaningful and effective. There are other, less comprehensive and more organic ways of arriving at the same thing. As Mumford put it, in his treatment of the medieval city,

> Organic planning does not begin with a preconceived goal: it moves from need to need, from opportunity to opportunity, in a series of adaptations that themselves become increasingly coherent and purposeful, so that they generate a complex, final design, hardly less unified than a pre-formed geometric pattern. Towns like Siena illustrate this process to perfection. Though the last stage in such a process is not clearly present at the beginning, as it is in a more rational, non-historic order, this does not mean that rational considerations and deliberate fore-thought have not governed every feature of the plan, or that a deliberately unified and integrated design may not result.[36]

This approach is something like the opposite of that of the grid, but it is precisely the openness of the structure to subsequent generations' free movement from opportunity to opportunity that marks it as exemplary. Once again, we are talking about a plan that enables spontaneity and growth rather than micromanaged details.

A key factor in this openness is the recognition that the making of place must have a participatory dimension if it is to be genuine and enduring. Place is not something that can be manufactured by others or handed over intact from generation to generation. On the contrary, each generation faces the task anew. One thinks of Goethe's famous adage, placed in the mouth of Faust: *Was du ererbt von deinen Vätern hast, Erwirb es, um es zu besitzen* ("What you have inherited from your fathers, you must earn or appropriate for yourself, and only then will it be yours").[37] It is made ours in the very way that John Locke described the act of taking possession of land or some other thing in his *Second Treatise*: a thing becomes our property, fully possessed by us, when that thing has been "mixed with our labor," with the wealth of experiences we have had in our "land of living," and the efforts we have expended on it and for it.[38]

Subsequent generations must be given this opportunity too, a need that may require a special kind of imagination, one that deliberately leaves avenues to be explored, tasks for others to do, heritages to be appropriated freshly, and sufficiently low-hanging fruit to encourage the young to try their own energies on the world. The imperative requirement to respect such future needs is yet another reason to resist the megaproject syndrome, with its conviction that all change must be systemic and revolutionizing, so that in order to change one thing you must change all things at once. How much better to learn to begin where you are, and learn to cherish what you already have. And while historic preservation can easily degenerate into a form of fetishism, treating the past as something to be exhibited rather than something to be lived in, the experience of the century just past should have taught us the importance of not tearing things down unless we absolutely have to. You never know what the future will find to be of use in the past. Consider the examples of Greenwich Village and the New Orleans French Quarter, both areas that were once consigned to the backwaters of urban life, little more than slums, and now are prized (perhaps even overprized) neighborhoods.

But the most important element in fostering a sense of place is to teach ourselves, or let ourselves be taught, to see with fresh eyes the place where we find ourselves. This is the task that the citizens of Mesa, and Chattanooga, and every other city that yearns for an invigorated sense of itself as a place, are facing. It is a great and worthy effort, and few objectives could be more conducive to the common good. Let a thousand planning flowers bloom, and let every reasonable expedient be tried. But we should be mindful that there is likely to be a large admixture of the spontaneous and the unexpected in our successes. Sometimes the "land of our living" can surprise us.

To leave you with a better sense of what that might mean, let me quote one last time from Lewis Mumford, this time from his autobiography. He is describing the house that he and his wife Sophia purchased and lived in for many decades in Amenia, New York—a tiny village far away, one may note with amused interest, from the densely urban locales of which he wrote so beautifully and pungently. That irony is an insight into the complexity of the man, just as Thomas Jefferson's ecstatic descriptions of Paris throw his own professed agrarianism into a more complex light. But such ironies need not detain us here, because the core of what Mumford is saying applies across the board, to all habitations and all human affairs, and all places.

Notice first how precisely Mumford's opening sentence echoes the image with which Frost begins "The Gift Outright":

> We took possession of our property in the autumn of 1929, though it would be more correct to say that our land gradually took possession of us. The house itself was in a state of utter disrepair: the trappers had hung their pelts on big nails that broke what plaster still remained on walls and ceilings. There was a small weedy patch outside the kitchen on the south side that indicated there might once have been a vegetable garden there, and there was a clump of peony bushes and a few old-fashioned roses; but the remaining land was bare of almost everything but burdock and plantain.[39]

A candidate for rural slum clearance, you might say! But then something uncanny happened:

> . . . we gradually fell in love with our shabby house as a young man might fall in love with a homely girl whose voice and smile were irresistible. As with faces—Abe Lincoln bears witness—character is more ingratiating and enduring than mere good looks. No rise in our income has ever tempted us to look elsewhere for another house, still less to build a more commodious or fashionable one. In no sense was this the house of our dreams. But over our lifetime it has slowly turned into something better, the house of our realities. In all its year-by-year changes, under the batterings of age and the bludgeonings of chance, this dear house has enfolded and remodeled our family character—exposing our limitations as well as our virtues.[40]

That undistinguished house in Amenia had not been theirs for very long before the tables turned, and they became the house's. We too will find, if we are lucky, that though we may conjure the house of our dreams, it is the house of our realities that shapes us in the end. And, *pace* Le Corbusier, such a house will never be merely a machine for living, not unless we agree to be machines ourselves. A house becomes a *home*, one of the ultimate expressions of place, not only by being congenial and familiar and comfortable, but by taking on a life of its own, a presence that no amount of forethought could have created, and that no machine could ever mimic. Such is the everyday magic of place-making, and it is the kind of everyday magic that cannot be planned, though it can certainly be planned for, and hoped for, and sought. And cherished when found.

ACKNOWLEDGEMENTS

WE DIDN'T PLAN on it happening this way. But the book you have before you has turned out to be an example of the organic and participatory approach to planning and place-making advocated by so many of its contributors. We say this because the book is something very different from, and something better and more ambitious than, what we its editors envisioned at the outset of this project. There is a hopeful lesson in that.

Indeed, we had no clear notion that any book at all, let alone this one, would be the result of our efforts. Instead, we set out at first hoping merely to stimulate a conversation about the diminishing sense of place in modern life, and about the possible consequences of that change for our lives in community. Our initial plan involved the organizing of a conference on the subject of "place," held in Malibu, California, at Pepperdine University's School of Public Policy, under the auspices of Pepperdine's Davenport Institute for Public Engagement and Civic Leadership. We felt that Pepperdine's School of Public Policy, which is unique among policy schools in having a strongly humanistic and philosophical orientation in its curriculum, would be the perfect venue for such a conversation, and Pepperdine's spectacular location along the Pacific coast would attract the interest of a wide swath of participants and audience members. We were right on all counts.

The conference was held on March 11–12, 2011, and was entitled "A Place in the World: Geography, Identity, and Civic Engagement in Modern America," a title meant to suggest the growing tenuousness of our sense of place in a globalizing world economy and culture, and to explore what the consequences of that change might be, and what should be done in response to it. Thanks to the generous support provided us by several donors, we had sufficient funds to mount a follow-up conference, entitled "Why Place Matters: Moving From Theory to Practice," on March 22, 2012.

In both conferences, we made every effort to direct the conversation toward issues of general interest, explored in accessible, jargon-free language that would engage the attention of a broader public. We endeavored to include a wide range of academic disciplines and perspectives on the subject of place. But we were especially active in seeking the input of public officials and other practitioners, both on panels and in the audience, an effort that was rewarded by a consistently high and stimulating level of discussion—the kind of discussion that would become stale and even sterile if conducted among academics alone. Our Practitioner Roundtables included as participants the city managers of Ventura and Palo Alto, the planning commissioner of the city of Santa Monica, prominent local architects and planners, journalists, and notable local civic and environmental activists. Members of the general public also attended both conferences, and were enthusiastic about the quality and accessibility of the conversation.

We have a long list of people to thank. The conferences themselves, which laid the foundation for the book, were made possible by generous support from the Lynde and Harry Bradley Foundation of Milwaukee, Wisconsin and the Earhart Foundation in Ann Arbor, Michigan, as well as the indispensable support provided by Pepperdine University and particularly by Dean James Wilburn of the School of Public Policy there, whose leadership has made that School such a standout among schools of public policy. Without his support, and support from the SunTrust Chair of Excellence in Humanities at the University of Tennessee at Chattanooga, this book could not have been published. Ashley Trim of the Davenport Institute at Pepperdine deserves special recognition; she worked tirelessly on both the conference and the book, keeping everyone informed of the progress, tracking down information, doing editorial work, and altogether being indispensable.

For advice about the direction of the book, we are indebted to our wise and generous friend Steve Wrinn, Director of the University Press of Kentucky, one of the very finest people in the book trade—or in any other trade for that matter.

We are grateful to Roger Kimball of Encounter Books for giving the book such a distinguished home, and to him, Heather Ohle, Carl W. Scarbrough, and the rest of the Encounter team for their splendid professionalism in bringing this project to fruition. In addition, we thank the American Enterprise Institute in Washington, D.C., for permission to publish Roger Scruton's "Manifesto for a New Urbanism," which first appeared in the form of an AEI "Outlook" paper.

We must reserve a special category of thanks for Adam Keiper, editor of *The New Atlantis* and its New Atlantis Books series, for his role in shepherding this book into publication, and doing so with both efficiency and love. His contribution was a *sine qua non*; the book could not have taken the form it did without him. For one thing, several of the book's most important contributions began life as essays in *The New Atlantis*. But just as importantly, Adam and his dedicated young staff of editors, though in reality only a small platoon, performed as formidably as a battalion, poring over the text and proofs, and checking dates, citations, quotations, and other references with the zeal and skill of champions, and all on a very tight, sleep-depriving schedule. Our thanks go to the members of that platoon: Caitrin Nicol Keiper, Ari N. Schulman, Samuel Matlack, and Brendan P. Foht, as well as *New Atlantis* interns Michael Begun, Christopher Coles, Maximilian de la Cal, Danielle Nelson, and John Paul Spence. Special thanks as well to Maximilian de la Cal for the preparation of the book's index. Their work on the book was supported by the Earhart Foundation, the Center for the Study of Technology and Society, the Ethics and Public Policy Center, and the Witherspoon Institute.

And finally, we thank all the people who took part in our conferences, and our students, all of whom have richly confirmed our intuition that the subject of place has become an urgent one, a subject that a great many people are eager to think about more deeply and discuss more seriously. This book is meant to initiate just such thought and discussion.

ABOUT THE CONTRIBUTORS

WILFRED M. MCCLAY (Editor) is the G. T. and Libby Blankenship Chair in the History of Liberty, and Director of the Center for the History of Liberty, at the University of Oklahoma. He is also a senior fellow at the Ethics and Public Policy Center, a senior fellow at the Trinity Forum, and a contributing editor to *The New Atlantis*. His books include *The Masterless: Self and Society in Modern America* (University of North Carolina Press, 1994), which won the Merle Curti Award of the Organization of American Historians.

TED V. MCALLISTER (Editor) is the Edward L. Gaylord Chair and an Associate Professor of Public Policy at Pepperdine University's School of Public Policy. He is the author of *Revolt Against Modernity: Leo Strauss, Eric Voegelin, and the Search for a Postliberal Order* (University of Kansas Press, 1995).

JOSEPH A. AMATO is Professor Emeritus of History and Rural and Regional Studies at Southwest Minnesota State University, where he was a founder of the Center for Rural and Regional Studies. The most recent of his many books is *Surfaces: A History* (University of California Press, 2013).

PHILIP BESS is the Director of Graduate Studies at the University of Notre Dame's Department of Architecture, where he teaches graduate urban design and theory, and works as a design consultant for municipalities, architects, and community-development corporations through the office of Thursday Associates. He is the author of *Till We Have Built Jerusalem: Architecture, Urbanism, and the Sacred* (ISI, 2006).

BRIAN BROWN is the principal and CEO of Narrator, a company that helps nonprofits and campaigns retool their fundraising strategies to capitalize on long-term social changes. He is also the founder and editor of Humane Pursuits, a web publication dedicated to helping Millennials explore how to live the good life in a modern context.

DANA GIOIA is an internationally acclaimed and award-winning poet and former Chairman of the National Endowment for the Arts, where he launched a series of national initiatives aimed at reaching underserved communities. In 2011, he became Judge Widney Professor of Poetry and Public Culture at the University of Southern California.

RUSSELL JACOBY, a historian, is a professor in residence at the University of California, Los Angeles. He is the author of numerous books, including, most recently, *Bloodlust: On the Roots of Violence from Cain and Abel to the Present* (Free Press, 2011).

MARK T. MITCHELL is the chairman of the Department of Government at Patrick Henry College where he teaches courses in political theory. He is the author, most recently, of *The Politics of Gratitude: Scale, Place, and Community in a Global Age* (Potomac Books, 2012).

PETE PETERSON teaches public policy at Pepperdine University's School of Public Policy, where he is the Executive Director of the Davenport Institute for Public Engagement and Civic Leadership, a program dedicated to helping solve California's public problems by promoting citizens' participation in governance.

CHRISTINE ROSEN is a senior editor of *The New Atlantis*, where she writes about the social and cultural impact of technology, as well as bioethics and the history of genetics. She is also a Future Tense Fellow at the New America Foundation, and the author, most recently, of *The Extinction of Experience* (W. W. Norton, 2014).

WITOLD RYBCZYNSKI is emeritus professor of urbanism at the University of Pennsylvania. An architect and critic, he has worked on practical experiments in low-cost housing in Mexico, Nigeria, India, the Philippines, and China. He served on the U.S. Commission of Fine Arts from 2004 to 2012. The author of many books, including a prize-winning biography of Frederick Law Olmsted, Rybczynski's latest is *How Architecture Works: A Humanist's Toolkit* (Farrar, Straus and Giroux, 2013).

WILLIAM A. SCHAMBRA is the director of the Bradley Center for Philanthropy and Civic Renewal, a program at the Hudson Institute that aims to encourage foundations and charitable donors to direct more resources toward support of the small, local, and often faith-based grassroots associations that are the heart of a vital civil society. He was previously a program officer at the Lynde and Harry Bradley Foundation in Milwaukee, Wisconsin.

ARI N. SCHULMAN is the executive editor of *The New Atlantis*, where he writes on artificial intelligence, rationalism, bioethics, and questions of science and culture. He is the creator of the Austin Map Project.

ROGER SCRUTON is an English philosopher, writer, and public commentator widely known for his work on aesthetics, culture, and politics. He is a senior fellow at the Ethics and Public Policy Center and a contributing editor to *The New Atlantis*. In addition to more than thirty nonfiction books, he has written three novels, the most recent of which is *Underground Notes* (Beaufort Books, 2014).

GARY TOTH is Director of Transportation Initiatives with the Project for Public Spaces, a nonprofit planning, design, and educational organization dedicated to helping people create and sustain public spaces that build stronger communities. He previously spent more than three decades at the New Jersey Department of Transportation, eventually as Director of Project Planning and Development.

YI-FU TUAN is an emeritus professor at the University of Wisconsin-Madison. A widely acclaimed cultural geographer, his many honors include the Vaudrin-Lud Prize from the International Festival of Geography, the inaugural Stanley Brunn Award for Creativity in Geography from the Association of American Geographers, and the Cullum Geographical Medal from the American Geographical Society. The most recent of his many books is *Religion: From Place to Placelessness* (Center for American Places, 2010).

NOTES

INTRODUCTION: WHY PLACE MATTERS (MCCLAY)

1 Gertrude Stein, *Everybody's Autobiography* (New York: Cooper Square Publishers, 1971), 289.

2 The sculpture was installed in 2005 by artists Steve Gillman and Katherine Keefer, as part of the "Gateway Series" of public art commissioned by the Berkeley Civic Arts Commission. "The South Berkeley Gateway Project," Official Web Site of the City of Berkeley, California, www.ci.berkeley.ca.us/ContentPrint.aspx?id=19660.

3 Carolyn Jones, "Berkeley: No tea cozy for 'There' sculpture," *San Francisco Chronicle*, June 2, 2010, available at www.sfgate.com/bayarea/article/Berkeley-No-tea-cozy-for-There-sculpture-3263028.php.

4 Verlyn Klinkenborg, "Remembered Spaces," *New York Times*, July 17, 2007, A20, available at www.nytimes.com/2007/07/17/opinion/17tue4.html.

5 *Ibid.*

6 Robert Wiebe, *The Search for Order: 1877–1920*, (New York: Hill & Wang, 1967), xiii.

7 William Leach, *Country of Exiles* (New York: Pantheon Books, 1999), 30.

8 Simone Weil, *The Need for Roots: Prelude to a Declaration of Duties Towards Mankind*, trans. Arthur Wills (New York: Routledge, 2001), originally published as *L'Enracinement: prélude à une déclaration des devoirs envers l'être humain* (Paris: Éditions Gallimard, 1949).

9 George Santayana, *The Genteel Tradition* (Lincoln, Neb.: University of Nebraska Press, 1998), 157.

GPS AND THE END OF THE ROAD (SCHULMAN)

1 Jack Kerouac, *On the Road* (New York: Penguin, 1999, orig. 1957), 110.

2 Randall Stross, "When GPS Confuses, You May Be to Blame," *New York Times*, September 1, 2012, BU3, www.nytimes.com/2012/09/02/technology/gps-and-human-error-can-lead-drivers-astray-digital-domain.html.

3 Berg Insight, "GPS and Mobile Handsets: Summary," *LBS Research Series 2013*, www.berginsight.com/ReportPDF/Summary/bi-gps4-sum.pdf.

4 Antoine de Saint-Exupéry, *Wind, Sand and Stars* (San Diego: Harcourt, 2002, orig. 1939).

5 Dire Straits, "Tunnel of Love," *Making Movies*, 1980, Vertigo.

6 Michael Gormley, "NY State Seeks to Crack Down on Wayward Truckers," Associated Press, October 14, 2009.

7   "Swedish Tourists Miss Island Due to GPS Typo," Associated Press, July 28, 2009.

8   Jeff Barnard, "Couple Stranded 3 Days After GPS Leads Them Astray," Associated Press, December 29, 2009.

9   Gilly Leshed, *et al.*, "In-Car GPS Navigation: Engagement with and Disengagement from the Environment," *Proceedings of the SIGCHI Conference on Human Factors in Computing Systems* 2008: 1675–1684, doi:10.1145/1357054.1357316.

10 Thomas A. Ranney, "Driver Distraction: A Review of the Current State-of-Knowledge," National Highway Traffic Safety Administration, 2008, available at www.nhtsa.gov/DOT/NHTSA/NRD/Multimedia/PDFs/Crash%20Avoidance/2008/810787.pdf.

11 Brit Susan Jensen, Mikael B. Skov, and Nissanthen Thiruravichandran, "Studying Driver Attention and Behaviour for Three Configurations of GPS Navigation in Real Traffic Driving," *Proceedings of the SIGCHI Conference on Human Factors in Computing Systems* 2010: 1271–1280, doi:10.1145/1753326.1753517.

12 "SatNav Danger Revealed: Navigation Device Blamed for Causing 300,000 Crashes," *Mirror News*, July 21, 2008, www.mirror.co.uk/news/uk-news/satnav-danger-revealed-navigation-device-319309.

13 "Navigation Systems Seriously Undermine Road Safety," Stichting Onderzoek Navigatiesystemen (Navigation System Research Foundation), December 10, 2007, www.stichtingonderzoeknavigatiesystemen.nl/_files/son_nav001_20071210_en_Navigation_systems_seriously_undermine_road_savety.pdf.

14 Giuseppe Iaria, *et al.*, "Cognitive Strategies Dependent on the Hippocampus and Caudate Nucleus in Human Navigation: Variability and Change with Practice," *Journal of Neuroscience* 23 (July 2, 2003), 5945–5952, available at www.jneurosci.org/content/23/13/5945.

15 Scott Adams, "Dilbert Pocket," *The Scott Adams Blog*, December 10, 2009, www.dilbert.com/blog/entry/dilbert_pocket/.

16 "Chrysler advert: Dodge Challenger Freedom commercial," *The Telegraph*, July 19, 2010, www.telegraph.co.uk/motoring/motoringvideo/7899056/Chrysler-advert-Dodge-Challenger-Freedom-commercial.html.

17 Martyn Williams, "Nissan Car Brakes Automatically to Avoid Collisions," *Tech Hive*, July 28, 2010, www.techhive.com/article/202067/nissan_brakes_woot.html.

18 Michael Taylor, "No Doze: Mercedes E-Class alerts drowsy drivers," *Autoweek*, December 24, 2008, www.autoweek.com/article/20081224/FREE/812249991.

19 John Staddon, "Distracting Miss Daisy," *The Atlantic* 302:1 (July/August 2008), 102–105, www.theatlantic.com/magazine/archive/2008/07/distracting-miss-daisy/306873/3/.

20 Nick Paumgarten, "Getting There," *The New Yorker* 82:10 (April 24, 2006), 86–101, www.newyorker.com/archive/2006/04/24/060424fa_fact.

21 John Markoff, "Google Cars Drive Themselves, in Traffic," *New York Times*, October 9, 2010, A1, www.nytimes.com/2010/10/10/science/10google.html.

22 John Markoff, "Google Lobbies Nevada to Allow Self-Driving Cars," *New York Times*, May 10, 2011, A18, www.nytimes.com/2011/05/11/science/11drive.html.

23 Alex Hutchinson, "Global Impositioning Systems," *The Walrus* 6 (November 2009), thewalrus.ca/global-impositioning-systems/.

24 *Ibid.*

25 Ryan Avent, "Another Fine Mess I've Gotten Myself Into," *The Bellows*, November 8, 2010, www.ryanavent.com/blog/?p=2353.

26 Markoff, "Google Cars Drive Themselves, in Traffic."

27 Quoted in Yi-Fu Tuan, *Space and Place: The Perspective of Experience* (Minneapolis: University of Minnesota Press, 2001, orig. 1977), 4.

28 Brad Templeton, "The Finger of AI: Automated Electrical Vehicles and Oil Independence," lecture, Singularity Summit 2009, New York, October 4, 2009, archive.org/details/SingularitySummit2009Talks. See also futurisms.thenew atlantis.com/2009/10/robo-cars-and-energy-independence.html.

29 Ian Mount, "New for '09: GPS Tour Guides," CNN Money, December 30, 2008, money.cnn.com/2008/12/29/smallbusiness/virtual_tour_guide.fsb/index.htm.

30 Nick Statt, "Foursquare touts 40M users in bid for renewed relevancy," *CNET News*, September 5, 2013, news.cnet.com/8301-1023_3-57601522-93/foursquare-touts-40m-users-in-bid-for-renewed-relevancy/.

31 Kathleen Fennell, "Dating apps like Grindr sex up smartphones," *The Pitt News*, September 29, 2013, www.pittnews.com/news/article_6ea99c4a-296b-11e3-ac9e-0019bb30f31a.html.

32 Yoshio Nakatani, Ken Tanaka, and Kanako Ichikawa, "A Tourist Navigation System that Promotes Interaction with Environment," *Engineering Letters* 18 (May 13, 2010), www.engineeringletters.com/issues_v18/issue_2/EL_18_2_08.pdf.

33 Ari N. Schulman, "The Austin Map Project," austinmap.org.

34 Kerouac, *On the Road*, 38.

35 T. S. Eliot, "Introduction to Adventures of Huckleberry Finn," in *Adventures of Huckleberry Finn*, ed. Thomas Cooley (New York: W. W. Norton & Company 1999), 348. Originally printed in Mark Twain, *The Adventures of Huckleberry Finn* (London: Cresset Press, 1950), vii–xvi.

36 Kerouac, *On the Road*, 126.

37 Henry Shukman, "Walking Into the Earth's Heart: The Grand Canyon," *New York Times*, TR1, November 25, 2009, travel.nytimes.com/2009/11/29/travel/29canyon.html.

38 William Least Heat-Moon, *Blue Highways: A Journey into America* (Bay Back Books, 1999, orig. 1983), 172.

39 Yi-Fu Tuan, *Space and Place: The Perspective of Experience* (Minneapolis: University of Minnesota Press, 2001, orig. 1977), 18.

40 Alain de Botton, *The Art of Travel* (New York: Vintage, 2004, orig. 2002), 111.

41 Tuan, *Space and Place*, 146.

42 Walker Percy, "The Loss of the Creature," in *The Message in the Bottle* (New York: Picador, 2000, orig. 1975), 47.

43 *Ibid.*, 48.

44 *Ibid.*, 49.

45 Shukman, "Walking Into the Earth's Heart."

46 Percy, "The Loss of the Creature," 49–51.

47 *Ibid.*, 48.

48 *Ibid.*, 46.

49 Least Heat-Moon, *Blue Highways*, 288.

50 De Botton, *The Art of Travel*, 242.

51 Walker Percy, "The Man on the Train," in *The Message in the Bottle* (New York: Picador, 2000, orig. 1975), 86.

52 George Orwell, "In Front of Your Nose," reprinted in *The Collected Essays, Journalism, and Letters of George Orwell*, vol. 4: *In Front of Your Nose, 1945–1950* (Boston: David R. Godine, 2000), 125.

53 Edward S. Casey, "How to Get from Space to Place in a Fairly Short Stretch of Time: Phenomenological Prolegomena," in *Senses of Place*, eds. Steven Feld and Keith H. Basso (Santa Fe: School of American Research Press, 1996), 14–17.

54 *Ibid.*, 18.

55 Edward S. Casey, *The Fate of Place: A Philosophical History* (Los Angeles: University of California Press, 1998), 213.

56 Mathew Honan, "I Am Here: One Man's Experiment With the Location-Aware Lifestyle," *Wired*, January 19, 2009, www.wired.com/gadgets/wireless/magazine/17-02/lp_guineapig.

57 Tift Merritt, "Broken," *Another Country*, 2008, Fantasy Records.

58 Fatality Analysis Reporting System Encyclopedia, National Highway Traffic Safety Administration, www-fars.nhtsa.dot.gov.

59 Walker Percy, "The Message in the Bottle," in *The Message in the Bottle*, 119.

60 Amy A. Kass, "The Homecoming of Penelope," in *Apples of Gold in Pictures of Silver: Honoring the Work of Leon R. Kass*, eds. Yuval Levin *et al.* (Lanham, Md.: Lexington Books, 2010), 4.

61 Walker Percy, *The Moviegoer* (New York: Vintage International, 1998, orig. 1961), 202.

62 *Ibid.*, 98–99.

63 Jack Neff, "Is Digital Revolution Driving Decline in U.S. Car Culture?," *Advertising Age* 81:22 (May 31, 2010), adage.com/article/digital/digital-revolution-driving-decline-u-s-car-culture/144155/.

64 Alvin Toffler, *Future Shock* (New York: Random House, 1970).

PLACE-CONSCIOUS TRANSPORTATION POLICY (TOTH)

1 Federal Aid Road Act, 1916, 39 Stat. 355, 64th Cong., July 11, 1916. Also see Richard Weingroff, "Federal Aid Road Act of 1916: Building the Foundation," *Public Roads* 60:1 (Summer 1996), www.fhwa.dot.gov/publications/publicroads/96summer/p96su2.cfm.

2 U.S. House of Representatives, National Interregional Highway Committee, "Interregional Highways" (report), 78th Cong., January 12, 1944, ntl.bts.gov/lib/33000/33400/33441/final_report/volume_3_html/09_historical_documents/content9bda.htm.

3 David Schrank and Tim Lomax, "The 2005 Urban Mobility Report," Texas Transportation Institute, May 2005, www.apta.com/resources/reportsandpublications/Documents/urban_mobility.pdf.

4 "Overweight and Obesity—Adult Obesity Facts," Centers for Disease Control and Prevention, www.cdc.gov/obesity/data/adult.html.

5 Richard F. Weingroff, "The Genie in the Bottle: The Interstate System and Urban Problems, 1939–1957," *Public Roads* 64 (Sep/Oct 2000), www.fhwa.dot.gov/publications/publicroads/00septoct/urban.cfm.

6 Tim Lomax et al., "Real-Timing the 2010 Urban Mobility Report," Texas Transportation Institute, February 2011, utcm.tamu.edu/publications/final_reports/Lomax_10-65-55.pdf.

7 Joe DiStefano, "Envision Utah: Producing a Vision for the Future of the Greater Wasatch Area," Calthorpe Associates, Envision Utah, and Fregonese Calthorpe Associates, April 2000, www.ecotippingpoints.org/resources/download-pdf/ETP_Envision-Utah.pdf.

8 "Context Sensitive Solutions," U.S. Department of Transportation Federal Highway Administration, contextsensitivesolutions.org.

"I CAN'T BELIEVE YOU'RE FROM L.A.!" (GIOIA)

1 Woody Allen and Marshall Brickman, *Annie Hall*, directed by Woody Allen (Los Angeles: Rollins-Joffe Productions, 1977).

2 H. L. Mencken, *A Mencken Chrestomathy* (New York: Vintage, 1982), 290.

3 "*Paradies und Hölle können eine Stadt sein.*" Bertolt Brecht, "Hollywood Elegies," from *Gedichte* (Poems), ed. E. Hauptman and B. Slupianak (Frankfurt: Suhrkamp, 1976), vol. 6, 58.

4 Westbrook Pegler, "Fair Enough," *The Evening Independent*, November 13, 1938, 11.

5 F. Scott Fitzgerald, *The Last Tycoon* (Des Plaines, Il.: Bantam Books, 1976), 13.

6 Charles Simic, interview, *The Cortland Review*, August 1998, www.cortlandreview.com/issuefour/interview4.htm.

7 For 1900 figure: Campbell Gibson, "Table 13: Population of the 100 Largest Urban Places: 1900" in "Population of the 100 Largest Cities and Other Urban Places in the United States: 1790 to 1990," U.S. Census Bureau, Population Division

Working Paper 27 (June 1998), www.census.gov/population/documentation/twps0027/tab13.txt. For present-day figure: U.S. Census Bureau, "Incorporated Places and Minor Civil Divisions Datasets: Subcounty Resident Population Estimates: April 1, 2010 to July 1, 2012," www.census.gov/popest/data/cities/totals/2012/files/SUB-EST2012_6.csv.

8 For 1900 figure: Richard L. Forstall, "Population of Counties by Decennial Census: 1900 to 1990," U.S. Census Bureau (March 1995), www.census.gov/population/cencounts/ca190090.txt. For present-day figure: U.S. Census Bureau, "Table 2. Annual Estimates of the Population of Combined Statistical Areas: April 1, 2010 to July 1, 2011" in "Vintage 2011: Metropolitan and Micropolitan Statistical Areas Tables" (July 1, 2011), www.census.gov/popest/data/metro/totals/2011/tables/CBSA-EST2011-02.csv.

9 "List of Cities by GDP," Wikipedia, en.wikipedia.org/wiki/List_of_cities_by_GDP.

10 "List of United States cities by population," Wikipedia, en.wikipedia.org/wiki/List_of_United_States_cities_by_population.

11 For "largest Catholic diocese": "Parishes," website of the Archdiocese of Los Angeles, www.la-archdiocese.org/Pages/Parishes/.

12 "Los Angeles (city), California" in "State and County QuickFacts," U.S. Census Bureau, quickfacts.census.gov/qfd/states/06/0644000.html.

13 Robert Bruegmann, "L.A. the King of Sprawl? Not at All," *Los Angeles Times*, October 23, 2005, M5, articles.latimes.com/2005/oct/23/opinion/oe-bruegmann23. See also Sandra O'Flaherty *et al.*, "Is Los Angeles More Crowded Than New York?" (white paper), Livable Places, 2006, www.livableplaces.org/news/documents/LANYDensity_report_000.pdf.

14 Jan Morris, *The World: Life and Travel 1950–2000* (New York: Norton, 2003), 228.

15 Quentin Crisp, "A Bigger Splash," in *How to Go to the Movies* (New York: St. Martin's Press, 1989), 194.

16 Randy Newman, "I Love L.A.," *Trouble in Paradise*, 1983, Warner Bros.

COSMOPOLITANISM AND PLACE (JACOBY)

1 Diogenes Laërtius, *Lives and Opinions of Eminent Philosophers*, trans. Robert Drew Hicks, VI:63 (Loeb Classical Library, 1925), vol. 2, 65.

2 Laërtius, *Lives and Opinions*, VI:38, vol. 2, 41.

3 *The Dissertations of Maximus Tyrius*, trans. Thomas Taylor, vol. 1 (London: R.H. Evans, Pall-Mall, 1804), 203–204.

4 John L. Moles, "Cynic Cosmopolitanism," in *The Cynics: The Cynic Movement in Antiquity and Its Legacy*, ed. R. Bracht Branham and Marie-Odile Goulet-Cazé (Berkeley: University of California Press, 1996), 106–121.

5 Yuri Slezkine, *The Jewish Century* (Princeton: Princeton University Press, 2004), 1.

6 Kwame Anthony Appiah, *Cosmopolitanism: Ethics in the World of Strangers* (New York: Norton, 2005), xv.

7 Robert J. Holton, *Cosmopolitanisms: New Thinking and New Directions* (New York: Palgrave Macmillan, 2009), 117.

8 Walter D. Mignolo, "The Many Faces of Cosmo-Polis: Border Thinking and Critical Cosmopolitanism," in *Cosmopolitanism*, ed. Carol A. Breckenridge, et al. (Durham, N.C.: Duke University Press, 2002), 182.

9 "Some Materials on the Recent Attacks against Cosmopolitanism," *Soviet Studies* 1:2 (October 1949), 179, www.jstor.org/stable/148598.

10 *Ibid.*, 180.

11 *Ibid.*, 181.

12 Fuyuki Kurasawa, "A Cosmopolitanism from Below: Alternative Globalization and the Creation of a Solidarity without Bounds," *European Journal of Sociology* 45 (2004), 233–255. Kurasawa argues for a political cosmopolitanism "from below" that supplements that "from above."

13 Joel S. Kahn, "Other Cosmopolitans in the Modern Malay World," in *Anthropology and the New Cosmopolitanism: Rooted, Feminist and Vernacular Perspectives*, ed. Pnina Werbner (Oxford: Berg, 2008), 273.

14 Jonathan Parry, "Cosmopolitan Values in an Indian Steel Town," in *Anthropology and the New Cosmopolitanism*, 340.

15 Appiah, *Cosmopolitanism*, 109–110.

16 *Ibid.*, 110.

17 Appiah, *Cosmopolitanism*, 111.

18 René Girard, *Violence and the Sacred*, trans. Patrick Gregory (Baltimore: Johns Hopkins University Press, 1977), 49, originally published as *La violence et le sacré* (Paris: Éditions Grasset, 1972).

19 *Ibid.*, 56–79.

20 *Ibid.*, 147.

21 *Ibid.*, 169–192.

22 *Ibid.*, 49 and 51.

23 Eugen Weber, *Peasants into Frenchmen: The Modernization of Rural France, 1870–1914* (Palo Alto: Stanford University Press, 1976).

24 René Girard (interview), "René Girard, philosophe et anthropologue: 'Ce qui se joue aujourd'hui est une rivalité mimétique à l'échelle planétaire,'" *Le Monde*, November 5, 2001. English translation ("What Is Occurring Today Is a Mimetic Rivalry on a Planetary Scale") by Jim Williams for the Colloquium on Violence and Religion, www.uibk.ac.at/theol/cover/girard/le_monde_interview.html.

25 René Girard, *Celui par qui le scandale arrive* (Paris: Desclée de Brouwer, 2001), 23–24.

26 "Hundreds Flee Nigerian City Swept by Riots," *New York Times*, November 25, 2002, www.nytimes.com/2002/11/25/world/hundreds-flee-nigerian-city-swept-by-riots.html.

27 Jean-Pierre Dupuy, "Anatomy of 9/11: Evil, Rationalism and the Sacred," *Sub-Stance* 37:115 (2008), 42.

28 Malise Ruthven, *A Fury for God: The Islamist Attack on America* (London: Granta, 2002).

29 Cited in Cordula Meyer, "Die Täter: Der Professor und der Terrorist," *Spiegel Online*, July 2006, www.spiegel.de/spiegelspecial/a-435654.html.

30 Dittmar Machule, interview, *Four Corners*, October 18, 2001, www.abc.net. au/4corners/atta/interviews/machule.htm.

31 Daniel Brook, "The Architect of 9/11," *Slate*, September 10, 2009, www.slate.com/id/2227245/.

32 Evan Thomas, "The Day that Changed America," *Newsweek*, December 30, 2001, www.thedailybeast.com/newsweek/2001/12/30/the-day-that-changed-america.html. Cited in Ruthven, *A Fury for God*, 260–261.

33 Slezkine, *The Jewish Century*, 44.

34 Simone Weil, *The Need for Roots: Prelude to a Declaration of Duties towards Mankind*, trans. Arthur Wills (New York: Routledge, 2001), 45, originally published as *L'Enracinement: prélude à une déclaration des devoirs envers l'être humain* (Paris: Éditions Gallimard, 1949).

35 Weil, *Roots*, 40.

36 Francine du Plessix Gray, *Simone Weil* (New York: Viking/Penguin, 2001), 169 ff.

37 Theodor W. Adorno, *The Jargon of Authenticity*, trans. Knut Tarnowski and Frederic Will (Evanston: Northwestern University Press, 1973), 53.

38 Ben Kiernan, *Blood and Soil: A World History of Genocide and Extermination from Sparta to Darfur* (New Haven: Yale University Press, 2007).

MAKING PLACES: THE COSMOPOLITAN TEMPTATION (MITCHELL)

1 Cicero, *The Republic* III:xxii (renumbered III:33), trans. Niall Rudd (Oxford: Oxford University Press, 1998), 68–69.

2 Marcus Aurelius, *Meditations* IV:4, trans. C. R. Haines (Cambridge, Mass.: Harvard [Loeb edition], 1994, orig. 1916), 71–73.

3 Immanuel Kant, *Perpetual Peace: A Philosophical Sketch* in *Kant: Political Writings*, ed. Hans S. Reiss, trans. H. B. Nisbet (Cambridge: Cambridge University Press, 1991), 107–8. Italics appear in both the English translation and German original.

4 Jürgen Habermas, "Kant's Idea of Perpetual Peace, with the Benefit of Two Hundred Years' Hindsight," in James Bohamn and Matthias Lutz-Bachmann, eds, *Perpetual Peace: Essays on Kant's Cosmopolitan Ideal* (Cambridge, Mass.: M.I.T. Press, 1997), 130.

5 Jürgen Habermas, *Between Facts and Norms: Contributions to a Discourse Theory of Law and Democracy* (Cambridge: Polity Press, 1996), 515.

6 Martha Nussbaum, "Patriotism and Cosmopolitanism," *For Love of Country?*, ed. Joshua Cohen (Boston: Beacon Press, 1996), 4.

7 *Ibid.*, 13.

8 *Ibid.*, 13.

9 *Ibid.*, 15.

10 Fyodor Dostoevsky, *The Brothers Karamazov*, trans. Richard Pevear and Larissa Volokhonsky (New York: Farrar, Straus and Giroux, 2002, orig. 1992), 57.

11 Martha Nussbaum, "Toward a Globally Sensitive Patriotism," *Dædalus* 137:3 (Summer 2008), 80.

12 *Ibid.*, 79–80.

13 *Ibid.*, 82.

14 *Ibid.*, 83.

15 *Ibid.*, 82.

16 This is in striking contrast with Grotius, who argued that the natural law would retain all of its force even if God did not exist.

17 James Madison, "Federalist #51," in *The Federalist: The Gideon Edition*, eds. George W. Carey and James McClellan (Indianapolis: Liberty Fund, 2001), 267–272.

18 Cf. Barry Allan Shain, *The Myth of American Individualism: The Protestant Origins of American Political Thought* (Princeton: Princeton University Press, 1994).

19 David Miller, "Cosmopolitanism: A Critique," *Critical Review of International Social and Political Philosophy* 5:3 (Autumn 2002), 84.

20 Robert Nisbet, *The Present Age: Progress and Anarchy in Modern America* (Indianapolis: Liberty Fund, 2003), 87ff.

PLACE / SPACE, ETHNICITY / COSMOS: HOW TO BE MORE FULLY HUMAN (TUAN)

1 Charles Lamb (writing as "Elia"), "New Year's Eve," *London Magazine* III:xiii (January 1821), 6–7.

2 Philip Larkin, *Required Writing* (Ann Arbor: University of Michigan Press, 1999), 55.

3 Burr Shafer, *The Wonderful World of J. Wesley Smith* (Vanguard Press: New York, 1960).

4 Victor Turner, *The Ritual Process: Structure and Anti-Structure* (Ithaca: Cornell University Press, 1977, orig. 1969).

5 Hannah Arendt, *The Human Condition* (Garden City, NY: Doubleday Anchor Books, 1959).

6 Kenneth Clark, *Civilization* (New York: Harper & Row, 1969), 3.

7 "Cities are a product of time.... In the city, time becomes visible.... Layer upon layer, past times preserve themselves in the city." Lewis Mumford, *The Culture of Cities* (New York: Harcourt, Brace, Jovanovich, 1970, orig. 1938), 4.

8 Nicholas Carr, *The Shallows: What the Internet Is Doing to Our Brains* (New York: Norton, 2010).

9 T.S. Eliot, "Four Quartets 1: Burnt Norton," *Collected Poems: 1909–1962* (New York: Harcourt Brace & Co., 1963), 176.

10 Bertrand Russell, *Portraits from Memory and Other Essays* (New York: Clarion, 1969), 175.

11 Uno Holmberg, "Siberian Mythology," in *Mythology of All Races* vol. 4, ed. J. A. MacCulloch (Boston: Marshall Jones Co., 1927).

12 Stanley Diamond, ed., *Primitive Views of the World* (New York: Columbia University Press, 1964); Karl A. Nowotny, *Beiträge zur Geschichte des Weltbildes* (Vienna: Verlag Fredinand Berger, 1969).

13 Milan Kundera, *The Unbearable Lightness of Being*, trans. Michael Henry Heim (New York: Harper and Row, 1984).

14 Gareth B. Matthews, *Philosophy and the Young Child* (Cambridge, Mass.: Harvard University Press, 1980).

15 Oscar Wilde, "The Happy Prince," in *The Complete Works of Oscar Wilde: Stories, Plays, Poems, and Essays*, ed. J. B. Foreman (London: William Collins Sons & Co., 1966), 285–291.

THE DEMAND SIDE OF URBANISM (RYBCZYNSKI)

1 Irving Kristol, "Urban Civilization & Its Discontents," *Commentary* 50:1 (July 1970), 31, www.commentarymagazine.com/article/urban-civilization-its-discontents/. Emphasis in original.

2 According to the U.S. Census, the total number of people living in cities larger than 250,000 was 39.4 million in 1960, 42.3 million in 1970, and 52.1 million in 2006. The corresponding figures for cities between 25,000 and 250,000 were 36.6 million in 1960, 45.8 million in 1970, and 81.7 million in 2006. Measured as a percentage of the total population living in cities (115.9 million in 1960, and 186.1 million in 2006), the big cities' share dropped from 34.0 percent in 1960 to 28.0 percent in 2006, whereas the small cities' share rose from 31.6 percent in 1960 to 43.9 percent in 2006. See census.gov.

3 Paul Taylor *et al.*, "Denver Tops List of Favorite Cities: For Half of America, Grass Is Greener Somewhere Else," Pew Research Center, Washington, D.C., January 29, 2009, 5, pewsocialtrends.org/files/2011/04/Community-Satisfaction-POSTED-updated.pdf.

4 *Ibid.*, 5.

5 David Brooks, "I Dream of Denver," *New York Times*, February 17, 2009, A29, www.nytimes.com/2009/02/17/opinion/17brooks.html.

6 Witold Rybczynski, *Last Harvest: How a Cornfield Became New Daleville: Real Estate Development in America from George Washington to the Builders of the Twenty-first Century, and Why We Live in Houses Anyway* (New York: Scribner, 2007), 41–48.

7 *Reston Town Center: A Downtown for the 21st Century*, ed. Alan Ward (Washington, D.C.: Academy Press, 2006).

8 *The New Urbanism: Toward an Architecture of Community*, ed. Peter Katz (New York: McGraw-Hill, 1994).

METAPHYSICAL REALISM, MODERNITY, AND TRADITIONAL CULTURES OF BUILDING (BESS)

1 Alasdair MacIntyre, *After Virtue* 2nd edition (Notre Dame, Ind.: University of Notre Dame Press, 1984), 57–58.

2 Karl Marx and Friedrich Engels, "The Communist Manifesto," in *The Marx-Engels Reader* 2nd edition, ed. Robert C. Tucker (New York: W. W. Norton & Co., 1978), 475–477.

3 Wendell Berry, *Sex, Economy, Freedom & Community: Eight Essays* (New York: Pantheon, 1994), 128.

4 Max Weber, "Politics as a Vocation" in *The Vocation Lectures* (Indianapolis: Hackett Publishing, 2004).

5 Bertrand de Jouvenal, *The Pure Theory of Politics* (Cambridge: Cambridge University Press, 1963), 45.

6 Léon Krier, *Houses, Palaces, Cities* (New York: St. Martin's Press, 1985), 70–71, reproduced in Philip Bess, *Till We Have Built Jerusalem* (Wilmington: Intercollegiate Studies Institute, 2006), 116.

7 Alexis de Tocqueville, *Democracy in America*, trans. and ed. Harvey C. Mansfield and Delba Winthrop (Chicago: University of Chicago Press, 2000), 482 ff.

A PLEA FOR BEAUTY: A MANIFESTO FOR A NEW URBANISM (SCRUTON)

1 Friedrich Hayek, *The Constitution of Liberty* (Chicago: University of Chicago Press, 1978), 340.

2 Jane Jacobs, *The Death and Life of Great American Cities* (New York: Modern Library, 2001 [Fiftieth Anniversary Edition]).

3 Peter Hall, *Great Planning Disasters* (London: Weidenfeld and Nicolson, 1980).

4 "In 2004, the median duration of current residence for the U.S. population 15 years and older was 5.9 years." Matthew C. Marlay and Alison K. Fields, "Seasonality of Moves and the Duration and Tenure of Residence: 2004," *Current Population Reports* (Washington, D.C.: U.S. Census Bureau, July 2010), 6, www.census.gov/prod/2010pubs/p70-122.pdf.

5 Edward C. Banfield, "The Logic of Metropolitan Growth," in *The Unheavenly City Revisited* (Boston: Little, Brown and Company, 1974).

6 Joel Kotkin, *The Next Hundred Million: America in 2050* (New York: Penguin Books, 2010); Robert Bruegmann, *Sprawl: A Compact History* (Chicago: University of Chicago Press, 2005).

7 Robert Putnam, *Bowling Alone: The Collapse and Revival of American Community* (New York: Simon & Schuster, 2000).

8 Alexis de Tocqueville, *Democracy in America*, trans. and ed. Harvey C. Mansfield and Delba Winthrop (Chicago: University of Chicago Press, 2000), 489–492 ff.

9 Joel Garreau, *Edge City: Life on the New Frontier* (New York: Doubleday, 1991).

10 Steven Hayward, "Fixing the Dysfunctional City," in *Smarter Growth: Market-Based Strategies for Land-Use Planning in the 21st Century*, eds. Randall G. Holcombe and Samuel R. Staley (Westport, Conn.: Greenwood Publishing Group, 2001), 235–250.

11 George L. Kelling and James Q. Wilson, "Broken Windows," *Atlantic Monthly* (March 1, 1982), 29–38, www.theatlantic.com/magazine/archive/1982/03/broken-windows/304465/.

12 *"Les Sept vieillards"* ("The Seven Old Men"), in *Fleurs du mal* (*Flowers of Evil*), fleursdumal.org/poem/221.

PLACE AND POVERTY (SCHAMBRA)

1 It was long held that the Progressives sought for a reassertion of institutions close to citizens, as opposed to political bosses and powerful corporations. But considerable scholarship over the last three decades has raised serious doubts on this point. The democratic reforms that the Progressives introduced (such as direct-ballot initiatives and referenda) were meant to break the power of political "machines"—that is, the Catholic and immigrant institutions that kept the "best" from ruling efficiently and scientifically. Along with those reforms were others (such as the city-manager form of urban governance, the municipal research bureau, expert commissions, blue-ribbon panels, at-large elections, the short ballot) that would insure that the democratic voice, once freed from the machine, would become entirely malleable to the will of the elites. The kind of localism Progressives would tolerate was a localism that had been taken out of the hands of the locals and put into the hands of those trained in the sciences who happened to live in a given locale. *The Progressive Revolution in Politics and Political Science*, John Marini and Ken Masugi, eds. (Lanham, Md.: Rowman and Littlefield, 2005).

2 Thomas Haskell, *The Emergence of Professional Social Science: The American Social Science Association and the Nineteenth-Century Crisis of Authority* (Champaign: University of Illinois Press, 1977), 14.

3 Herbert Croly, *Progressive Democracy* (New Brunswick: Transaction Publishers, 1998, orig. 1914), 370.

4 Edward A. Ross, *Principles of Sociology* (New York: The Century Co., 1920), 422.

5 Nathan Glazer, *The Limits of Social Policy* (Cambridge: Harvard University Press, 1988), 3.

6 John McKnight, "Regenerating Community," *Social Policy* 17 (Winter 1987), 55.

7 Lynn Vincent, "Family Helpline of Los Angeles: Community-based Solutions—

One Person at a Time," *Philanthropy, Culture, and Society* (newsletter), Capitol Research Center, February, 1999, 7, capitalresearch.org/pubs/pdf/Philanthropy%20 Culture%20&%20Society%20February%201999.pdf.

THE RISE OF LOCALIST POLITICS (BROWN)

1 Le Corbusier (Charles-Édouard Jeanneret-Gris), *Towards a New Architecture*, trans. Frederick Etchells (New York: Dover Publications, 1986), 4, orig. published as *Vers une architecture* (Paris: L'Espirit Nouveau, 1923).

2 Stephanie R. South, "Making the Move from Shouting to Listening to Public Action: A Student Perspective on Millennials and Dialogue," *Journal of Public Deliberation* 6:1 (2010), www.publicdeliberation.net/jpd/vol6/iss1/art1/.

3 John Kay, *Why Firms Succeed: Choosing Markets and Challenging Competitors to Add Value* (New York: Oxford University Press, 1995), 8.

4 Howard Schultz, *Onward: How Starbucks Fought For Its Life Without Losing Its Soul* (New York: Rodale Books, 2011).

5 Gary Hamel, "Who's Really Innovative?" (blog post), WSJ.com, November 22, 2010, blogs.wsj.com/management/2010/11/22/whos-really-innovative/.

6 Heather Gowdy *et al.*, "Convergence: How Five Trends Will Reshape the Social Sector," (James Irvine Foundation, 2009), 10, irvine.org/images/stories/pdf/eval/ convergencereport.pdf.

7 Robert D. Putnam, *Bowling Alone: The Collapse and Revival of American Community* (New York: Simon & Schuster, 2000).

8 Mike McGrath, "The New Laboratories of Democracy: How Local Government is Reinventing Civic Engagement" (white paper), Philanthropy for Active Civic Engagement, May 2009, 8, www.pacefunders.org/publications/NewLaboratories ofDemocracy.pdf.

9 *Ibid.*

10 See BostonCompleteStreets.org.

11 Saul Alinksy, *Reveille for Radicals* (Chicago: University of Chicago Press, 1946), 14.

12 M. William Sermons and Peter Witte, "State of Homelessness in America 2011" (report), National Alliance to End Homelessness, January 2011, www.endhome lessness.org/content/article/detail/3668. See also "Hunger and Homelessness Survey: A Status Report on Hunger and Homelessness in America's Cities" (report), U.S. Conference of Mayors, December 2009, usmayors.org/pressre- leases/uploads/USCMHungercompleteWEB2009.pdf.

13 "2010 Annual Update: Year Five" (report), Denver's Road Home, November 10, 2010, 2, denversroadhome.org/files/DRH_AnnualReport2011_vF_crops.pdf.

14 "Big Society," Wikipedia, en.wikipedia.org/wiki/Big_Society.

15 Rod Dreher, *Crunchy Cons: The New Conservative Counterculture and Its Return to Roots* (New York: Three Rivers Press, 2006).

16 Mark T. Mitchell, "What our Hands Have Wrought" (blog post), Front Porch Republic, March 2, 2009, www.frontporchrepublic.com/2009/03/734/.

THE NEW MEANING OF MOBILITY (ROSEN)

1 Tanzina Vega, "AT&T Begins Service to Text Users in Certain Locations" (blog post), NYTimes.com, February 27, 2011, mediadecoder.blogs.nytimes.com/2011/02/27/att-begins-service-to-text-users-in-certain-locations/.

2 Holman W. Jenkins Jr., "Google and the Search for the Future," *Wall Street Journal*, August 14, 2010, online.wsj.com/article/SB10001424052748704901104575423294099527212.html.

3 Sherry Turkle, *Alone Together: Why We Expect More from Technology and Less from Each Other* (New York: Basic Books, 2011).

4 Simone Weil, *The Need for Roots: Prelude to a Declaration of Duties towards Mankind*, trans. Arthur Wills (New York: Routledge, 2001), 43, originally published as *L'Enracinement: prélude à une déclaration des devoirs envers l'être humain* (Paris: Éditions Gallimard, 1949).

5 The term "continuous partial attention" was coined by technologist Linda Stone; it caught on in the press in 2007. Stone writes about it at lindastone.net/qa/continuous-partial-attention/.

6 Anja Boenicke, "The Opt-out Marriage," Policy Innovations (a publication of Carnegie Council), November 30, 2007, www.policyinnovations.org/ideas/briefings/data/marriage, discussing Hans-Peter Blossfeld and Heather Hofmeister, "Globalife—Life Courses in the Globalization Process: Final Report," 2005, oldsite.soziologie-blossfeld.de/globalife/pdf/final_report.pdf.

7 Keith Gessen, *All the Sad Young Literary Men* (New York: Penguin Group, 2008), 230.

8 Matthew C. Marlay and Alison K. Fields, "Seasonality of Moves and the Duration and Tenure of Residence: 2004," *Current Population Reports* (Washington, D.C.: U.S. Census Bureau, July 2010), 6, www.census.gov/prod/2010pubs/p70-122.pdf.

9 Brian McKenzie, "Out of State and Long Commutes: 2011," *American Community Survey Reports* (Washington, D.C.: U.S. Census Bureau, February 2013), 2, www.census.gov/hhes/commuting/files/2012/ACS-20.pdf.

10 Galia Solomonoff, "Of Knowledge, Content, Place, and Space," in *Is the Internet Changing the Way You Think? The Net's Impact on Our Minds and Future*, ed. John Brockman (New York: HarperCollins, 2011), 383–385.

MAKING AMERICAN PLACES: CIVIC ENGAGEMENT RIGHTLY UNDERSTOOD (MCALLISTER)

1 G. K. Chesterton, "The Toy Theatre," in *Tremendous Trifles* (New York: Dodd, Mead & Co., 1909), 182–183, archive.org/stream/cu31924013463140#page/n195/mode/2up.

2 Edmund Burke, "Reflections on the Revolution in France," in *The Writings and Speeches of Edmund Burke—Volume VIII: The French Revolution 1790–1794*, ed. L. G. Mitchell (New York: Oxford University Press, 1998), 97–98.

3 Jean Bethke Elshtain, *Democracy on Trial* (New York: Basic Books, 1995), 1–5.

4 Alexis de Tocqueville, *Democracy in America*, trans. and ed. Harvey C. Mansfield and Delba Winthrop (Chicago: University of Chicago Press, 2000), 7. See also 661–673 (the closing chapters of volume II), where Tocqueville explores these savage instincts when unmoderated.

5 *Ibid.*, 458–463 (volume II, part 1, chapter 17).

6 Ted V. McAllister, "The Tocqueville Problem and the Nature of American Conservatism," *Anamnesis* 1:1 (2011), 75–79.

7 Tocqueville, *Democracy in America*, 63–65 ff.

8 *Ibid.*, 64–65.

9 *Ibid.*, 65 (emphasis added).

10 *Ibid.*, 663.

11 Burke, "Reflections," 129.

PLACE AS PRAGMATIC POLICY (PETERSON)

1 Robert Nisbet, *The Quest for Community* (Wilmington: Intercollegiate Studies Institute, 2010, orig. 1953), 250.

2 Robert D. Putnam, *Bowling Alone: The Collapse and Revival of American Community* (New York: Simon & Schuster, 2000); Robert D. Putnam and David E. Campbell, *American Grace: How Religion Divides and Unites Us* (New York: Simon & Schuster, 2010).

3 Robert D. Putnam, "*E Pluribus Unum*: Diversity and Community in the Twenty-First Century," *Scandinavian Political Studies* 30:2, (June 2007), 137–174.

4 *Ibid.*, 150–151 (emphasis in original).

5 *Ibid.*, 147–149.

6 *Ibid.*, 164–165.

7 James Q. Wilson, "Bowling with Others," *Commentary* (October 2007), 30–33, www.commentarymagazine.com/article/bowling-with-others/.

8 *Ibid.*, 31.

9 *Ibid.*, 33.

10 The following story is taken from my article Pete Peterson, "The Citizen Returns," *National Civic Review* (Spring 2010), 12–18, ncl.org/publications/ncr/99-1/Peterson.pdf.

11 Mallory Simon, "Island DIY: Kauai Residents Don't Wait for State to Repair Road," CNN.com, April 9, 2009, www.cnn.com/2009/US/04/09/hawaii.volunteers.repair/.

12 "Polihale State Park Still Closed," The Garden Island (website), February 12, 2009, thegardenisland.com/news/local/polihale-state-park-still-closed/article_924055 00-7edc-50ec-afaa-a99e800b17db.html.

13 Simon, "Island DIY."

14 *Ibid.*

15 "DLNR, Volunteers Reopen Polihale State Park" (press release), State of Hawaii government website, April 2009, archive.lingle.hawaii.gov/govgallery/news/files/2009/april/dlnr.

16 Simon, "Island DIY."

17 "An act to add and repeal Section 5080.42 of the Public Resources Code, relating to state parks," California Assembly Bill 42 (approved by governor, October 4, 2011), leginfo.ca.gov/pub/11-12/bill/asm/ab_0001-0050/ab_42_bill_20111004_chaptered.pdf.

18 Pete Peterson, "Creative Californians Redefine Rahm's 'Rule One,'" *The American*, March 7, 2012, www.american.com/archive/2012/march/creative-californians-re define-rahms-rule-one/.

19 Emily Charrier-Botts, "Nonprofit to Run Jack London: First State Park to Be Run by Nonprofit," *Sonoma Index-Tribune* (April 13, 2012), A1.

20 *Ibid.*

21 For comprehensive reporting on the Bell scandal, see "Crisis in Bell: High Salaries Stir Outrage" (collection of articles), *Los Angeles Times* (2011–2013), www.latimes.com/news/local/bell/.

22 Jeff Gottlieb and Ruben Vives, "D.A. Looks into City of Bell's Salaries," *Los Angeles Times*, June 24, 2010, AA1, www.latimes.com/news/local/la-me-bell-council-interactive,0,5213462.htmlstory.

23 "Bell (city), California" in "State and County QuickFacts," U.S. Census Bureau, quickfacts.census.gov/qfd/states/06/0604870.html.

24 Jeff Gottlieb, "336 Voters Opened Bell's Wallet; Tiny Turnout Approved Change Allowing City to Avoid State Salary Limits," *Los Angeles Times*, July 23, 2010, A1, articles.latimes.com/2010/jul/23/local/la-me-0723-bell-charter-20100723.

25 *Ibid.*

26 *Ibid.*

27 Hector Becerra, "Bell Scandal May Spur a Civic Shift; In Nearby Cities, Residents Rose up to Oust Corrupt Officials with Mixed Results," *Los Angeles Times*, July 22, 2010, A1, articles.latimes.com/2010/jul/22/local/la-me-0722-bell-democracy-20100722.

28 Rick Cole, "Plundered Cities; Systematic Reform Is Needed to Prevent Another Bell in L.A. County's Rust Belt," *Los Angeles Times*, July 30, 2010, A21, articles.latimes.com/2010/jul/30/opinion/la-oe-cole-bell-scandal-20100730.

29 Pete Peterson, "Liberty ... Bell?" (online article), Fox & Hounds, January 24, 2012, www.foxandhoundsdaily.com/2012/01/libertybell/.

30 Stephen Goldsmith, "The New Political Reality" (online article), *Governing*, February 8, 2010, www.governing.com/blogs/bfc/The-New-Political-Reality.html.

31 Alexis de Tocqueville, *Democracy in America*, trans. and ed. Harvey C. Mansfield and Delba Winthrop (Chicago: University of Chicago Press, 2000), 503.

32 Putnam, "*E Pluribus Unum*," 163–164.

33 Mancur Olsen, *The Logic of Collective Action: Public Goods and the Theory of Groups* (Cambridge, Mass.: Harvard University Press, 1965).

34 John McKnight, *The Careless Society: Community and Its Counterfeits* (New York: Basic Books, 1995), 49.

35 Goldsmith, "The New Political Reality."

LOCAL HISTORY: A WAY TO PLACE AND HOME (AMATO)

1 Much of the substance of this essay in based on the introduction and conclusion of my *Rethinking Home: A Case for Writing Local History* (Berkeley: University of California Press, 2002).

2 Joseph A. Amato, *Jacob's Well: A Case for Rethinking Family History* (St. Paul: Minnesota Historical Society Press, 2008).

3 Paul Valéry, "Remarks on Intelligence," in *The Outlook for Intelligence*, trans. Denise Folliot and Jackson Mathews, ed. Jackson Mathews (New York: Harper & Row, 1962), 79 (emphasis in original).

4 Constance McLaughlin Green, "The Value of Local History," in *The Pursuit of Local History: Readings on Theory and Practice*, ed. Carol Kammen (Walnut Creek, Calif.: AltaMira Press, 1996), 90–91.

5 For an introduction to thinking about nostalgia, see Fred Davis, *Yearning for Yesterday: A Sociology of Nostalgia* (New York: Free Press, 1979).

6 Charles Péguy, "A nos amis, a nos abonnés," in *Œuvres en prose, 1909–1914* (Paris: Éditions Gallimard, 1957), 48–49 (trans. Joseph A. Amato).

7 Lewis Mumford, "The Value of Local History," in *The Pursuit of Local History: Readings on Theory and Practice*, ed. Carol Kammen (Walnut Creek, Calif.: Altamira Press, 1996), 88.

8 *Ibid.*, 89.

9 For a useful introduction to environmental history, see Dan Flores, "Place: An Argument for Bioregional History," *Environmental History Review* 18 (Winter 1994), 1–18; for additional works, see "Acknowledgments and Sources."

10 For a single example, see Carlo Ginzburg, *The Cheese and the Worms: The Cosmos of a Sixteenth-Century Miller* (Baltimore: John Hopkins University Press, 1980).

11 The three nearest towns are Worthington (population 12,800), New Ulm (population 13,500), and Willmar (population 19,600). "List of cities in Minnesota," Wikipedia, en.wikipedia.org/wiki/List_of_cities_in_Minnesota.

12 For recent anthropological definitions of region, see Eric Wolf, *Europe and the People without History* (Berkeley: University of California Press, 1982); John Comaroff, *Ethnography and the Historical Imagination* (Boulder, Col.: Westview Press, 1992); Richard Fardon, ed., *Localizing Strategies: Regional Traditions of Ethnographic Writing* (Washington, DC: Smithsonian Institution Press, 1990).

13 Jeremy Black's *Maps and History: Constructing Images of the Past* (New Haven:

Yale University Press, 1997), Dava Sobel's *Longitude* (New York: Penguin, 1995), and Anne Marie Claire Godlewska's *Geography Unbound: French Geographic Science from Cassini to Humboldt* (Chicago: University of Chicago Press, 1999) are three recent testimonies to the notion that places are discovered, imagined, invented, and contrived by mapmakers as well as historians.

14 One ecological work based a distinct aspect of a region is Dan Flores, *Caprock Canyonlands: Journeys into the Heart of the Southern Plains* (Austin: University of Texas Press, 1990).

15 See, for example, Daniel Worster, *Under Western Skies: Nature and History in the American West* (New York: Oxford University Press, 1992), and Patricia Limerick, *The Legacy of Conquest: The Unbroken Past of the American West* (New York: Norton, 1987).

16 In his essay "Reading the Landscape," prominent geographer D. W. Meinig shows the importance of place in the thought of the two contrasting founders of landscape studies, British thinker W. G. Hoskins and American thinker and founder of the journal *Landscape* J. B. Jackson, in *The Interpretation of Ordinary Landscapes: Geographical Essays* (New York: Oxford University Press, 1979), 195–244.

17 For the influence of Eric Hobsbawm and Terence Ranger's *The Invention of Tradition* (Cambridge: Cambridge University Press, 1983), see the introductory pages of Witold Rybczynski, *Home: A Short History of an Idea* (New York: Viking, 1986), esp. 9–10; and Joseph A. Amato and Anthony Amato, "Minnesota, Real and Imagined," *Dædalus* 129 (Summer 2000), 55–80.

18 William Cronon, *Nature's Metropolis: Chicago and the Great West* (New York: Norton, 1991); John Hudson, *Making the Cornbelt: A Geographical History of Middle-Western Agriculture* (Bloomington: University of Indiana Press, 1994); John Borchert, *America's Northern Heartland* (Minneapolis: University of Minnesota Press, 1987); and Andrew R. L. Cayton and Peter S. Onuf, eds., *The Midwest and the Nation* (Bloomington: University of Indiana Press, 1990).

19 Guy Thuillier and Jean Tulard, *Histoire locale et régionale* (Paris: Presses. Universitaires de France, 1992), 119.

20 Paul Valéry, "The Crisis of the Mind," in *The Outlook for Intelligence*, trans. Denise Folliot and Jackson Mathews, ed. Jackson Mathews (New York: Harper & Row, 1962), 35.

21 This insight is drawn from Thuillier, especially *Histoire locale et régionale*.

22 Valéry, "The Crisis of the Mind," 23.

THE SPACE WAS OURS BEFORE WE WERE THE PLACE'S (MCCLAY)

1 Scott Carlson, "Sprawling Mesa, Ariz., Aims to Become College Town," *Chronicle of Higher Education*, March 18, 2012, chronicle.com/article/Sprawling-Mesa-Ariz-Aims-to/131230/.

2 "Mesa (city), Arizona" in "State and County QuickFacts," U.S. Census Bureau, quickfacts.census.gov/qfd/states/04/0446000.html. "List of United States cities by population," Wikipedia, en.wikipedia.org/wiki/List_of_United_States_cities_by_population.

3 Carlson, "Sprawling Mesa, Ariz."

4 June Scobee Rodgers, *Chattanooga: River City Renaissance* (Memphis: Towery, 1998); John Parr, "Chattanooga: The Sustainable City" in *Boundary Crossers: Case Studies of How Ten of America's Metropolitan Regions Work*, eds. John Parr and Bruce Adams (College Park, Md.: Academy of Leadership, 1998), 68–80; "Chattanooga: A City Reinvented Through Vision," Southeast Natural Resource Leadership Institute (date unknown).

5 Yi-Fu Tuan, *Space and Place: The Perspective of Experience* (Minneapolis: University of Minnesota Press, 2001, orig. 1977).

6 Robert Frost, "The Gift Outright" in *The Poetry of Robert Frost*, ed. Edward Connery Lathem (New York: Henry Holt, 1923), also available at www.poetryfoundation.org/poem/237942.

7 I leave out of account here, but not out of mind, the fact that the land they encountered was *not* empty, and that indeed one of the tasks for recent historical scholarship has been the recovery and incorporation of knowledge about the ways that the land had already been settled and storied, by the indigenous peoples, and how those elements managed to persist. Our sense of place is never finished, not only because of the constant emergence of things that are new, but also because of the re-emergence of the old, and the challenge of coming to terms with it.

8 Jane Jacobs, *The Death and Life of Great American Cities* (New York: Modern Library, 2001 [Fiftieth Anniversary Edition]).

9 Lewis Mumford, "Revaluations I: Howard's Garden City," in *New York Review of Books*, April 8, 1965, 10–12.

10 Lewis Mumford to Erik Wensberg (letter), in the Jane Jacobs Papers, box 13 folder 11, John J. Burns Library, Boston College, quoted in Anthony Flint, *Wrestling with Moses: How Jane Jacobs Took on New York's Master Builder and Transformed the American City* (New York: Random House, 2009), 126.

11 Jacobs, *The Death and Life*, 50.

12 *Ibid.*, 35.

13 Flint, *Wrestling with Moses*.

14 An excellent précis of this history, and much else about the Village's early heyday, is in Kenneth S. Lynn, "The Rebels of Greenwich Village," in *The Air-Line to Seattle: Studies in Literary and Historical Writing about America* (Chicago: University of Chicago Press, 1983), 60–92.

15 The full title of Reed's poem is: "The Day in Bohemia, Or, Life Among the Artists: Being a *Jeu D'esprit* Containing Much that is Original and Diverting. In which the Reader Will Find the Cognomens and Qualities of Many Persons Destined

One Day to Adorn the Annals of Nations, in Letters, Music, Painting, the Plastic Arts, and Even Business; Together with Their Foibles, Weaknesses, and Shortcoming. And Some Account of the Life Led by Geniuses in Manhattan's Quartier Latin," (New York: Hillacre Bookhouse, 1913), www.bohemianlit.com/full_text/reed/day.htm.

16 Bonnie Kavoussi, "Jane Jacobs' Old Hudson Street Townhouse for Sale in West Village Jane Jacobs Probably Wouldn't Have Wanted to Live In," *New York Observer*, June 8, 2009, observer.com/2009/06/jane-jacobs-old-hudson-street-townhouse-for-sale-in-west-village-jane-jacobs-probably-wouldnt-have-wanted-to-live-in/.

17 David Brooks, *Bobos in Paradise: The New Upper Class and How They Got There* (New York: Simon and Schuster, 2000).

18 Matthew Schuerman, "What Would Jane Jacobs Think?," *New York Observer*, September 19, 2007, observer.com/2007/09/what-would-jane-jacobs-think/.

19 Joel Kotkin, "The Triumph of Suburbia," *Daily Beast*, April 29, 2013, www.thedailybeast.com/articles/2013/04/29/the-triumph-of-suburbia-despite-downtown-hype-americans-choose-sprawl.html; Joel Kotkin and Wendell Cox, "Cities and the Census," *City Journal* 21 (Spring, 2011), www.city-journal.org/2011/eon0406jkwc.html.

20 Richard Thaler and Cass Sunstein, *Nudge: Improving Decisions About Health, Wealth, and Happiness* (New York: Penguin, 2009).

21 Lewis Mumford, "The Ideal Form of the Modern City," *The Lewis Mumford Reader*, ed. Donald L. Miller (New York: Pantheon, 1986), 162.

22 Winston Churchill, "A Sense of Crowd and Urgency," presented to the House of Commons, London, October 28, 1943, found in *Winston S. Churchill: His Complete Speeches*, ed. Robert Rhodes James (New York: Chelsea/Bowker, 1974), 6869.

23 Robert Fishman, "The American Planning Tradition: An Introduction and Interpretation," in *The American Planning Tradition: Culture and Policy*, ed. Robert Fishman (Washington, D.C.: Woodrow Wilson Center Press, 2000), 1–29.

24 Alexis de Tocqueville, *Democracy in America*, trans. and ed. Harvey C. Mansfield and Delba Winthrop (Chicago: University of Chicago Press, 2000), 234.

25 Fishman, "The American Planning Tradition," 4.

26 *Ibid.*, 19.

27 Charles R. Van Hise, Address to the Wisconsin Press Association in February 1905, quoted in Merle Curti and Vernon Carstensen, *The University of Wisconsin: 1848–1925* volume 2 (Madison, Wisc.: University of Wisconsin Press, 1949), 88, digital.library.wisc.edu/1711.dl/UW.UWHist18481925v2.

28 Daniel Nelson, *Frederick W. Taylor and the Rise of Scientific Management* (Madison: University of Wisconsin Press, 1980).

29 Daniel Bell, *The End of Ideology: On the Exhaustion of Political Ideas in the Fifties* (Glencoe, Il.: Free Press, 1960).

30 John F. Kennedy, Commencement Address at Yale University, June 11, 1962, www. presidency.ucsb.edu/ws/?pid=29661.

31 *Ibid.*

32 Fishman, "The American Planning Tradition," 5.

33 Witold Rybczynski, *City Life* (New York: Scribner, 1995), 44–46.

34 John A. Kouwenhoven, *The Beer Can by the Highway: Essays on What's American about America* (Baltimore: Johns Hopkins University Press, 1988), 41–58.

35 This description is not meant to deny the title of "jazz" to "free jazz" and other avant-garde elaborations, only to insist that they be understood as later elaborations of early forms fitting the general description provided here.

36 Lewis Mumford, *The City in History: Its Origins, Its Transformations, and Its Prospects* (New York: Harcourt, Brace, and World, 1961), 302.

37 Johann Wolfgang von Goethe, *Faust*, lines 682–683 (author's translation).

38 "Whatsoever then he removes out of the state that nature hath provided, and left it in, he hath mixed his labour with, and joined to it something that is his own, and thereby makes it his property." John Locke, *Second Treatise of Civil Government* (1690), chapter 5, section 27.

39 Lewis Mumford, *Sketches from Life: The Autobiography of Lewis Mumford : The Early Years* (New York: Dial Press, 1982), 485.

40 *Ibid.*

INDEX

COPYRIGHT ACKNOWLEDGMENTS

A NOTE ON THE TYPE

WHY PLACE MATTERS *has been set in Minion, a type designed by Robert Slimbach in 1990. An offshoot of the designer's researches during the development of Adobe Garamond, Minion hybridized the characteristics of numerous Renaissance sources into a single calligraphic hand. Unlike many early faces developed exclusively for digital typesetting, drawings for Minion were transferred to the computer early in the design phase, preserving much of the freshness of the original concept. Conceived with an eye toward overall harmony, Minion's capitals, lowercase letters, and numerals were carefully balanced to maintain a well-groomed "family" appearance—both between roman and italic and across the full range of weights. A decidedly contemporary face, Minion makes free use of the qualities Slimbach found most appealing in the types of the fifteenth and sixteenth centuries. Crisp drawing and a narrow set width make Minion an economical and easygoing book type, and even its name evokes its adaptable, affable, and almost self-effacing nature, referring as it does to a small size of type, a faithful or favored servant, and a kind of peach.*

SERIES DESIGN BY CARL W. SCARBROUGH